For

Katherine Finn

With best wishes

Helen Sandrich.

DEAR DARK HEAD

HELEN LANDRETH

DEAR
DARK HEAD

An Intimate Story of Ireland

New York **WHITTLESEY HOUSE** London

McGRAW-HILL BOOK COMPANY, INC.

SIXTH PRINTING

PUBLISHED BY WHITTLESEY HOUSE
A division of the McGraw-Hill Book Company, Inc.

To the poets and scholars of Ireland who have done so much through all the ages to keep the seeds of fire aglow.

Acknowledgments

➼➺⧽⧽⧼⧼⭠

"ALAS, O hand, how much white vellum hast thou written. Thou wilt make famous the vellum, while thou thyself wilt be the bare top of a faggot of bones."

So wrote one of the Irish scribes a thousand years ago, with unhappy accuracy. For his fingers have long been fleshless, and his name is lost in the mist of time. Lost, too, are the names of many of the old poets and historians whose tales have been recounted in this book. Were it not so, in gratitude their names would be mentioned here.

But the names of the scholars who translated those old tales and poems are known, and the author of this book is glad to acknowledge her indebtedness to them. Her deep gratitude goes to these scholars, living or dead: John O'Donovan, who translated the *Annals of the Four Masters;* Whitley Stokes, translator of the *Tripartite Life of St. Patrick* and many other tales; Standish H. O'Grady, whose *Silva Gadelica* was used many times and whose translation of *The Triumphs of Turlough* was also used; John Fraser, who translated the *First Battle of Moytura;* Joseph Dunn, who translated *Táin Bó Cúalnga, The Cattle Raid of Cúalnga;* Kuno Meyer, from whose *Selections from Ancient Irish Poetry* and translations in many scholarly magazines the author has used *Instructions of King Cormac Mac Art*, *On the Flightiness of Thought*, three selections from *The Triads of Ireland*, and two adaptations of poems; Lady Gregory, for her rendering of Dallan Forgaill's *Lament* for Columcille, and Columcille's *Lament on Leaving Ireland*, from *A Book of Saints and Wonders*, and for her version of two tales of the *Fenian Cycle*, which, with other translations, were used as a basis for a description of the life of the men of the Fianna; Douglas Hyde, Alexander Cameron, A. A. Carmichael, T. O'Flanagan, and Whitley Stokes, whose translations of various versions of the legend of Deirdre were the basis for the version of the tale as it appears in this book; James H. Todd, for his translation of *Wars of the Gael and Gall;* Gerard Murphy, for his translation of *The Lays of Finn;* John O'Mahoney, for his translation of Geoffrey Keating's *History of Ireland;* Charles Plummer, for his translation of colophons and marginalia; Daniel Corkery, for translations of poems in his *Hidden Ireland* and for permission to use prose extracts from the same; Denis Murphy, for his translation of O'Clery's *Life of Hugh Roe O'Donnell;* P. W. Joyce, Patrick O'Kelly, William Hennessy, Edward Gwynn, Walter Purton, Stephen Gwynn, James MacPherson, Richard O'Duffy, J. H. Lloyd, O. C. Bergin, G. Schoepperle, A. O'Kelleher, W. Reeves, J. J. Lawlor, for translations used briefly or indirectly.

The author is indebted to the Council of the British Academy for permission to use material from *Colophons and Marginalia of Irish Scribes*, by Charles Plummer, published in *Proceedings of the British Academy;* to the British Museum, for permission to use abstracts of poems translated by Standish H. O'Grady in the *Catalogue of Irish Manuscripts in the British Museum;* to the Irish Texts Society for permission to use Standish H. O'Grady's translation of *The Triumphs of Turlough,* and Gerard Murphy's translation of *Lays of Finn,* published by the Society; to Thornton Butterworth, Ltd., London, and the Literary Executors of the late Sir Alfred Robbins, for permission to use quotations from *Parnell—The Last Five Years;* to Constable and Company, London, and Fraulein A. Meyer, for permission to use the translations of the late Kuno Meyer as mentioned above; to the Executors of Lady Gregory's estate, John Murray, London, and Charles Scribner's Sons, New York, for permission to use such parts of Lady Gregory's works as have been mentioned above; to David Nutt, London, for the use of portions of Joseph's Dunn's *Táin Bó Cúalnge;* to The Talbot Press, Ltd., Dublin, for their permission to use quotations from *Political Writings and Speeches* by Padraig Pearse; to the same firm and to the authors, for concurring in giving permission to use quotations from *White Light and Flame* by L. Mac Manus, and *The Victory of Sinn Fein* by P. S. O'Hegarty; to the same firm, Mrs. Clement Shorter, and Mitchell Kennerly, New York, for permission to quote *Sixteen Dead Men,* by Dora Sigerson Shorter, published in *The Tricolor;* to G. P. Putnam's Sons, for permission to quote Alcuin's letter from *The Vikings in Western Christendom,* by Charles Keary; to George Bernard Shaw, for permission to quote from a letter by Mr. Shaw published in the London *Daily News;* to the anonymous author of *Who Fears to Speak of Easter Week.*

The author extends her most grateful thanks to Dorothy Macardle for the use of the manuscript of several chapters of *The Irish Republic,* about to be published by Gollancz and Company, London.

⇛ x ⇚

The author gladly acknowledges her indebtedness to Dr. William Cornog for several translations from Medieval Latin made especially for *Dear Dark Head*.

To the Trustees of the New York Public Library, to Dr. Richard I. Best, Director of the National Library of Ireland, Dublin, and to Miss Roisin Walsh, Director of the Public Library, Dublin, the author is deeply grateful for their kindness in extending library privileges to her.

Countless pleasant memories mingle with the gratitude the author feels for the friends who motored her through Ireland and helped her to know the country more intimately.

After many years the labor of forming this book is coming to an end. Already the author has written Finis to the story of Ireland itself, and to the Afterword. But there is one more quotation which seems appropriate, a colophon one of the old Irish scribes appended to his manuscript a thousand years ago: "The names enjoined on me to enter in this book, but omitted by carelessness, sloth or forgetfulness of mine, I commend to Thee, O Christ, to Thy Mother, and all the heavenly host, that here or in life eternal their happy memory be kept in honor."

HELEN LANDRETH.

FALLS CHURCH, VIRGINIA,
August, 1936.

Contents

Dear Dark Head

FOREWORD

➤➤➤〰〰〰

HE *Caronia* sailed from New York for Liverpool on November 7, 1925, with Queenstown listed as a port of call.

It was a bitter, unwelcoming wind that met me as I went on deck to see what Ireland looked like. The peddling women with their baskets who had come out on the tender were red-faced and shivering, and their clothes beat about them as they climbed the ladder to the ship. The land that circled the cove was barren, with only a few leaf-stripped trees silhouetted against the sky. Queenstown, a mile away, was barely discernible in the dusk. It was all bleak, all gray.

And yet, I had a sense of home-coming. Never had I set foot on Irish soil. I had only one ancestor, a great-grandmother, who had been Irish. Kathleen O'Kelly, her name was. I knew little of her. I knew less of Ireland. And still I yearned to it.

"It is strange," I said to my father, "that I feel so at home here. I know very little of Ireland. It comes down to this. There were kings, and fairies, and jaunting cars. There is the Blarney Stone, and I suppose the Lakes of Killarney are real. But Brian Boru is only a name, and so is the Easter Rising. Of Ireland today I know no more than that somewhere in Dublin is the Abbey Theatre, and William Butler Yeats with a broad ribbon on his eyeglasses."

3

I was not alone in my ignorance. "The misfortune is," said Gilbert Chesterton, in his *Irish Impressions*, "that men know the name too well, and the thing too little."

There is good reason for this. Long ago England put her hand on Ireland's mouth. At the end of the sixteenth century the young Earl of Essex, in Ireland to subdue it for the queen who would soon cut off his head, wrote home to Elizabeth, " 'Twere as well for our credit that we alone have the exposition of our quarrel with this people, and not they also." That policy kept the story of Ireland's past from her own people as well as outsiders. Irish poets were even forbidden to write poems in their country's honor. But their praise for her could not be stilled. So a woman symbolized Ireland in the poems they wrote for her, a woman to whom they gave little names, poetic, endearing names. She was to them Dark Rosaleen, and Kathleen ni Houlihan, and Brown-Haired Maid. She was The Harp. She was their Dear Dark Head.

Things are better now, and Ireland has found her voice. But to outsiders, to strangers, it is still hard to find a comprehensive story of Ireland's past. Indeed some scholars say her history has never been written. Certainly an honest and accurate picture of the Irish people, from their shadowy beginning to this day, has never been presented to the casual reader in such a way that the facts of history have not smothered entirely the charming and distinctive qualities which the source materials possess.

To know the Irish people as well as Irish history through all the ages, one has to search through countless tomes, through Keating, and the O'Gradys, and Patrick Joyce, and O'Curry, and assemble a likeness as one would a jigsaw puzzle. One has to find translations of the old annals, *The*

Annals of the Four Masters, the *Annals* of Clonmacnoise, of
Loch Cé, and Tigernach, the *Books* of Ballymote, and Lien-
ster, and Lecan, the *Book of the Dun Cow*, the *Book of Invasions*. One has to consult State Papers. One has to unearth
back issues of scholarly magazines published in many lands,
Eriu, and *Revue Celtique*, and *Irische Texte*, and *Zeitshrift für
Celtische Philologie*, and many others.

All this takes time and patience and a great love for
Ireland. But when one has read these, and the picture of
Ireland has been formed, there comes the great desire to have
others know of her, too; of her great warriors, Conn of the
Hundred Battles, and Finn Mac Cool, and Cuchulain; of her
poets, with their mantles of birdskins, and their tinkling
musical branches; of hermits in little huts, looking up from
their manuscripts to watch gray cuckoos, and then to write
of them on the margins of their vellum; of warrior queens,
sweeping into battle in their chariots, of fleets of Danish
ships on the Boyne; of scholars who studied Greek under
the hedges; of the happy time when Ireland was the center
of learning of the world; of great soldier princes, outside
whose tents thick king-torches flared through all the
night; of the tarred heads of Irish patriots which decorated
the battlements of Dublin Castle when Elizabeth was bringing Ireland to her knees.

That means a book, a book which would be not history
alone, not social history only, but a combination of both:
a book, most of all, which would record the changing
temper of the Irish people.

That such a book should include both history and legends
perhaps requires some explanation. There are no written
records of pagan Ireland. But when Patrick brought the
light of Christianity to the land of his boyhood captivity

he found a people devoted to the memory of their ancestors. From one generation to another their poets and historians had handed down brave tales of old battles, accounts of the reigns of kings and queens, and genealogies which reached back to the dawn of time.

Not acceptable as history, these old tales, which were transmitted to manuscript in the Middle Ages, still give a vivid picture of the ancient ways of these people. What matter whether Nuada of the Silver Hand ever lived or not? The legend of his life illustrates three important facets of the Irish nature: their Platonistic love of beauty, which would tolerate no king who was maimed or blemished; their reverence for the words and bodies of poets; their craftsmanship in metals, which began so far back in the past that they claim it for their first ancestors.

These legends have been the basis for many scholarly works on social history. Scholars have picked them to pieces, and sorted and classified their component parts. Then from these scattered fragments they have built up pictures of the old times. The fantastic details which had been embroidered into them through the centuries were of course dropped out with the thread of narrative on which they were strung. But those fantastic details were sometimes both charming and illuminating, and the narratives were generally amusing. By not dissecting the tales, by presenting them just as they were told by generations of Irish poets, one achieves the result which the social historians sought, with more ease and greater vividness.

At the end of one of the manuscripts of the Cattle Raid of Cualnge, an epic which centers about Queen Maeve of Connaught at the time of Christ, the scribe has added a footnote in Latin: "I, who have copied this history, or more truly legend, give no credence to various incidents narrated in it. For some things therein are the feats of jugglery of demons, sundry others poetic figments, a few are probable, others improbable, and even more invented for the delectation of fools."*

The author believes that an intelligent reader will be able to separate for himself the poetic figments and the feats of jugglery of demons from the probable realities of the past as they are presented in the legends, and that a reader less severe than the scribe will enjoy them all, and find them valuable.

The real history of Ireland begins about the fourth or fifth century. But so accurate are many details of the legends which came into being about the time of Christ that a surprising amount of archaeological corroboration for them has been found. They cannot be lightly dismissed as pure fiction.

When the time of actual history is reached, the legends are used no more, except occasionally to illustrate national customs or the Irish temperament, and then their fictional nature is always indicated.

This book does not profess to be complete or critical. Greater works are in progress. True scholars, true historians, will give the world the works on Ireland which are so sorely needed. But one who loves Ireland has wanted to do something for her, too; to bake a little cake before the large loaves are ready, a little cake compounded of the same ingredients as the ones to come. One who has had the great pleasure of reading of old saints and scholars, and warriors naïve enough to wait battle till their opponents could make

* See sources on page 351.

proper weapons and prepare themselves for attack, has wished to make available for many people the loveliness she found only by hundreds of hours of research.

If this book has many quotations, it is with a purpose. Can you read of Columcille, whose death was "not the sorrow of one house, or the grief of one harp-string," and not want to know more of him? Can you read of the Great Plain of the Curragh, in whose "clearer fairer aire the falcon goes to a higher pitch, or mounts so high as to be scarce visible," and not want to explore further the history of Irish sport? Can you learn of the three fair things which hide ugliness, the three sparks which kindle love, the three preparations of a good man's house, and not want to know more of the Triads?

There will be few, I think, who will read these things without having their respect for Ireland increased, and their affection kindled.

As for the *Instructions of King Cormac MacArt*, imparted by that learned and lusty monarch, it is difficult to decide whether their likeness to the philosophies of the present are more amusing than their difference. "Honor poets" and "Do not dress elegantly unless you possess sheep" are surely dated. But "Every lover likes a dainty bed" was as timeless when Ciarnait's admirer expounded it as when its classical ancestor was gathered into the Greek Anthology.

She is a queer country, Ireland, the problem child of the nations, if a nation so old can still be called a child. She is precocious, willful, temperamental. Like all misunderstood children of the past she has had much punishment. It is not over. She has been beaten and bloody. She may be again. She, who has had so many riches and lost them so cruelly, recovers her heritage dearly, and with disheartening slow-ness. Meanwhile she suffers, she sings, she makes friends, she makes enemies. But her people are valiant, as they have always been, and the shades of her heroes support her. Their voices sound through all this book, telling the story of Ireland.

Chapter I

NUADA OF THE SILVER HAND

THE SLEEP of the High King of Ireland was troubled by a dream. Filled with wonder and perplexity he pondered over it for a while, then sent for his wizard to interpret it for him.

"I saw a great flock of birds," said the high king, "coming from the depths of the ocean. They settled over all of us, and destroyed us. One of us, I thought, struck the noblest of the strange birds, and cut off one of its wings. Tell me, Cesard, is there a meaning to this vision, and what does it portend?"

Cesard the Wizard employed his skill and knowledge, and by means of ritual the meaning of the king's vision was revealed to him.

"This is a warning," he said, "a warning for you and our country. Warriors are coming across the sea; a thousand heroes covering the ocean. Speckled ships will press in upon us. All kinds of death they announce. A new people will overtake us; a people skilled in every art and magic spell. An evil spirit will overtake us and be our doom. The strangers will be victorious in every strife."

"That," said Eochaid the High King, "is a prophecy of the coming to Ireland of enemies from far distant countries."

Even as he spoke the strangers were setting out for noble Ireland. They had bold, hardy chiefs, and men proficient in every art, and they determined to go to Ireland, which had been the home of their ancestors in ages past. Fierce and gray with foam was the sea, hazardous the journey, but with care and watchfulness it was accomplished. As soon as they had landed in Ireland the strangers broke and burnt all their ships on the shore, that they might not be tempted to retreat to them, and then proceeded to the Red Hill of Rain, where they halted and encamped. At last their hearts and minds were filled with contentment that, after long exile and oppression by foreign masters, they had reached once more the home of their ancestors.

It was reported to Eochaid the High King, and his people the Fir Bolgs, that the Tuatha de Danann had arrived in Ireland.

"It is a great disadvantage to us," said the King of Ireland, "that we have no knowledge or report of where yon host came from, or where they mean to settle. Let Sreng set out to visit them, for he is big and fierce and bold to spy on hosts, and interview strangers, and uncouth and terrifying to behold."

Thereupon Sreng the champion rose and took his strong brown shield, and his two thick-shafted javelins, his death-dealing sword, his fine, four-cornered helmet, and his heavy iron club, and went on his way to the Hill of Rain.

The Tuatha de Danann saw this huge, fearsome man approaching them.

"Here comes a man all alone," they said. "It is for information he comes. Let us send someone to speak to him."

So Bres, the great warrior of the Tuatha de Danann, went from the camp to inspect and parley with the stranger. He carried with him his shield and his sword, and his two great flesh-seeking spears. The two men approached each other warily till they were within speaking distance. Each looked keenly at the other without speaking a word. Each was astonished at the other's weapons and appearance. Sreng wondered at the great spears he saw, and rested his shield on the ground before him, so that it protected his face. Bres, too, kept silent, and from behind his shield peered at the huge broad-pointed weapons of the other.

The inspection over, the two men greeted each other, for their origins were the same and they spoke the same language. Each recited the names of his ancestors.

"It is glad I am to know we are of the same race," said Sreng. "Now is the time to remember it. Our temper is high, lordly and fierce is our pride against our foes. It would be well for you to humble yourselves to prevent the destruction of your own men. A battle between our people would be no pleasant entertainment, but a gathering where many would be crushed."

"It would be no gay amusement," agreed Bres, impressed with the other's fierceness and weapons. "Take down that shield from before your face, that I may be able to tell the Tuatha de Danann of your appearance."

"I will do so," said Sreng, "for it was for fear of that sharp spear you carry that I placed my shield between us."

"Show me your weapons," said Bres.

"I will," Sreng answered gladly, and he unfastened his thick-shafted javelins. "What do you think of them?"

"I see," said Bres, "huge weapons, broad-pointed, stout and heavy, mighty and keen-edged. Woe to him whom they

should smite, against whom they should be cast. Death is
in their mighty blows, destruction is in but one descent of
them; wounds are in their hard plying; overwhelming is
the horror of them. What do you call them?"

"Battle javelins are these," said Sreng proudly.

"They are good weapons," said Bres. "Bruised bodies
they mean, gushing gore, broken bones and shattered
shields of the hosts that go against them. It would be well
for us to make a covenant and compact."

They did so. Before they parted Bres gave to Sreng one of
the two long spears he had brought with him as a warning
to the Fir Bolgs. "Take this," he said, "and show it to
your people. Tell them it is a specimen of the weapons of
the Tuatha de Danann. Tell them they must give my people
battle, or the half of Ireland."

"On my word," said Sreng, "I would prefer to give you
half of Ireland rather than face your weapons. But ours
have sharp blades, too. Take this javelin to show your
people how well the Fir Bolgs are armed."

They parted from each other with respect.

Sreng of the Fir Bolgs hurried to Tara, and told his story.
"Stout are their soldiers, manly and masterful their men,
bloody and battle-sure their heroes. Very great and strong
their shields, and hard and broad their blades. Hard it is
to fight with them. Better to make a fair division
of the land, and to give them half of Ireland as
they desire."

"We will not grant that, indeed," said the Fir Bolgs,
"for if we do the land will all be theirs."

That message was carried to the Tuatha de Danann. After
much parley they demanded of the Fir Bolgs when they
wished to give battle.

"Some delay is called for," said the Fir Bolg nobles, cunningly. "We shall have to prepare our spears, and mend our mail, and shape our helmets, and sharpen our swords and make suitable attire, for this will be an important battle, and we would not wish to enter it hastily. And you, too, will prepare your weapons, and make such javelins as we have shown you."

So they arranged an armistice till their equipment should be ready and they were prepared for battle. Six weeks of summer, half the quarter, had gone when the appointed day of combat came.

The Fir Bolg hosts arose on that day with the first glimmer of sunlight. The painted, perfectly wrought shields were hoisted on the arms of brave warriors, the tough, seasoned spears and battle javelins were grasped in the right hands of heroes. In firm, close-packed companies they advanced to give battle to the Tuatha de Danann. Their poet Fathach went before them to describe their fury, and recount the story of the battle. The Tuatha de Danann formed a compact, well-armed host, marshaled by fighting warriors, and provided with deadly weapons and stout shields. Every one of them pressed on his neighbor with the edge of his shield, the shaft of his spear, or the hilt of his sword, so closely that they wounded each other. As the two forces met and their warriors paired in combat, the sunbeams shimmered on the swords' graven grooves, the duels were a dazzle of shattered light. For a whole day the combat continued, and great numbers were destroyed.

On that day the Tuatha de Danann were defeated and returned to their camp. The Fir Bolgs did not pursue them across the battlefield, but returned in good spirits to their own camp. They each brought with them into the presence of their king a stone and a head, and made a great cairn of them. Their wounded they healed in the thick green waters of the wells of healing that their physicians had prepared.

At the battle next day, strong mighty blows were dealt by the battalions on both sides. Their swords were twisted by continual smiting. In the hand-to-hand combats the swords broke on splintered bones. The warding was well timed, the guarding was gallant, and rapid the rending blows. There was straining of spears, and shivering of swords, and shattering of shields, and battering of bodies. When the night fell, the Fir Bolgs were driven across the battlefield.

After the conflict next day the Fir Bolgs were neither happy nor cheerful, and the Tuatha de Danann were sad and dispirited.

The battle on the fourth day was a flaming mass full of changing colors, many feats and gory hands, of swordplay and single combat. Fierce and pitiless and terrible the work of spears, and cruel swords and javelins. The furies and monsters and hags of doom that hovered over the battle-field cried aloud, so that their voices were heard in the rocks and waterfalls, and in the hollows of the earth. The warriors fixed pillars on the ground, and chained them-selves to them to prevent anyone fleeing till the stones should flee. They lunged at each other with their keen sharp spears till the short shafts were twisted through the quivering of the victims on the points. The edges of the swords turned on the lime-covered shields, the curved blades were tempered in boiling pools of blood in the thighs of warriors.

Loud was the singing of the lances as they cleft the shields, loud the noise and din of the fighters as they battered bodies and broke bones. Boiling streams of blood took the sight from the gray eyes of resolute warriors. It was then that Bres made an onset on the Fir Bolg army, and killed a hundred and fifty men. Then Sreng, the mighty champion of the Fir Bolgs, dealt a blow with his sword at Nuada, the king of the Tuatha de Danann, and cutting away the rim of his shield, severed his right arm at the shoulder. The king's arm with a third of his shield fell to the ground, and the king fell beside it. It was then that he called aloud for help, and his warriors hearing him rushed to protect him.

So weary were the warriors on both sides that neither was capable of attacking the other. Their swift blows had grown feeble through all the slaughter, and their spirits had fallen because of all their ills, and their courage faint through the vastness of their disaster, and so they parted.

The Fir Bolgs were wounded and full of heavy reproaches. They considered what it was their interest to do, whether they should leave Ireland in defeat or undertake to share it with Tuatha de Danann.

The Tuatha de Danann took counsel, and their decision was to offer the Fir Bolgs their choice of the provinces of Ireland, while a compact of peace and goodwill was made between the two people. The Fir Bolgs chose Connaught, and took possession of the province.

As for the triumphant De Danann, King Nuada had lost his swordhand, and with it his throne, for the Tuatha de Danann—and all Irishmen after them—would not be ruled by a man who was maimed or blemished in any way. So the sovereignty went to the warrior Bres.

But his seven-year rule was full of arrogance and injustice, and the people murmured against him. He stripped them of their jewels and their treasures, and even their food. He made vassals of his warriors, and servants of his captains. Moreover, his court was not sumptuous and hospitable as a king's court should be. The knives of his people were not greased at his table, nor did their breath smell of ale from the banquet. Neither poets nor bards nor pipers nor trumpeters nor jugglers nor buffoons were engaged in entertaining the assemblies of the court.

Once upon a time the high poet Corpre came a-guesting to Bres's house. But the king did not offer him the hospitality to which he was entitled, or the honor which was his due. Instead he was given a cabin, narrow, dark, and poor, wherein was neither fire nor furniture nor bed. Three small cakes, and they dry, were brought him on a little dish. On the morrow he arose, and he was not thankful. As he went across the garth he composed a satire on the stingy king, and that was the first satire made in Ireland. From that hour naught save decay was on Bres, till finally the people rose against him, and again made Nuada their ruler. The artificers had made him a silver hand so cunningly contrived that it had all the movements of a hand of flesh, and so lovely that none could call it a blemish.

Out of the misty Celtic past has come this legend, which begins the story of Ireland. Sometime in the centuries before Christ strange ships touched Irish shores, strange men fought with the people who were already there for possession of the land. Who were they, and from whence did they come? Ask that question of a sage, and have a cautious answer. The newcomers, says the sage, were probably part of the Celtic inhabitants of Central Europe.

"And when did they come, O Sage?"

"Perhaps four or five centuries before Christ. Surely no longer ago than that."

"And whom did they find in Ireland, O Sage?"

"They found the Picts, my child, a people so sturdy and stubborn that it was hundreds of years, well into the Christian era, before they were subdued."

The legends tell a gaudier tale, and in them birth is given to names that live in Ireland today. Three thousand years ago, they say, there was discontent in Ireland. Heavy tribute was laid on the people by the Fomorians, the fierce people of a neighboring island. So the sons of Nemed consulted their wizard, and asked his advice.

"Depart if you feel the time is ripe," said the wizard, "do not suffer wrong, pay no more tribute. Your sons or your sons' sons will recover the land from which you are now fleeing."

"Is that your advice to us, Fintan?" asked the sons of Nemed.

"It is," said Fintan, "and I have yet more counsel for you; you must not go by one route or in one direction, for a fleet cannot be brought together without outbreak of fighting; a large number means quarreling, strangers provoke challenge; and an armed host, conflict. You do not find it easy to live together in any one spot in Ireland, and it would not be any easier for your hosts in seeking new homes."

Immense was the fleet, eager the gathering, that set out for the east. They spread in different directions, as Fintan had advised. One group was storm driven to the dry strands of Thrace and the sandy shores of Greece, where they settled. Thereupon the inhabitants and champions of the land visited them, and made a compact of peace and concord with them. Territory was apportioned them, but on the seashore, on the distant borders, on cold rough stretches and rugged rocks, on the hillsides and mountain slopes, on inhospitable heights and in deep ravines, on broken lands and ground unfit for cultivation. But the strangers transported great quantities of soil to the smooth, bare rocks, and made them into smiling, clover-covered plains.

When the chiefs and the powerful men of the land saw the smooth broad and grassy fields, and the wide expanses of fruitful, cultivated land, they expelled the newcomers, and gave them in exchange wild, rugged regions, hard, stony lands infested with poisonous serpents. And again they carried earth in their leather sacks, and made of the wilderness good fruitful fields. And for this reason they were called Fir Bolgs, or Men of the Bags.

Their numbers increased and multiplied, till they counted many thousands. The tribute grew heavier and their labors harder. But now they had grown to be a powerful company and they resolved to make wide, curved boats of their woven bags that they used for carrying soil, and sail again to Ireland.

Two hundred years had passed in exile. It was the same time that the famous warlike children of Israel were leaving Egypt in search of the Land of Promise.

The Fir Bolgs made boats of their sacks, and stole some of the galleys of the Greeks. They killed every one of the Greeks worth killing that they could get hold of, and devastated their land. They brought plunder and spoil to the place where the galleys were, and the smooth, black-prowed boats they had made of their sacks and bags. One thousand, one hundred and thirty was the number of their ships that put out for Ireland. They reached the land of their fathers, and were masters of it for thirty years.

It was then that their high king dreamed of strange birds, and that dream came true with the return of the Tuatha de Danann to Ireland, those other descendants of the sons of Nemed, whose exile had been spent in northern lands. They defeated the Fir Bolgs at the battle of Moytura, and made themselves rulers of the land.

But as they ruled, new conquerors sailed toward them. From the flat, hot sands of Egypt they came, descendants of Scota and Gaedhal Glas. Their wanderings took them to Spain, and from there they set out for Ireland. Eight sons of a captain named Milesius were leaders of the new invaders, and from them the people were given the name of Milesians.

They battled with the De Danann for the possession of Ireland, and routed with great slaughter. It was at the battle of Tailtenn, in Meath, that the Milesians gained supremacy. Legend says that the victors claimed half the land, and took as their share everything aboveground. The De Danann were given everything underground, and it was under the hills they went, and became the ancestors of the fairies, the Little People, whom superstitious Irishmen of today still think they see on moonlight nights.

Chapter II

MACHA OF THE RED HAIR

⋙⋘

HE GAELS loved this green new land to which they had come. Isle of the Woods, they called it, and Inis Elga, the Noble Island. They made a division of it between themselves, the surviving sons of old Milesius casting lots for their share of the land. Eremon took the northern half of the island, and his brother Eber the southern. The children of their brothers Ir and Ith, who had been slain in conflict, were sent to the far eastern corners of the land.

The kings Eremon and Eber cast lots, too, for the poet and the harper who had come with them. To Eber of the south went the tuneful, accomplished harper, and to Eremon of the north the professor of poetry. And it is a matter of boast with the north to this day that it has always excelled in poetry, just as the south of Ireland has been noted for the sweetness of its stringed music.

Sumptuous and orderly were the courts of these legendary kings. Seven reigns after Eremon gold was first smelted in Ireland, and ever after the old tales are bright with gleam of great brooches, and goblets for brown ale. And red and brown and crimson dyes, it is said, were found in the island in this reign, so that clothes were now gaily stained. And when in the reign of the next king other dyes had been found, the Gaels adopted a code of colors for their clothes. One color only could be used in the garment of a slave; two in the clothes of rent-payers; three in those of soldiers; four in the habits of goodly heroes or young lords of territories; five could be used in the uniform of an army leader. A chief poet or professor of learning might wear six colors, and kings and queens dressed proudly in garments of seven hues.

A king had seven occupations. On Sunday he was at ale drinking; Monday the government of the tribe took his time; Tuesday he played at chess; Wednesday he watched greyhounds coursing. Thursday was dedicated to the pleasures of love, Friday to horse racing; Saturday he sat in judgment on his people.

These were the occupations of petty kings. At Tara ruled one who claimed fealty from them all and whose glory outshone them as the sun outshines the stars. Historians say that the eminence of Tara began about the time of Christ, and that before that there were no high kings in the land. But legends say that Ireland was always divided into fifths, and that a king at Tara dominated them all.

But Tara's glory was once rivaled by another royal seat, and Emain Macha was its name. How came it to be called that? Not hard to tell, the old tales say.

Three kings were over Erin in cosovereignty some three centuries before Christ. Their father had been king before them, and to his three sons he left the sovereignty in turn. So the brothers, namely Dithorba and Cimbaeth, and Aedh Ruadh, which means Red Hugh, arranged that each should rule for seven years in turn.

And they gave guarantees between them, seven druids, seven poets, and seven captains. The seven druids were to scorch them by incantations, the seven poets to satirize and denounce them, the seven captains to wound and bruise them if each man of them did not vacate the throne at the end of his seven years. They reigned three times, each man of them, that is, sixty-three years. Then Red Hugh was drowned, and the Ass-an Roe, Red-Haired Man's Cataract, the place of his drowning is still called.

He left no children but one daughter, Macha Mong Ruad, and that red-haired amazon demanded her father's turn of ruling. But her uncles said that the throne would not be given to a woman.

A battle was fought between them, and Macha was victor. Seven years she spent on the throne, and Dithorba her uncle was killed in the Corann in that time. So his five good sons thought to take the rule in his place, but Macha would not resign it to them, saying that it was not from securities she had obtained it, but on the battlefield by force. So on the battlefield they tried to take it from her. But again Macha gained the victory, so that a slaughter of heads was left upon the field. Macha kept the throne, and her five cousins she sent into banishment in the wilderness of Connaught.

After that she took Cimbaeth to be her husband, and she gave him the command of her soldiers. When they had formed this union, Macha sent out to discover the sons of Dithorba. With dyes and dough she disguised herself as a leprous woman, and she traveled alone till she found her quarry in the Bairenn of Connaught, busy cooking a wild hog. The men asked news of her, and shared their supper with her at their fire.

Then, warm and fed, their thoughts became amorous. Said a man of them, "Beautiful are the eyes of the hag. I would go apart with her." He took her with him into the woods alone, but when they were far from the others Macha tied that man by main strength, and she left him in the woods. When she came again to the fire his brothers asked for him.

"He was ashamed to come back to you after walking with a leprous woman," said Macha.

They said to her, "That is no shame, and we will all of us do the same."

Each man of them took her into the wood, and she tied each of them by main strength, and carried them in one tie to Ulster.

The men of Ulster proposed to have them killed, but Macha Mong Ruad would not have it so. "It would be the defilement of the righteousness of a sovereign," she said, "but they shall be condemned to slavery, and shall raise a rath around me which shall be the chief city of Ulster forever."

So she marked for them the outlines of the fort with the brooch of gold from her neck, and Emain Macha, or the Brooch of Macha, the great fort was henceforth called. The Navan fort is the name it is known by now, and visitors to Armagh may still trace the double enclosures of its ramparts.

The right to rule in Ireland has always rested largely on the sword. Kings' sons have followed their fathers on the throne for generation after generation, but never was it inheritance alone that put them there, but strength and cunning, too. And all too often the line of succession was broken by someone whose strength was greater, and whose sword was sharper.

Two generations after red-haired Macha had won renown as a warrior, and as the only woman who ruled over all Ireland, Cobtach the Slender murdered the King of Ireland, his own brother, and his brother's son, and usurped the throne. Labraid, the grandson of the slain king, was saved only because he had been dumb from childhood, and so was not eligible to rule. But while playing at hurley one day with some comrades he happened to be hit on the side of the head with a caman. The blow restored the use of his speech to Labraid and, blemished no longer, he was fit to rule. This fact did him little good, however, since he had no means of seizing the throne. But he possessed one quality, not uncommon with Irishmen, which was to be worth an army to him.

He had grown up to be a handsome young man, but was still in poverty and exile, when his great-uncle Cobtach summoned the men of Erin to the Feast of Tara, and Labraid went, like everyone, to partake of it. When they were happily consuming the banquet provided by the king, the eulogists on the floor were lauding the kings and queens, the princes and nobles of the gathering.

"Tell us," said the king ingenuously, "who is the most hospitable man in Erin?"

Craipthene the Harper answered him. "It is Labraid Loingsech, the grandson of your brother. I went to him in the spring, and he killed his only ox for me."

Said Ferchertne the Poet, "It is true that Labraid is the most hospitable man in Erin. I went to him in winter, and though he possessed only one cow, he killed her for me."

"Go away all of you, then," said Cobtach in anger, "since you think him more hospitable than I."

So the three men went to the west, and found refuge with Scoriath, the king of the land of Morca.

"You shall have good comradeship here as long as I live," said the king, welcoming them. "Prince and harper and poet are welcome to my court."

The king had a daughter, Moriath, beautiful and young. The mother's two eyes never slept at the same time for guarding her, and no stolen hour of dalliance was to be had with her. But Moriath and Labraid came to love each other, and they made a plan between them. The king was to hold a great feast for the men of Morca, and Craipthene the Harper would be there to play for them. Now there were three tunes which every chief harper had to be knowing. There was the slumber tune, which from its deep murmuring caused all who heard it to fall fast asleep, and the laughing tune, which from its merriment made everyone who heard it to break into laughter, and the tune which because of its plaintiveness caused everyone within hearing to weep bitterly.

So for the sake of the young lovers, when the feast was over Craipthene picked up his harp, and the strains which came from it were not the gay ones usual for a banquet, but the soothing sounds of the slumber tune. Before they could know what was happening to them, the whole court was asleep, and the young lovers came together.

Not long afterward the queen awoke, and aroused the king. "This is an ill slumber which has fallen on us, indeed. Our daughter has now a woman's breath. Hearken to her sigh after her lover has gone from her."

But the anger of the royal pair was calmed when they learned that it was Labraid who had taken their daughter's love. They called another feast, a wedding feast this time, and Labraid and Moriath sat side by side as husband and wife. Then Labraid went abroad, and found friends and soldiers in the country beyond the sea, and when he returned to Ireland it was at the head of troops. The high king was at Dind Rig, the royal residence of Leinster. There Labraid marched, and he burned the Dind when the high king and thirty other kings of Erin were within it, and he made himself king over all Ireland.

His foreign soldiers had brought with them to Ireland broad spears called laighen (len) and from them Leinster is said to have received its name. Ferchertne the Poet said it was as far as the Ictian sea that Labraid went on his journey, and that the number of foreigners he brought back with him was two thousand and two.

Do not regard this testimony too lightly. Scholars whose work is with the past have found the tale plausible, though it is here embroidered with fantasy and fiction.

Even in the old days, the poets of Ireland were people of great learning, and the right to a poet's training was a hereditary one, jealously guarded by certain ancient families. There were seven orders of poets, and twelve years was the time it took to reach the highest rank. A chief poet had to be master of the hundreds of metrical forms which Irish verse might take, he had to know by heart more than three hundred of the old tales which were told by generation after generation of poets, he must needs be versed in the secret language of poets.

But when the years of study were over, honor and riches awaited a chief poet. He ranked next to the king, and like a king his banquet share of meat was a fine steak. He practiced his art only before kings and nobles, in the great courts of the land; lesser poets sang for lesser people. His journeys were made on horseback, and over him tinkled a little musical branch of gold, whereas the musical branch carried by poets of lower rank was only of silver or bronze. And his most prized perquisites were the chief poet's chair, and the poet's mantle, worn only on state occasions, made of the soft crests of bright-colored birds.

At about the time a certain star was shining over Bethlehem, and a mighty king, Conor Mac Nessa, was ruling in Ireland, the son of Erin's chief poet went to Scotland to study. Legend says that one day when he was by the sea a wave whispered to him of his father's death. So the young poet Nede hurried to Emain Macha, and there met Bricriu of the Evil Tongue. And for the gift of his purple tunic, with its adornment of silver and gold, Bricriu promised him his advice and intercession in becoming chief poet.

And Bricriu told Nede falsely that Ferchertne, the second of his name to be a renowned poet, and the likely successor to Nede's father, was cold in death, when in truth Ferchertne was to the north of Emain Macha, bringing wisdom to his pupils. And he gave Nede advice regarding his appearance, since Nede was boyish as regards age.

"No beardless man is ever made chief poet in Emain Macha," he said. So the boy took a handful of grass and cast a spell upon it, so that everyone would suppose it was a beard that was on him. And he went then and sat in the poet's chair, and wrapped the mantle of honor around him. These were the colors of that robe: golden crests on the upper half of the mantle, and white and speckled skins of birds from the girdle downward.

Thereafter Bricriu went to where Ferchertne was teaching, and said to him, "Sad it is for you that a young boy has taken the chair of chief poet. A young and honorable man is wearing the soft mantle that his father wore before him."

So Ferchertne hurried to the palace, and complained to the king that a youth whose beard was made of grass had taken the seat that belonged to one of many years and long training. Conor Mac Nessa then decreed that the two poets should compete for the post of chief poet, and the court gathered to hear their learned reasoning. And learned it was, and clever, but the court knew nothing of what was said, for the whole discourse was in the ancient language of the poets, and what was said was known to the two contestants alone. Then Conor became angered, and he decreed that hereafter the poets' training should be given to all who sought it, and that it should not be the monopoly of a few.

The greatness of Ferchertne's wisdom had overcome young Nede, and he wrapped the older poet in the mantle, and knelt to him, and acknowledged him as chief poet. Graciousness was in Ferchertne's reply to him. "Stay with me, thou little in age and great in knowledge. May thou be a casket of poetry, may thou be a king's right arm. May thou be high in the land."

So the court of Emain Macha was glorified by two learned poets instead of one.

Chapter III

CONOR MAC NESSA, KING OF ULSTER

T THE time of Christ, Conaire the First was High King of Ireland, a ruler so noble, just, and mild that men's voices are said to have sounded as melodious as lutes during all his reign. And while Conaire ruled at Tara, Ulster's king was Conor Mac Nessa. But it is the name of the lesser king that has been in the mouths of men since those times, and the reason for it was partly for a deed that was no credit to him, the sadness that he put on Deirdre of the Sorrows. But he was a princely man, too, and at his court of Emain Macha he had the greatest jewel in all Ireland, the champion Cuchulain, whose sword was ever ready to sing battle music. And besides this, Conor had for an enemy the covetous Queen Maeve of Connaught, and the story of the war she made against him will never have its last telling.

The legends say he was named from his mother, Nessa, daughter of Eochaid Yellowheel, King of Ulster. This was why she was called Nessa. In those days it was the custom for children to be placed in fosterage, that they might have many parents to cherish them. There were twelve foster fathers fostering the girl according to Eochaid's desire.

Assa was the name they had for her at first, for it was easy (assa) to foster her.

Now one day there happened to come to the house where Eochaid's daughter lived a champion who was also a wizard, Cathbad, son of Ross. The girl's fosterers were all slain by Cathbad in a single night, and no one knew who had wrought the slaughter. After this the girl went a-championing, and took arms, and fared forth with two comrades, throughout all Ireland, that she might know who it was had killed her fosterers. And she laid the tribes waste: she devastated all equally, because she knew not her foes in particular. "Let her be called Ni-hassa" (not easy), said everyone. Henceforth Nessa was her name.

Then she went a-soldiering into the province of Ulster. She went one day there alone to bathe, when there came to her the same champion Cathbad. He came between her and her spear shafts, and she became his beloved wife, and bore him a son, whose name was Conor Mac Nessa.

He grew into dignity and wisdom, and mingled with the nobles of the land. His mother was then in widowhood, and desired by Fergus, son of Ross, who had the throne of Ulster. As a bride price she asked that her son be given the kingship for the space of one year, that it might be said that his children were the descendants of a king. "That is fair enough," said Fergus.

Then Nessa began to instruct her son and his fosterers, and his household, to strip every second man, and to give his wealth to another. And her gold and her silver were given to the champions of Ulster, for the benefit of her son.

At the end of the year, Fergus claimed his pledges. "A colloquy about it," said the Ulstermen, and took counsel in an assembly. They deemed it a great dishonor that Fergus

had given them to Nessa as a bride price. But they were
thankful to Conor for his goodly gifts to them. This then
was their suffrage: "What Fergus sold, let it part from him.
What Conor bought, let it stay with him."

So then Fergus parted from the kingship of Ulster,
and Conor became its king. Ulster, Leinster, Connaught, and
Munster were the provinces of Ireland in those days, and
their kings' courts were goodly in the manner of the court
of the high king at Tara. Poets and historians told the court
their tales, harpers played for them, physicians cured them,
cupbearers served them, strong men guarded them. By his
very look did fierce, shaggy-haired Triscadal kill any who
came into Conor's presence without a welcome. It was
needful to hearken to the decision of the house steward,
who ruled seat and bed and board for all. Treasure keepers
hoarded the king's jewels and golden chessmen. Swift
runners, both men and women, who could "circle Erin in
a single day," were ready to carry his word throughout
the island. Charioteers, horsemen and kitcheners, swine-
herds and waiters all had their place in the king's household. And for amusement the king kept buffoons and jesters
and jugglers. Nine swords a keen juggler could take in his
hand, and nine silver shields, and apples of gold. When he
threw them all upward, none fell to the ground, and only
one of them was on his palm at a time. Each of the play-
things rose and fell past one another like bees bearing honey
to their hives on a day of beauty.

So there was much dignity and delight and fame and
conspicuousness in the household of Conor Mac Nessa.

And his fame was made greater by the valor of his battle
heroes, the Knights of the Royal Branch, though the Red
Branch Knights is the name that others give them. They

were great heroes for guarding Ulster, and when their chariots swept into battle, loud was the clamor of wheels, the clash and rattle of arms, and like thunder the hoofbeats of their horses.

The Red Branch was the name of their house, and it was like to the king's house in the manner of its making: that is, its walls were of red yew, with copper rivets making them strong and beautiful. Thrice fifty were the number of rooms in that house, and three couples in every room. In the Speckled House were the warriors' shields and spears and swords, and the name was given it because the house was speckled with the brightness of the hilts of the swords, with their bands of silver and gold, and the gold and silver rims of the shields that sparkled in the firelight, and the brightness of the goblets and drinking horns.

This is why the weapons were taken from the warriors. Whenever they heard any rude thing, or a word not to their liking, unless they took vengeance for it at once, every man would rise up against another, so that each of them was smiting his head and his shield on another throughout the house. Wherefore their weapons were taken from them and kept safe apart from them.

These men, and many others, hung their shields in the Speckled House: Conall the Victorious, who never slept without the head of a Connaughtman beneath his knee, Laegaire the Battle Winner, Dubtach the Beetle of Ulster, and Eoghan his son, and Naoise, Ainnle, and Ardan, the three sons of Usnach. But the greatest and bravest of them was Cuchulain, son of Sualtam. His fame was a shout that could be heard in every land.

He was nephew and foster son to Conor Mac Nessa. When he was seven years old he heard the king's druid say,

"Who takes arms on this day will have a short span of life, but his fame will be greater than any other." So Cuchulain put off his playing suit, and went to the king. "What I want is to be taking arms this day," he said. And when he had the king's permission he picked up a spear, and went out to seek combat with friend or foe.

All the fighting men in Ulster had a hand in his bringing up, and when he was at an age to learn them he was sent to study battle feats with the woman-warrior Scathach in Scotland. Young men went to her from many countries, and many an Irish champion learned from her how to hurl a spear and swing a sword. She taught Cuchulain all the arts of war, and all the feats of a champion, so that there was no warrior in all Ireland better with weapons. It was said that when his strength in fighting was weakest he could defend himself against twenty, and that when his full strength was in him he could fight alone against forty. For dread of him fighting men turned from battle, and whole armies went backward from fear of his face.

Fleet, and brave, and beautiful the legends have him. The ease of his running was like water from a high cliff; like the rapid thunder was the speed of it. And his sad, dark face was so beautiful to the women of Ireland that they were forever setting their love upon him. Three fifties of them in Emain Macha loved him, and that was not pleasing to the other men of the land. So Conor sent out nine messengers to search throughout Ireland for a bride for Cuchulain. His equal in rank and age and skill was the requirement Cuchulain set. And it was Cuchulain himself who found such a woman, when all the messengers failed. She was Emer, daughter to Forgall the Wily, who kept one of the six great houses of hospitality in Ireland.

Of all the maidens in Ireland Emer was the one Cuchulain chose to court. The gifts which made her pleasing to him were her lovely face, her sweet voice, her skill with a needle, her wisdom, and her chastity. And besides these, he saw over the bosom of her gown the whiteness of her breasts, and for this he loved her, too. So he took her as a bride to Emain Macha, and for honor to Cuchulain the king did not claim his right of her.

Now at this time Connaught was ruled by Queen Maeve, and her husband Ailill. Maeve had once been married to Conor himself, but they were too large for one nest, and Maeve had married in turn the King of Leinster, and Ailill of Connaught. Both Maeve and Ailill were children of kings, and each of them had pride enough for many. As they were having pillow-talk one night they began to compare their possessions, because Maeve was angered that Ailill called her a rich man's wife.

"I was as well off before ever I saw you," said Maeve. "High King of Erin was my sire, and of his six daughters myself was the noblest and seemliest and the goodliest of them in bounty. I was the best of them in battle and strife and combat. 'Twas I had fifteen hundred mercenaries of the sons of aliens exiled from their own lands, and as many more sons of freemen of this land. It was I plighted thee, and gave purchase price to thee, which of right belongs to the bride: namely, the raiment of twelve men, a chariot worth thrice seven bondmaids, the breadth of thy face in red gold, the weight of thy left forearm in bronzed silver. I am a rich man's wife! Hagh! A man dependent upon a woman's bounty is what thou art!"

So each one ordered that their possessions were to be brought to them, even the least, that they might know

which had the most treasures and riches and wealth. Their
pails and their caldrons and their wrought-iron vessels
were brought to them; their jugs and their keeves and
their eared pitchers were fetched in to them. Likewise their
rings and bracelets and thumb rings and their golden treasures, the fillets of gold for their hair, and the crowns they
wore only in battle.

Their flocks of sheep were led in; horses and steeds and
studs were brought from pasture and paddock; their droves
of cattle and swine and the roaming flocks were led from
the brakes and waste places of the province.

All these were counted and numbered and claimed, and
were the same for both, except that Ailill had a special
brown bull that Maeve could not equal, and the White-
Horned was its name. And it was the same to Maeve as
if she had not owned a pennyworth, forasmuch as Ailill
could exceed her in the matter of the bull.

So she sent out messengers throughout all Ireland to
find her a bull the equal of the White-Horned. They
returned and said that a man of Cualnge, in Ulster, had a
bull better than any in the land. The Brown Bull of Cualnge
was the best animal on four hoofs. So when Maeve could
not hire the bull peacefully, she set out, with her husband,
and her army, and her court, to make a raid into Ulster.
And she rallied the other provinces of Ireland to her, so
that four-fifths of Ireland was against Ulster alone. And
they brought with them men of music, and of amusement,
and of eulogy, that the more conspicuous might be the
ravages.

Now because of an old curse Macha Mong Ruad had put
on the men of Ulster there was a sickness that used to
weaken the warriors of the province whenever danger was

upon them, and this sickness came on them all, except the boy-troop of Emain Macha, and Cuchulain, because one of his ancestors was said to be out of the elf-mounds. So Cuchulain alone stood in the Gap of Ulster, and hindered Maeve's forces. A hundred warriors every night was what he used to destroy.

"Our hosts will not last long in this fashion," said Maeve. She sent terms to Cuchulain, that he should have treasure, and bondmaids, and chariots, if he would stop his fighting. But what Cuchulain said was that the bondmaids should be sent to the kneading troughs, and to the querns to grind corn; that he would have none of them. His terms were that a single champion of the men of Erin be sent to contend with him each day. The while he stayed that man, Maeve's army would be permitted to continue its march. When he would have slain that man, another warrior should be sent to meet him at the ford of battle. And whatever Ulstermen were injured or wounded near by him, Maeve's leeches should heal them, and be paid no price for the healing. And whatever daughters of kings or of princes should love him, Maeve should provide the bride prices.

"Better one man a day, than a hundred every night," said Maeve. But Cuchulain quickly killed all that met him in conflict, so that it became hard for Maeve to find one to face him. It was then she sent for Ferdaid, head of the fighters of Connaught, that she might persuade him to go against Cuchulain. But Cuchulain and Ferdaid were friends, having learned their feats of arms together with the lady Scathach in Alba, and Ferdaid was loath to cast a spear at a comrade. But Maeve dispatched druids and poets of the camp, and lampoonists, to Ferdaid, to the end that they might make satire and scoffing speeches against him, and mock and revile and disgrace him if he did not come to the tent of Maeve and Ailill.

Ferdaid went to them for the sake of his honor, forasmuch as he deemed it better to fall by shafts of valor and bravery and skill than to fall by the shafts of satire, abuse, and reproach.

Ferdaid was honored and waited on in Maeve's camp, and choice, well-flavored strong liquor was poured out for him, till he was drunk and merry. Finnabair, daughter of Ailill and Maeve, was seated by his side. It was Finnabair who placed her hand on every goblet and every cup Ferdaid quaffed, and gave him three kisses with every cup. It was she who passed him sweet-smelling apples over the bosom of her tunic. And she ceased not to say that her darling and her chosen sweetheart, of all the world's men, was Ferdaid. And when Maeve had him drunken and merry, great rewards were promised him if he would make the fight and combat against Cuchulain.

She promised him a chariot worth twenty-eight bond-maids, and the apparel of twelve men, and land and wine and gold, and Finnabair to be his wife, if he would make the combat.

In the morning Ferdaid's charioteer put horses to his chariot, and Ferdaid drove to the ford of battle. Heavy were the reproaches which Cuchulain cast on him for making the fight against a friend.

"Do not be remembering our friendship," said Ferdaid, "for it will be no protection to you."

Each of them was very busy casting spears from morning's early twilight till noon at midday. However great the excellence of throwing on either side, equally great was the excellence of the defense so that during all that time neither of them bled or reddened the other. But from the middle of day to the hour of evening's sundown, each of them bled and wounded and reddened the other all that time.

"Let us leave off now," said Ferdaid.

They threw their arms from them into the hands of their charioteers. Each went toward the other in the middle of the ford, each of them put his hands on the other's neck, and gave him three kisses. Their horses were in one and the same paddock that night, and their charioteers by the same fire. And their charioteers made ready a litter-bed of fresh rushes for them, with pillows for wounded men on them.

Then came healing and curing folk to care for them, and they laid herbs and grasses and curing charms on their cuts and stabs, their gashes and many wounds.

Early on the morrow they rose and went to the ford of combat. In their chariots they engaged that day. And when the hour of evening's close was come, their horses were spent, their drivers wearied, and they themselves—the heroes and warriors of valor—were exhausted.

They threw their arms away from them into the hands of their charioteers. Each of them went toward his fellow. Their horses were in the same paddock that night, and their charioteers by the same fire.

The curing and healing men came to attend and watch and mark them that night, for naught else could they do, because of the deepness of their cuts and stabs, but apply philters and spells and charms to stanch their blood and lighten their deadly pain.

Early on the morrow Ferdaid rose in evil mood and with a dark mien. Cuchulain also had no happiness in him. The warriors resorted to swords that day, and were engaged in smiting each other from the twilight of early morning to the hour of evening's close. They parted without a kiss or blessing or other sign of friendship that night. Their horses were not in the same paddock, and their charioteers were not at the same fire.

Great was the rage of the warriors next day, and that he might surely win the victory, Cuchulain's charioteer prodded him with sharp words. "The battle warrior that is against thee shakes thee as a fond woman shakes her child. He washes thee as a cup is washed in a tub. He grinds thee as a mill grinds soft malt. He pierces thee as a sharp tool bores an oak. He binds thee as the woodbine binds the tree. He pounces on thee as a hawk pounces on fledglings, so that no more hast thou the right or title or claim to valor or skill in arms, thou little imp of an elf-man."

At this Cuchulain made for Ferdaid with the violence of a dragon and the speed of a bloodhound. And his great Spear of the Feats cut through Ferdaid's shield into him, till every joint and every limb was filled with its barbs.

"Ah, now that sufficeth," said Ferdaid. "I am fallen by that blow, indeed." Whereupon Cuchulain cast his shield from him, and hastened toward Ferdaid. He clasped him in his arms and bore him northward over the ford, so that he should die in honor, on the land to the north. And Cuchulain mourned that through him Ferdaid had come to his death.

"There shall not be found the hand of a hero who wounds warriors' flesh, like cloud-colored Ferdaid. None held up shields on the field of battle that was the equal of the ruddy son of Daman. No sons of kings had better fame than he. Sorrowful am I that through treachery of a queen he is brought to his death." And the funeral games of Ferdaid were held.

Then Cuchulain sent word to Conor Mac Nessa that help should be sent to him, since he was no longer able to protect all the gaps and passes of the mountains against Maeve's folk. The measure of his wounds was such that he could not bear any garments to touch his skin, so that spancel hoops held his cloak from him. There was not the space of a needle point from his crown to his soles without wound or sore.

Thereafter Conor rallied his warriors, and with thirty hundred spear-bristling chariot fighters proceeded to the Ford of the Spearpoints. For a whole day the earth was not naked with their passing.

"I do not make much of them," said Maeve, when she heard of the hosting. "We have goodly warriors and stout youths to deal with them."

When the morning of battle came all the men of Ulster arose at one time, in the train of their king. And in this wise they rose, stark naked all of of them, their weapons in their hands. Each one whose door looked to the east went through the tent westward, for he deemed it too long to go round by it.

And when Cuchulain heard the noise of battle he burst his bonds of healing, and he set out to attack the men of Erin. He drove his chariot at Maeve's captain, and the captain turned in his course from him, and the men of Erin turned with him, and broke their ranks westward over the hill. At the time of sunset when man and tree were no more to be known apart, Maeve and the last company of the men of Connaught fled in rout westward over the hill. Then Ailill and Maeve made peace with the men of Ulster, and with Cuchulain. For seven years there was no killing of men among them.

It was during this time that Conor and his nobles went to the house of the king's chief storyteller to enjoy a feast. Fedlimid, son of Dall, was the name of the man. And while the king and his people were lighthearted and merry, soothed by the gentle music of the harpers, and the melody of the voices of the bards and poets, and the excellence of the food and ale, it happened that the storyteller's wife brought forth a daughter.

And Cathbat the druid named the girl Deirdre, and made a prophecy about her, that hurt and harm and evil would come to the province because of her, and that sorrow would be her lot. When that prophecy was heard by the warriors of Ulster they designed to kill the girl on the spot. "Let it not be done," said Conor. "It is foolish to fight against fate, and evil comes to one who would destroy a babe. I will take the child under my own protection, and I assure the men of Erin by the securities of moon and sun that anyone who ventures to destroy her, either now or again, shall neither live nor last if I outlive him."

And Conor took the child under his protection, and placed her in a moat apart, in a fortress of the Red Branch. Lavarcham, the king's conversation woman, was sent to care for her. For fourteen years the nurse-mother was teaching Deirdre all the knowledge she herself had, and a poet's training had been hers. There was no plant springing from root, nor star gazing from heaven, nor bird singing from spray, for which Deirdre had not a name. A drop of blood in bodily form was never lovelier than that girl, who grew to be as lithe and fair as a sapling, and as straight and graceful as a moorland rush. Her skin was white as the swan on the lake, and her movements like the hind on the hill.

A high tremendous wall guarded this treasure, and no man could come near her, for Conor designed her for himself. But once on a snowy day a calf was killed outside her window, and the blood of the calf was poured out on the snow. Then, as Deirdre watched, a raven bent down to drink the blood.

"That is the appearance of the man I would marry," said Deirdre. "The color of the raven on his hair, the color of the calf's blood on his cheek, and his skin as white as the snow."

"There is a man the like of that in Conor's household," said Lavarcham. "His name is Naoise. He is son of Usnach, and his brothers, from whom he never parts, are Ainnle and Ardan."

When Deirdre heard this, great melancholy and sleeplessness came on her, so that for love of her foster child Lavarcham brought the girl and Naoise together. When Deirdre saw the young warrior, her blood became warm within her, and she gave him three kisses, and a kiss to each of his brothers. And Naoise gave her love that he never had for another living thing.

One island could not hold Conor and any who went against him, so Deirdre and the sons of Usnach set out for Alba, and the brothers took military service under the ruler of that land, who took them into his friendship.

Deirdre's beauty was still a curse to her, and the King of Alba came to desire her. But Deirdre's flame was all for Naoise, and the thing was not accomplished. Then the King of Alba gave commands to the sons of Usnach to go into dangers and battles and difficulties, in expectation that they would be slain. And besides this, the men of Alba were assembled to slay them. This was clear to Deirdre, and she warned the others. They all departed that night, and went to a sea-girt isle.

At this time Conor was lamenting that he had lost both his intended bride and three of his best warriors, and he sent a message to Naoise promising him welcome in Erin. The messenger brought guarantees of peace and friendship, but Deirdre distrusted that it was with treacherous design that the king sent for them.

Their journeyings are not told of till they came to the plain of Emain. Then Deirdre said to the sons of Usnach that, if Conor asked them into the house with himself and his nobles, he did not mean to deal treacherously with them, but if they were sent to the House of the Red Branch it would be ill for them. "Great are thy fears, woman," said Naoise. "Conor sends us to the House of the Red Branch and we go."

Conor himself began to long for Deirdre and he sent a messenger to see if her old beauty of form remained to her. "I give you my word, Conor," said the messenger, "that Deirdre has the best form and appearance of all the women of the world."

It was then that Conor said, "Arise, ye men of Ulster. Surround the House of the Red Branch, and set it in crimson flames of fire."

When Deirdre and the sons of Usnach saw that they were betrayed, the three brothers came out to the Ulstermen, and great numbers fell by them. They made an enclosure by joining their shields together, and placed Deirdre between them, and made an assault upon the troop. Then Conor's command was that the sons of Usnach be slain, and when their blood had gone from them, the Ulstermen raised three great shouts of sorrow on their account.

As for Deirdre, whose beauty has caused these deeds to be done, she did not smile for the space of the year she shared Conor's couch. The strings of her heart were broken, and she gave no smile to her mouth during all that time. And when the king saw that he was not pleasing to her, his love for her left him, and he gave her over to Eoghan. After the king himself, there was no one Deirdre liked less than this man, since it was he whose sword had pierced Naoise. And Conor knew that this was true.

The two men placed her in a chariot to take her to Murthemn, where Eoghan had his home. Conor sat at her right side, and Eoghan by her left hand. One look of sorrow and despair she gave them, and they laughed.

"That is the look of a ewe between two rams," said Conor. Whereupon Deirdre's unhappiness overwhelmed her, and she hurled herself at a large stone by the chariot track, so that she broke her skull and killed herself.

After this Conor was wounded by a brainball that was in time the cause of his death. In those days the men of Erin used to take the brains of their slain enemies, and mix them with lime, that they might keep them for trophies. One of these balls, speeding from the sling of an enemy, pierced Conor's skull. His physician would not remove the ball, saying that if he did so the king's brains would fall out, and he would die. He cautioned the king not to let lust or anger overcome him, not to eat greedily, and not to mount a horse. In this manner the king lived seven years. For a third of the day he watched the boy-troop of Emain Macha, another third he spent in drinking ale till sleep should overcome him.

Legend says he died on the day Christ was crucified. On a spring afternoon he was sitting with his nobles when light turned to darkness, winds sprang up, and trees lashed about in fury. The king's druid was asked the meaning of this.

"Far away, in a strange land, a glorious Man is being nailed to a cross. Two thieves die beside him. He gives up his life for love of his fellow men, and his name will live forever," said the druid.

Anger filled the king at hearing of this terrible and unjust deed. He rushed from the house, pulling out his long-sheathed sword. As he hacked fiercely at a growth of saplings he hurled his voice against the rushing winds. "This, this, this," he shouted with every blow, "this is how I would avenge that sweet Man's death, could I but reach his murderers."

And his mounting anger caused the brainball to burst from him, and he died.

Chapter IV

PAGAN FIRES

➤➤〉〈〈〈

"WHAT IS the sweetest thing you have heard?" an Irish king was once asked.

"Not hard to tell," he replied. "The shout of triumph after victory, praise after labor, a lady's invitation to her pillow."

"What is best for a king?"

"Not difficult to answer. Best for him firmness without anger, patience without strife, affability without haughtiness, taking care of ancient lore, hostages in fetters, honoring poets, many alms, importing treasures from overseas, silken raiment, a sword-smiting troop to protect every tribe. Let him attend to the sick, crush criminals, give true judgment, foster every science, improve his soul, buy treasure, utter every truth, for it is through the truth of a leader that God gives all that."

It was nearly seventeen hundred years ago Cormac Mac Art asked those questions of himself, and had his answers ready. Were they honest answers, and did he live up to them? Any reader of Irish history will tell you that he did. He was the king who brought to the halls of Tara their brightest glory; under him the Fianna, the great band of

Irish warriors, reached their greatest strength; he built the first water mill in Ireland to grind corn for his Pictish mistress; he gathered together the old laws of Ireland for the first time; he wrote the *Instructions of King Cormac Mac Art*, from which two questions have been quoted. He was one of the great half-gods who moved through the dawn of actual Irish history. About his name there twines gray mist of legend, but the outlines of the great halls he built on Tara's hills are still visible, and no historian questions either his existence or his greatness.

It was in the middle of the third century that he lived. Many kings had ruled in Ireland since Conaire the Great had blessed the country with plentiful crops and clement weather. Many of them had been good kings, and Irish trees had bent from the weight of fruit, for in those days it was thought that the worthiness of the country's ruler influenced the weather. "His reign was not thunder-producing or stormy, and the wind did not take a hair off the cattle from the middle of autumn to the middle of spring," the annalists wrote of Conaire.

Evil was Ireland's state later in that first century, in the reign of Cairbre the Cat-Headed; fruitless her corn, for there used to be but one grain on the stalk, her cattle milkless, her rivers free of fish. Plentiless were Irish woods, for there used to be but one acorn on the oak.

The Cat-Headed One was a plebeian, of the rent-paying classes. These descendants of conquered people held no land by tribal right, and what little ground they had to till they paid for dearly. It was never plain-land of richest soil, or well-watered hilly land, or even axe-land that could be cleared for crops of corn and flax and herbs. The unfree tribes were not trained in use of arms, and what weapons they had were the crude knives and axes of the poor farmer. But led by Cairbre, who stirred them to revolt, they overthrew the government of the nobles, and were masters of Ireland for many years.

Tuathal the Desired was the king who overcame the revolutionists, and again put the nobles in power. So grateful were the people to him that they allowed him to take land from the four provinces of Ireland, and form the royal territory of Meath, the high king's own domain. He built for himself four royal residences in every part of the new province.

One he built at Tlactga, in the part that Munster had given him, and he ordered that the old festival of the Fire of Tlactga be held there every year. It was there that the druids of Ireland gathered on the eve of Samain, which is now called Halloween for the purpose of making a sacrifice to all the gods. While the Samain fire was blazing, and the sacrifices were burnt, no other fires burned in Ireland, under pain of punishment. When the ceremonies were over, the men of Erin were allowed to kindle no fire except from the sacred one, and for every fire kindled from it, the King of Leinster received a tribute.

In the part that Tuathal took from Connaught he built a residence at Usnach. There the men of Ireland came to the Fair of Usnach to exchange their goods and their wares and their jewels. The sacrificial fire they lit there was to the sun-god Bel, the archgod of their pagan faith. And it was also their custom at Beltain to light two fires in every district. Between these fires the men of the province drove a pair of each kind of cattle, that the animals might be protected against the cattle diseases of the year. And since the ground of Usnach had been taken from Connaught, it was ordained that the king of the province should receive as tax the horse and garment of every chieftain who came to the great convention.

Tailtenn was the name of the third chief residence that Tuathal built, Tailtenn, the place of the Marriage Fairs. The conduct of the meeting was most proper and becoming, the men on one side of the place of assembly, the women on the other, the while their fathers and mothers were arranging the contracts and agreements. No man came near the maidens, no damsel heard the soft sigh of a lover, till all was arranged for them. Tailtenn had been Ulster land, so Ulster's king was allowed to exact a tax of an ounce of silver for every couple united during the ceremony.

In that part of land which Tuathal had taken from Leinster was Tara, but Tara had been a royal residence for Irish kings for ages past, and Tuathal had no part in the making of its glory. Indeed, it would be a hundred years until Cormac Mac Art would build the great House of a Thousand Soldiers, and the House of Hostages, and the pleasant sunhouse of the women, and the Great Banqueting Hall, where the men of Ireland feasted.

Between Tuathal and Cormac there would rule a king, Felim the Lawgiver, whose fame lies in the fact that he died on his pillow. There would be Conn of the Hundred Battles, who rushed into battle as a wave rushes up the beach. Conn was a mighty warrior, but in his time he had to divide the kingship with another man, so that to this day the north of Ireland is known as Leath Conn, Conn's Half, and the south is Leath Mogh, Mogh's half. After him Conn's son would rule as Art the Solitary, and the usurper Lugaid Mac Conn would seize the throne, and

Fergus Blacktooth of Ulster would hold it for a while against the rightful ruler, Cormac Mac Art.

The land was replete with all that was good during Cormac's reign, the gifts of the sea were in abundance. From every river that was but knee-deep a salmon was got from every mesh of the net; a sack of wheat was produced from every ridge of land. Calves were commonly born after three months' gestation. Kine shed their milk without cessation, so that vessels enough could not be had for it. Then Ireland, say the *Annals*, was a land of promise, exempt from all necessity of herding and watching, free of theft and violence, and with no man perplexed in the matter of either meat or raiment.

Cormac was grandson of Conn of the Hundred Battles, and his father was Art the Solitary. But between the reign of Art and his son the throne was held by the usurper Lugaid Mac Conn, and Cormac was not suffered to be at court. The king did not know that the herdboy employed by the widow Bennaid was his nephew, who should have had the throne. But this knowledge came to him when the sheep that the boy guarded trespassed on the royal domain, and ate some greens used in dyeing cloth. Lugaid's queen, as owner of the greens, charged the widow Bennaid with the loss, and the case came before the king.

"Let the sheep be forfeit for the damage they have done," was the verdict of the king.

"Not so," exclaimed Cormac, who was present as herdboy. "That is an unjust decision for a king to give. The cropping of the sheep should be sufficient for the cropping of the greens, the wool for the woad, for both will grow again."

"That is a true judgment," cried all the people, "and he who makes it must surely be the son of a king." For in those days kings were the judges, and wisdom in judgment was held to be the gift of rightful kings only. So Cormac's identity became apparent, and in fear of the usurper he fled. Even when Lugaid died Cormac could not claim the throne, for the jealousy of Fergus Blacktooth caused him to have Cormac's beard burned by a candle, and this blemish kept him from the throne for another year.

Many good things besides clement weather came to Ireland in Cormac's time. It was he who first brought mills for grinding corn to the land. Some men of Ulster had made a raid into Scotland, and they brought back with them into captivity Ciarnait, daughter of a Pictish king. When Cormac heard reports of the fairness of the prize, he sent to demand her, and she was taken to his house. Of all women who lived in her time it was said she was fairest and none surpassed her in loveliness. Soon the measure of the king's love for her was great.

Cormac's wife, Ethne, heard of the girl, and was jealous. She said the two of them could not be with Cormac together. And while a king may be powerful in battle and in the government of the people, he cannot always rule his own household. In Ethne's presence Cormac became meek and gave Ciarnait into the queen's keeping. She put a thrall's work upon her. Nine bushels of corn a day ground at the quern was the weight of her thralldom. It was no task for an idler.

But Cormac still longed for her, and found means for them to come together secretly. Soon Ciarnait was great with child, and was unable to grind. Still the queen demanded her nine querns a day. Cormac took pity on his mistress, and brought a millwright across the sea from Scotland, so that a mill was made to help the beautiful slave girl. Until the memory of men now living a mill stood on the very place where the king's orders caused that first mill of all Ireland to be erected, and the keepers of it were proud to claim descent from the original millers.

Tara today shows other ruins of the grandeur of Cormac's days. On Tara hill he built a great sunhouse for the women, and a House of Hostages, for every king had hostages in fetters. In his time Cormac made three circuits of Ireland, and he took a hostage from every fort. The House of a Thousand Soldiers was built then. "A shining fort, not obscure to posterity. Seven hundred feet was its measure. Fierce folly did not hold sway over it, or strictness of harsh wisdom. Nine walls it had, which fierce fights could not demolish. Nine ramparts encircled the illustrious and impregnable fort.

"Commotion of lances was about the dwelling of the king, wherein was poured out sparkling wine. Thrice fifty warriors with coronets, and with gold gleaming from their weapons, guarded the king. Three hundred feet was the measure of that house, and seven cubits the measure of the great fireplace. Seven chandeliers blazed in the palace. Fifty heroes stood up in the presence of the king. Thrice fifty cup bearers carried ale in gold and silver goblets. Fifty above a thousand were enumerated in the household of the king."

And when he called the great feast of Tara, the greatest fair of all Ireland, great dignity was on the assembly.

Every third year was the great feast called, to preserve laws and rules, and to decide what was best for the country.

There came the men of Erin to one place, for three days before Samain and for three days afterward. They were constantly drinking throughout that week, but "without theft, without wounding, without feat of arms, and with rest from the exercise of horses. Whoever did any of those things was a wretched enemy with heavy venom. Gold was not received from him, but his soul in one hour."

At the nightly banquets, all were seated according to rank. Each man sat under his own shield, and these had been arranged before the great company entered the hall. Those with the greatest honor sat nearest the king, and those with lesser honor were in their proper places. Trumpeters called them to the hall when marshals had arranged all matters of seating, so that there was no question or disorder about the placing of the nobles. Each went without question of precedence to sit under his own shield.

All the men of Erin had meat according to their due. To king and chief of poets went a fine steak; minor poets had less tender cuts. The heads of the beasts went to physicians and stewards, and to stout smiths. Shanks were for jesters, chess players, sprawling buffoons, pipers, and jugglers. To musicians, artificers, and masons went the shins. Cupbearers and servants were given the broken meats to consume. Backs were eaten by druids and doorkeepers. The due of the strong, skilled folk was the fat underside of the shoulder.

At these gatherings the high king sat midway of the hall, his face to the west. A sword-length away to his right sat the King of Ulster, and an equal distance to the left the King of Munster. The King of Leinster faced him, and at his back was Connaught's king.

Beautiful was the appearance of Cormac in that assembly, according to the old tales. Flowing, slightly curling, and golden were his hair and his parted beard. A golden buckler, with stars and markings of gold and fastenings of silver, was upon him. Crimson his coat, with wide descending folds, and at his throat was set a brooch of precious stones. A torque of gold encircled the kingly throat. A white shirt entwined with golden threads was on him. Of gold, too, and set with precious stones was the girdle about his waist. Two spears with golden sockets in his hands, with many rivets of red bronze. Without blemish and without reproach, and beautiful of form and symmetrical was this great king.

Forty-two years was the length of Cormac's reign, and in spite of the freedom from violence which the annalists claim for it he fought thirty-one battles while he had the throne. The men of Ulster went against him, and forced him into retirement for the space of a year. And when he regained the throne he had trouble with the men of Leinster. They came to Tara, and invaded the House of the Virgins, where were kept alive the fires in honor of the sun and moon, and put the maidens to the sword. For that deed Cormac slew many Leinstermen, and he lifted with the sword an increase of the Boru tribute, which had first been exacted from Leinster by Tuathal. As eric-fine for the shameful death of his two daughters Tuathal had levied the tribute, to be paid every two years to the High King of Ireland. Many battles were fought over this tribute during the reign of forty kings, and in his time Cormac exacted it as often as the wealth of the province allowed. Great numbers of cattle and swine and sheep made up the tribute, and many articles of rich cloth, and chains of silver, and caldrons of brass.

The martial career of the great king was ended by an accident, and his life afterward was that of a scholar and writer. One day in the red Rath of Tara it became known that Cellach, son of Cormac, had violated a woman. In the disturbance which followed Cormac was blinded in one eye by Aengus of the Dreadful Spear.

Little did the avenger know what profit was to come from the blemish he inflicted on the king.

In his retirement he turned scribe, and collected in one great book all the laws and regulations of the land, which governed the people of Ireland till Elizabeth's English laws supplanted them. The *Book of Aicill* it was called, since the place of its writing was Aicill, close to Tara.

Cormac's name is also linked to the *Psalter of Tara*, but tradition claims an older authorship for it, and it is possible that he merely revised it, and put it in the form in which it has come down to us. "In this Psalter is all the best we have of history," says an old poem. "In it is set down what is the right of every king of a province, what is the right of the king of Tara in the East from the king of every songful province." Correlations and synchronizations it counted, and the limits of every province "marked by a stone-rick."

The *Book of Aicill* is the great monument of the old Irish legal system, and no one would say that the *Psalter of Tara* was without value to historians, but it is the third book of Cormac's writing which shows best the beliefs and customs of those remote days, and displays Cormac not only as a king but as a man. *Instructions of King Cormac Mac Art* it is called, with Cormac questioned by his son Cairbre, and the old king replying.

"For what is a prince selected over a country?" asks Cairbre of Cormac.

"Not hard to tell," answers Cormac. "By virtue of shape and race and knowledge, through wisdom and rank and liberality and honesty, by virtue of hereditary right, by strength of fighting and an army is kingship taken."

"O Cormac, Grandson of Conn, what is the true right of a king?"

"Not hard to tell, my son. Let him restrain the great, exalt the good, put down robbers, check theft, protect the just, and bind the unjust."

"O Cormac, grandson of Conn, what is best for the welfare of the country?"

"Not hard to tell, my son. Meeting of nobles, following ancient lore, keeping treaties, learning every art, listening to elders, turning a deaf ear to the rabble, guarding the frontier from every evil."

"O Cormac, grandson of Conn, what is best for me?"

"Not hard to tell, if you listen to my teaching. Do not give your honor for ale or for food, for it is better to save one's fame than it is to save one's food. Be not proud, unless you be a landowner, do not keep bridled steeds without a stud of horses, do not give banquets without brewing ale, do not dress elegantly unless you possess sheep, for pride without husbandry, luxury without horses, banqueting without ale, elegant dress without sheep are a crime in the gathering of the world."

"O Cormac, grandson of Conn, what is good for me?"

"Not hard to tell, if you listen to my teaching. Do not deride the old, though you are young, nor the poor, though you are rich, nor the naked, though you are clad, nor the lame, though you are swift, nor the dull, though you are clever. Be not too wise, be not too foolish, be not too conceited, nor too diffident, be not too haughty, be not too humble.

"If you be too wise they will expect much of you; if you be too foolish you will be deceived, if too humble you will be without honor; if too talkative you will not be heeded; if too silent you will not be regarded; if too harsh you will be broken; if too feeble you will be crushed.

"Do not race against a chariot, nor against the cast of a spear, nor up a great height, nor against the surf of the sea, nor against danger, nor a lance. Do not join blasphemy, be not sorrowful in an ale-house, be not forgetful of an assignation, do not be a bush of discord."

"O Cormac, grandson of Conn, what are the dues of a chieftain of an ale-house?"

"Not hard to tell," said Cormac. "Good behavior around a good chief, light to lamps, exerting oneself for the company, a proper settlement of seats, liberality of dispensers, a nimble hand at distributing, attentive service, music in moderation, short story-telling, a joyous countenance, welcome to guests, silence during recitals, harmonious choruses."

"O Cormac, grandson of Conn, what were your habits when you were a lad?"

"Not hard to tell," said Cormac. "I was a listener in woods, I was a gazer at stars, I was blind where secrets were concerned, I was silent in the wilderness, I was talkative among many, I was mild in the mead-hall, I was stern in battle, I was gentle toward allies, I was a physician of the sick, I was weak toward the feeble, I was strong toward the powerful, I was not close lest I should be burdensome,

I was not arrogant though I was wise, I was not given to promising though I was strong, I was not venturesome though I was swift, I did not deride the old though I was young, I was not boastful though I was a good fighter, I would not speak about any one in his absence, I would not reproach, but I would praise, I would not ask, but I would give, for it is through these habits that the young become old and kingly warriors."

"O Cormac, grandson of Conn, how do you distinguish the race of Adam?"

"I distinguish them all, both men and women, sons and daughters."

"How is that?" asks Cairbre.

"Every steadfast person is wise, every generous person is righteous, every patient person is persevering, every studious person is learned, every one who loves his kindred is gentle, every healthy person is joyous, every athlete is dull-witted, every madcap is a laughingstock, every uninformed person is quarrelsome, every lover likes a dainty bed, every wealthy person is fond of jewels, every genial person is generous, every horseman is nimble, every falsehood is bitter, every truth is sweet, skillful women are honey-mouthed, bad women are given to trysting, ill-met are their sons, woe to him who has them."

"O Cormac, grandson of Conn, what is the worst thing you have seen?"

"Not hard to tell, my son. Faces of foes in the rout of battle."

"O Cormac, grandson of Conn, what is the sweetest thing you have heard?"

"Not hard to tell. The shout of triumph after victory, praise after labor, a lady's invitation to her pillow."

"O Cormac, grandson of Conn, how do you distinguish women?"

"Not hard to tell. I distinguish, but I make no difference among them. They are crabbed as constant companions, they are haughty when visited, lewd when neglected, silly counselors, greedy of increase, steadfast in hate, forgetful of love, accustomed to slander, stubborn in a quarrel, not to be trusted with a secret, ever intent on pilfering, boisterous in their jealousy, slanderers of worth, scamping their work, stiff when paying a visit, disdainful of good men, viragoes in strife, sorrowful in an ale-house, tearful during music, lustful in bed, eager to go into society, exceeding all bounds in keeping others waiting. They utter what they do not perform, they attempt what they do not finish, they vow what they do not make true, they destroy what they do not save. Woe to him who humors them. Better to whip them than to humor them, better to scourge them than to gladden them, better to beat them than to coddle them.

"He will have neither honor nor life nor fame who listens to bad women," says Cormac to Cairbre.

"They are waves that drown you, they are fire that burn you, they are keen weapons that cut you, they are serpents for cunning, they are darkness in light, they are bad among the good, they are worse among the bad."

Almost forty years had been the time since Cormac's quarrel with Ethne about Ciarnait, but against which of the women his rancor stirred has not been told.

Tradition says that Cormac was one of three persons in Ireland to become a Christian before the advent of Patrick, and legends say that his conversion was the cause of his death. After being forty-two years in the kingship of Erin he died at Cletty, the bone of a salmon having stuck in his throat. Mailgenn the druid, it was said, was the one who caused the spirits to attack him in this manner, and to give him a painful death.

"Cormac had told his people not to bury him at Brugh, which was a cemetery of idolators, the resting place of those who adored stones and trees and sun and wind and fire, but to bury him at Ross-na-righ, with his face to the east. But when he was dead, his servants of trust held a council, and came to the resolution of burying him at Brugh, where his predecessors the kings of Tara were buried. Thrice they raised this body of the king to carry it over the Boyne to Brugh, and thrice the river rose so that they could not make the crossing. Then fear at violating the testament of a king came to them, and they dug Cormac's grave at Ross-na-righ as he had himself ordered."

Chapter V

FINN MAC COOL AND THE FIANNA

->>><<<-

OMETIMES AN Irish farmer of today, digging
deep into the soil, comes upon blackened
earth, and huge stones still crusted with
soot. He straightens his back then, and his
voice shrills with excitement as he calls
to whoever is near him, "Look at this now.
Here is a cooking-pit of Finn Mac Cool's men. Finn and the
Fianna feasted here." And his heart leaps within him, for
Finn Mac Cool was the greatest chieftain that the Fianna
of Ireland ever had, a famous tree for upholding battle,
and a bush of shelter for brave warriors.

The Men of the Fianna, what grand, brave fighters they
were, lithe, sunburned warriors who hindered robbers and
strangers from beyond the seas from coming into the island,
and from any bad thing finding root on her soil, men who
served their king as equals, and kept order and rule in the
land.

Perhaps it was the threat of a Roman invasion that
brought them into being. At any rate, Conn of the Hundred
Battles organized the famous fighting force at a time when
Roman legions held Britain, and looked for even more lands
to conquer. Seven battalions, with three thousand warriors

in each battalion, Conn could muster in time of war, but if peace was over the land only three battalions were kept in arms. Each of the provinces of Ireland contributed its own clan to the Fianna, and each clan had its own commander. Of these, the Clan Baskin, of Leinster, under the command of the mighty Finn himself, and the Clan Morna, captained by crafty old Goll Mac Morna, were rivals in the time of Cormac Mac Art, since Goll had slain Finn's father in the battle of Cnucha.

They were an infantry force always, and the chariots in which the Red Branch Knights had swept into battle were known to them, but formed no part of their equipment. Neither did they build enduring forts, since it was their plan to move easily over the island, camping out during the summer, and being quartered on the people in the winter. They loved a life of activity, and when they were not compaigning they constantly practiced their feats of running, leaping, wrestling, and hunting. It is no wonder they became great champions, and that they found fame for themselves and their leaders. It was in the time of Cormac Mac Art that they came to their greatest glory, and that glory lives after them, in the stories and songs that are known as the *Fenian Cycle*.

They were not common soldiers, trained simply to kill. Hard, indeed, were the tests one had to pass to join the band. No candidate was considered unless he, his family, and his clan were prepared to accept for him death or maiming in battle, without seeking satisfaction or vengeance, except what his brother warriors would give. No candidate was considered who was not a full poet. And no warrior was accepted who was less than six feet tall.

As to the strength, bravery, and agility of those who came to Finn, they were tested in many ways. Not a man of them was taken who could not ward off the blows of nine warriors, casting javelins at him from nine ridges away, and he in a trench to the depth of his knee. Not one was taken till he was started at a run through Ireland's woods, while men seeking to wound him followed in his wake, having between him and them at the start the interval of but one forest bough. Should he be overtaken, he was wounded, and not received into the Fianna. If his weapons quivered or trembled in his hands, he was not received. Should a branch in the wood be disturbed by him in his running, or a quivering leaf be left behind, he was no man for Finn. Neither was he taken should one lock of his braided hair be roughened by branch or bough. So light must his step be that in running he cracked no dry branch beneath his feet; so even his pace that he might pluck, without pause in his flight, the thorn that had lodged in his foot. And unless, at full speed, he could jump a stick the height of his brow, and stoop under one as low as his knee, he was no man for Finn.

And when the warrior had performed all these feats four vows of chivalry were laid on him as a final condition of his admission to the Fianna. He had to promise to marry his wife without dowry, choosing her for her manners, her beauty, and her virtue. He had to promise gentleness to all women, and the sharing of everything he possessed with anyone who stood in need. He was bound by his vows to fight at all odds, even nine to one.

But when he became one of Finn's men, what a life for a young man to live, making camp with his comrades at the end of the day, joyous from the hunt or from battle,

swimming with them, graceful as otters, in the Boyne or
the smaller streams of the inland, grouping themselves at
nightfall around their campfires, to feast and to sing songs
of bravery and love. Two crafts these heroes came to
with a will were fighting and love-making, and when
they were not busy at them, they liked to sing of their
conquests.

For six months of every year the Fianna lived in the open,
making their camp each night. From spring's beginning to
autumn's end they slept on triple beds of green branches,
new rushes, and fresh moss. All summer long they lived by
the chase, and the fruits and berries that grew in the woods.
All over the island were forests where none but Finn
and his men might hunt. They followed deer with hounds,
and hunted wild boar, and swift hares. Wild pigs they
chased with spears. Salmon they had from the Boyne, and
other fish from the coasts of Beare. Squirrels were brought
to their cooking pots, and birds out of the oak woods,
speckled eggs from the cliffs, otter from the hidden places
of the Doile, eels thick and green, and tender woodcocks,
and beside these, blackberries, haws of the hawthorns,
hazelnuts, cress in the early summer, and sprigs of wholesome gentian. Purple bogberries grew for their delight,
strawberries and raspberries ripened, sloes turned from
green to red-black.

Their ears loved the sounds of the forest, dogs' voices in
the glens following deer, the belling of mighty stags, the
calling of the foxes. Their music was the voice of the lin-
net, the sweet sadness of the thrush, the clamor of herons
at night, the martens' song in the mysterious wood. They
rested at noonday on the long hair of the heather, and
dreamed at night of white breasts of women.

"What music do you like best?" Finn asked of some of his chief men as they were gathered around a fire.

"To be playing at games," said Conan the Bald, who was a man with a good hand for an enemy, but of little sense elsewhere.

"The music I like best is to be talking to a woman," said Diarmuid of the Love Spot, and trouble enough that music brought him.

"My music is the outcry of my hounds," said Luigaidh's son, "and they putting a deer to its last stand."

"The music of the woods is best to me," said Finn's son Oisin. "The sound of the wind and the cuckoos and the blackbird, and the sweet silence of the crane."

But Oisin's son Osgar said, "The best music is the striking of swords in battle," and that was the answer that pleased Finn most.

What Finn himself had a mind for was to be listening to falling water, the cries of the blackbird, the waves of the ocean beating the strand, the scream of the sea gulls, the screech of crows over battle, and the little noise of ripples vexing the breast of a boat.

It was said that the three things which kept up the Fianna were Finn's knowledge, the swiftness of lean gray Caoilte, and the combativeness of Conan the Bald. There was great venom in Finn's sword, and anyone pierced by it never tasted food in his life again.

Finn was a king in his own right, and a poet, too, and his words of wisdom were sweet to his people. As a fighting man there was none better than Finn, and whatever good was said of him, he equaled it twice over. He never denied a hungry man food, or a woman her bride price. He never promised what he could not fulfill, and he never forsook a friend. He was gentle in peace and fierce in battle, and his sons, and his sons' sons followed him in that.

His father, Cool, too, had been a royal man, and head of the warriors of the Fianna before Finn was born. As he went to battle one day he passed by the house of a smith, but only the smith's daughter was within. Muirenn the Long-Haired she was called. Cool went in to her, and then passed on to battle.

When the smith returned he noticed a change in his daughter. "When I went away," he said, "you had the look of a maiden. Now you have the slow glance of a wife." Cool was killed in battle, but his seed lived after him, and the son born to the smith's daughter surpassed even his father in fame.

Finn had a great house at Almhain, and in winter when the men of the Fianna were quartered on the people of the country he lived there, with many of his captains around him. And it is said that everyone who stayed with him there had a golden helmet around his head, and a shield with gold markings, and soft garments of noble satin. Fifty of the best sewing women of Erin were kept busy making garments for the Fianna, and there was no warrior among them without a satin shirt, a clean, smooth, wadded tunic, and upstanding gilded headpiece. They each had a hard sword for splitting heads, and two spears for each man's hands. At the hunting each man loosed two swift, fierce hounds.

It was the people of Ireland and the king who had to pay for all this. The chief commander of the Fianna had the right to quarter his men, their hounds and attendants, free of charge on the country during the winter months. He had the right to have a whelp raised in every house in the island. He had the right to hunt all game, fish, fur, or feather. And besides, he had the right to claim any woman about to be married as a wife for one of his men.

In time the Fianna misused this power and became haughty in their demands. When they opposed the marriage of the daughter of the high king himself till tribute should be paid them, that monarch, Cairbre of the Liffey, son of Cormac Mac Art, disbanded one of the clans. Then strife arose between the king and the Fianna, and the two forces met in combat. Just before the battle the two armies kissed the ground in token that they would die on the field or leave it victorious. After rising they gave three great war shouts, and then rushed upon their enemies. So fierce was the combat, and so truly did the warriors keep their vows of victory or death, that the battle of Gowra practically annihilated the Fianna, and they never recovered their great power.

Were there women warriors in the Fianna? One might think so, after hearing Finn's daughter Luigtach, who put away her womanhood and hunted on the rough hills with the men; of Goll Mac Morna's famous woman runner, and of the death he dealt to the three daughters of Conara the Odd. There is the story of Crimora, the daughter of Rinval, bright in the armor of men, her bow in her hand, who followed her much-beloved Conall to battle. She drew her bowstring on one of the enemy, but her erring aim sent the arrow to Conall's heart. Like a rock from the shaggy hill he fell, and after a day and a night of mourning Crimora followed him in grief.

Women do not play very heroic parts in the tales of the *Fenian Cycle*. They were admired for the whiteness of their throats, the softness of their sides, the dimples of delight that played on their cheeks, but when it came to combat the laurels went to men. In an old tale called "The Little Brawl at Almhain" there is an account of a conflict in which women seem to have figured as fighters, without gaining any great glory. The story recounts the splendor of Finn's great house, the beauty of the golden goblets which served the guests, the formality with which they were seated at table. It tells of the old enmity of Finn for Goll Mac Morna, who had slain his father in battle. It tells of the little quarrel between the two men, which became a quarrel of both the leaders' clans, and which finally grew to a bloody battle.

"An ill place it had been for a feeble invalid, or delicate taper-fingered invalid, or aged senior of long date to be in the little brawl at Almhain on that night," says Standish O'Grady's translation, "a-listening to the groans of young and old, of high and low, as they lay, maimed and faint and infirm, or were stricken down and cut up. At this game they endured from the first of the night to rising of the morning' sun, nor ever gave each other quarter.

"In the morning the Fianna's losses were examined, and those of Finn's people were eleven hundred men and women, for many a most noble and hitherto fortunate lady, and lovely woman of many charms, gentle maid of sweet discourse, and gallant warrior, were fallen there, while many a slashed nose, many an eye ruptured, many an ear lopped, many a leg shorn through the bone, arm chopped, carcass mangled, and side bored in holes had such of Finn's people as still lived.

"As for Goll and his good folk, the clan Morna, of them were wanting none but fifty men and women; it was not that the women were slain, but that with fear they simply died. Every one of them that was curable was put to be treated, and for as many of them as on either side were slain, very deep and broad graves were dug. Then that great house of Almhain was cleansed, and again every one of them seated himself in order of nobility and patrimony, in which guise they passed fourteen days, and at such period's end they repaired to Tara."

The object of their journey was to have the high king, Cormac Mac Art, decide on the justice of the quarrel, which he did with a wisdom which pleased both sides.

And it was at Cormac's court at Tara that there began the romance of Cormac's daughter Grainne, and Diarmuid of the Love Spot, a romance which has lived in lovely words through all the centuries. One morning Finn Mac Cool rose up early. "And it is an early rising," he said, "when you cannot see the sun between your five fingers, nor distinguish the leaves of the oak from the beech."

Oisin, Finn's son, asked the cause of the early rising.

"I am without a wife since Maighneis died," said Finn, "and no man has slumber or sweet sleep who is without a fitting wife."

So Finn's people, loyal to him in love as in war, arranged a match between their chief and Grainne, the daughter of Cormac Mac Art.

But at the betrothal feast Grainne, who had set her love on Diarmuid, put bonds on him that he should take her away. He went reluctantly, his vows of honor making him do what any woman asked, his loyalty to his chief making his heart heavy within him. Each morning he left unbroken bread beside the place where he and Grainne had camped, as a sign to Finn that they were living in honor. And he reproached the woman, saying that he was like a deer or stag, passing his days along remote glens, or like the night owl, lamenting pleasure in every place. "From a king's palace you took me," he cried, "to be an exile all my days." From Tara to Athlone they fled, tracked by Finn's followers, who had no heart to be pursuing one of their comrades. And in time peace was made between Finn and the lovers, and Diarmuid and Grainne settled down to a life of happiness at the hill of Keshcorran.

But rancor lived in Finn's heart, and when the wild boar of Benbulben, which the men of the Fianna were hunting, injured Diarmuid, Finn would not use the healing power his hands possessed to cure the man of beauty. And when Diarmuid was dead, and his friends would have made war with Finn, the old chief, seeing his own people set against him and being a man of craft, wooed Grainne cunningly and with sweet words.

But she neither heeded nor hearkened to him, but told him to leave her sight, and straightway assailed him with her keen, sharp-pointed tongue. However, Finn left not plying her with sweet words and gentle, loving discourse, until he brought her to his own will, and he had the desire of his heart and soul of her.

When his people saw them together, they raised a cry of mockery and derision, so that Grainne bowed her head through shame.

But if dishonor cast its shadow on him there, Finn shines more brightly in other tales. The *Colloquy of the Ancients*, by far the finest collection of Fenian tales, is supposed to be an account of the Fianna's great deeds, given to Patrick by his son Oisin more than a hundred and fifty years later. They are legends only, but legends of a man who undoubtedly lived, and lived gloriously, in the third century after Christ.

After the overthrow of the Fianna, Oisin is supposed to have been carried away to the Land of Youth, under the Western Ocean. He returned to mortal existence, and to Ireland, when Patrick had brought Christianity to the land. Patrick converted him, but he was a somewhat reluctant convert, and his heart would often think with longing of the brave days of his youth. "Sad it is, Patrick," he would say to the saint, "to be thus feeble, a poor blind old man. After being a hero I now listen to clerics and to bells. If Finn were here, I would abandon them; I would follow the deer from the glen, and lay hold of its foot."

He was forever longing for bygone joys, the warbling of the blackbirds of Litir Lee, the sound of the waves of Rughraidhe lashing the shore, the resounding cries of the chase. He never ceased to glory in the prowess of his old comrades. To Patrick he would say innocently, when the cleric was telling him of God's power, "If I saw my son Osgar and God tussling hand to hand, and if I saw my son go down, then I would say your God was a stronger man." And all Patrick's scolding and talk of blasphemy would not disturb the old man's loyalty to his pagan days. "There never sat a cleric in a church," he would say, "though melodiously they chant psalms, more true to his word than the Fianna. They never shrank from combat, they were not niggardly in bestowing gold. By truth and the might of our hands we came safe out of every conflict. Inquire of thy God, holy Patrick, whether he recollects when the Fenians were alive, either in the east or in the west, men their equal in time of fight."

Chapter VI

THE COMING OF PATRICK

->>><<<-

HE SWEETEST music to my ears," said Osgar of the Fianna, "is the sound of swords striking in battle." That was a happy choice for him, for there was seldom a time in Ireland when the din of battle was not to be heard. The clash of spears on shields, the war cries of the heroes, the screams of the vultures hovering over the scenes of conflict, had mingled over battlefields almost without ceasing since the first invasion of the land.

But with the coming of Christianity the battle music was to be muted for a while, the sound of church bells and the chanting of monks would lull the martial spirit of the land, and love of learning would take the place of love of fighting. This change would come about gradually, and it is pleasantly ironical to note that the new manner of life would be due indirectly to a hostile act by a war-loving king, a man whose very name has a martial sound. Niall of the Nine Hostages was the king, who was not content to lift his sword against Irish enemies alone, but carried it to Alba and to Britain. From each of the five provinces of Ireland he took a hostage to Tara as

73

pledges of his power, and four more he carried from conquered Alba.

But countless Irish kings have fought and plundered without changing the destiny of the land. It was a boy brought by Niall in captivity from Britain who would do that, a swineherd who could become the greatest figure the land has ever known. His name would be changed from Succat to one so powerful that centuries later an English officer would report to his queen that it was held in more respect than that of the Savior himself: he would be a man who would quench pagan fires, win the submission of kings, and carry the cross to all corners of the land. So Niall's fame rests not only on his victories on the battlefield, but also on that momentous capture of the boy who would be Patrick.

Niall's predecessor, like many other Irish kings, was killed by treachery. Crimthann's own sister gave him poison, in the hope that her favorite son would succeed to the kingship. But there were many claimants for the throne, and Niall was to be the successful one. After much contention and swordplay it was Niall who stood on the Inauguration Stone at Tara, and his rival Corc had to be content with the victor's gifts. A thousand steeds, and half as many suits of armor, a hundred ninety gold rings, and fifty golden goblets Niall gave the defeated candidate, since such gifts were the custom when peace was made after a contested election.

But even after Niall was installed in the kingship another rival made an attempt to depose him. Eochaid, King of Leinster, came to Tara during Niall's absence and seized the throne. But after possessing the royal residence for nine days, the usurper was told by one of the learned druids of the court that it was not lawful for him to violate certain sacred restrictions of Tara. There was a prohibition, the druid declared, that no man should take the throne who had not received the degree of Knight of Chivalry, and who wore around his neck the chain or collar that was the symbol of that rank. So, lacking the necessary honor, Eochaid retired from Tara and relinquished his claim to the throne. Niall banished him to Alba, but not before many battles had been fought between them.

Those were the days when Gratianus was emperor at Rome, and his legions still held Britain and Gaul. But the Roman power was ebbing, and Niall was not lacking in enterprise to try his strength against them. He moved all Erin against Britain, and the sea, said the Roman poet Claudian, foamed with his hostile oars. He devastated many of the Roman-held provinces of Britain, and freed the Irish colonies in Scotland from submission to the Picts.

From the king's camp at Loegria Niall sent a plundering fleet along the coast. The raiders captured two hundred nobly born children and carried them to Ireland, where they were distributed as slaves throughout the land.

It was one of them, a boy later called Patrick, who fell to the lot of a petty chieftain of eastern Ulster, Milcho by name. For seven years this boy tended his master's swine on the rough hill of Slemish. But while his body was busy with the care of beasts, his soul was worshiping the Christian God. A hundred prayers was what he used to say each day, and nearly as many at night. He rose before daybreak, in the snow, in the frost, in the rain, and yet he received no damage, for he said, the spirit of God was warm within him. While he was there he perfected himself in the Gaelic tongue and made himself familiar with the habits and usages of the people.

After seven years of servitude he escaped, and made his way over land and sea to his home and his people.

There is neither record nor legend of how his young manhood was spent. But it is certain that while he was still with his parents in Britain he dreamed that he was summoned to Erin to convert the Irish to Christianity. His scholarship and religious training make it probable that he spent many years at study. It is also possible that he came again to Ireland as a missionary before he made his great entry as a bishop in the year 432.

Three men, tradition says, were converted to Christianity before the coming of Patrick, and Cormac Mac Art was one of them. Probably others had also been brought to the Church in the years between. But when Patrick landed at Wicklow the people in general were pagans. Druids and wizards were their holy men, and their gods were stone idols, and wind and sun and fire.

This, then, is the story of Patrick's coming, a tale that the years have made famous:

Twelve people were in Patrick's company when he landed in Ireland on his mission of converting the island to Christianity, twelve people in an open boat. They went first to the land of Patrick's captivity, and then made their way south. It was close to Easter time when they approached Tara, and when the high tide of that festival drew near Patrick went to the Graves of Fiacc's Men, and his tent was pitched in that place.

Now it happened that that was the night when all fires in Ireland were supposed to be extinguished, except the fires in honor of the archgod Bel. Neither gold nor silver could be taken from one who disobeyed that law, but his death was demanded as punishment. Many people of Ireland were gathered at Tara in celebration of Beltain, or May Day, and the High King of Ireland was himself by the pagan fire. Golden and fiery was the air around them, and dark and unlighted the surrounding plains. Then, while the people watched, the flame of another fire appeared, mounting from a faraway hill. Patrick had kindled the paschal fire in celebration of the Christian festival of Easter.

"That is a breach of a ban and a law of mine," said the displeased monarch, Loegaire, to his wizard. "Go and see who has made the flame."

"I see the fire," said the wizard, "and I know that, unless it is quenched on this the night when it is lighted, it will not be quenched till Doomsday. And moreover, he who kindled it will vanquish the kings and lords of Ireland unless he is restrained and forbidden."

"That will not be," said the high king, "for we will go and slay the man who made the fire."

Then his chariots and his horses were yoked for the king, and he took his company to the place where Patrick was. When he saw the company approach him, with the rims of their shields against their chins, Patrick came out to them, chanting the prophetic verse: "Some trust in chariots and some in horses, but we in the name of the mighty Lord."

Then Patrick and the king asked tidings of each other, and after they had spoken the king's wizard, Lochru, began an angry contention. Patrick answered his questions, but when the wizard went astray into blasphemy against the Trinity, Patrick looked wrathfully upon him, and called on the Lord to destroy him. Wherewith the wizard was raised into the air, and then cast down, and his brains were scattered on the stones, and he was broken in pieces. The heathen were adread at that, so it is said.

But there was no fear in the king, and in anger he called on his company to slay the cleric. When Patrick saw them rising against him, he prayed God to confound the heathen and to destroy them. "As the smoke vanishes, let them vanish. As the wax melteth in the fire, so let the ungodly perish in the presence of God."

Then a great earthquake and trembling of arms took place there. It seemed to the king's people that the sky fell on the earth, and the horses went off in flight. The wind whirled the chariots through the fields. Each man rose up against his neighbor, so that they were slain by their own comrades in the confusion, and the surviving fled on every side. Only three remained, unafraid: Loegaire and his queen and one of his household.

On the following day the men of Ireland went to Tara to feast. In the middle of the banqueting Patrick appeared among them in the Great Hall, though no door had opened for him. For Patrick had thought to himself, "It is not a candle under a vat that I will make of myself. I will see who will believe in me and who will not."

No man rose up in honor to him but Dubtach, the king-poet of Ireland, and a stripling of his household named Fiacc, and Dubtach was the first man who believed in Patrick on that day.

To the king's couch Patrick took his way, that he might partake of the banquet, and be proven in prophecy. And while he was eating and drinking with the king, another wizard of the king's household assayed to poison the cleric.

But Patrick, it is said, caused the wine to become sweet again. Then the wizard challenged Patrick to a match of their powers. They went out to the plain of Tara with all the people following, and were contending with each other at miracles.

"Let me see you cause snow to fall," said the wizard. "I would not wish to go against God's nature," answered Patrick. Whereupon the wizard made snow to fall to the depth of men's waists. "Now banish that snow," said Patrick. "That I cannot do," confessed the wizard. But at Patrick's word the snow melted away, quicker than speech, without rain, without sun, without wind.

At the wizard's command came darkness, but he could not dispel it. Patrick prayed to the Lord, and the darkness became day. So the two men were for a long time at this contention in the presence of the king and the people. Then Patrick's patience with the wizard ended, and he caused death to come to him, and destruction to many people, so that twelve thousand perished on that plain.

Patrick went to the king then, and said, "Unless thou believest now thou shalt die quickly, for God's anger will come on thy head."

But though Loegaire knelt to Patrick and gave him license to preach to the people of Ireland, he was unable to believe. "My father, Niall," he said, "when he heard of the coming of this faith, enjoined me not to believe in it, but to be buried in the topmost part of Tara, like warlike men." And that was the way Loegaire was buried, dressed in his armor, and facing the south where his foes were.

But Loegaire's wife believed, and after her her daughters. At one time Patrick went to the well on the hillside of Cruachan, and some of his followers were with him. That was the well where the daughters of the king used to go early every morning to wash their hands. Ethne the Fair and Fedelm the Ruddy were the names of the two maidens, and they were as beautiful and as eager as any in Ireland.

When they came to the well on that morning, and saw Patrick and his clerics, they wondered at the garments of the priests, with their books before them, and they thought that they were men of the elves, or apparitions. They asked tidings of Patrick, "Who are you, and whence do you come? Are you of the elves, or of the gods?" Patrick said to them that it was better for them to believe in God than to inquire of the strangers' race.

Said the girl who was elder, "Who is your God, and where is he? Is he in heaven or in earth, or under earth, or on earth? Is he in seas or in streams, or in mountains or in glens? Hath he sons and daughters? Is there gold and silver, is there abundance of every good thing in his kingdom? Tell us about him. How is he seen, how is he loved? How is he found? Is he in youth or in age? Is he everlasting? Is he beautiful? Have many fostered his sons? Are his daughters dear and beautiful to the men of this world?"

And Patrick answered them fervently: "Our God is the God of all things, the God of Heaven and earth and seas and rivers, the God of sun and moon and all the stars, the God of high mountains and low valleys, the God over heaven and in heaven and under heaven. He hath a dwelling both in heaven and earth and sea, and all that are therein. He inspires all things, he quickens all things, he surpasses all things, he sustains all things. He kindles the light of the sun and the light of the moon.

"He hath a son eternal like himself, and like unto him. But the son is not younger than the father, and the father is not older than the son. And the Holy Spirit breathes in them. Father and Son and Holy Spirit are not divided. It is my wish, as their servant, to unite you to the son of the heavenly king, for you are the dear daughters of a king of earth.''

And Loegaire's daughters asked Patrick to teach them the way to believe. And he baptized them, and blessed white veils on their heads. Then they asked to see Christ face to face. ''That you cannot do,'' said Patrick, ''unless you first taste of death, and receive Christ's body and blood.'' And the girls agreed, and received the sacrifice, and fell asleep in death. Patrick put them under one mantle on one bed, and their friends bewailed them greatly.

Now the wizards Moel and Caplait contended against Patrick because the girls had received the faith, and because of their death. Caplait came and was crying against Patrick, for Caplait had fostered the younger girl. Patrick preached to him, and he believed in God and in Patrick. Then Patrick put the shears around his hair, and he became a tonsured priest. Thereafter came the other wizard, Moel, and said to Patrick, ''No advantage or profit shall you get out of him, for I will bring him back to heathenism.'' But Patrick's faith prevailed on him also, and like his brother he submitted to Patrick's shears, and the two were together in their belief.

But though Patrick took two daughters from Loegaire in the name of Christ, one son of the king was restored to life because of Patrick. Patrick and his clerics came one time to the king's house, and a feast was prepared for them. Lugaidh, son of the king, began to consume it greedily. His haste was the cause of his death, for a piece of meat stuck in his throat and he immediately died. The queen cried out, and threw her son on the protection of Patrick. The saint then retired to a solitary house and ordered that the boy's body be brought to him. He made a prayer to God, and remained alone with the body for three days and three nights, without meat, without drink.

At the end of that time the boy lived, and Patrick told the queen that it was by the intervention of the Archangel Michael that the miracle had been wrought. Then the queen knelt joyfully at Patrick's feet, and took upon herself an obligation. Out of every flock she owned she promised a sheep to the poor, and a portion of each meal of her own to feed others, in honor of the archangel. And she instituted that same practice among other converts throughout the land. From that event arose the custom of the Michaelmas sheep and the Michaelmas portion, which is observed in Ireland down to the present day.

When many converts to the new faith had been made, the men of Ireland asked Patrick how they were to abide by its teachings, and also live under their ancient laws. They said that they would need an ordering of every rule that they had. So Patrick called to his presence every man to show his art. Then the evil laws concerning their crafts were cast from them, and proper ones in keeping with the new faith were arranged.

To Dubtach, the chief poet, was entrusted the correction of their old judgments, after he had been blessed by Patrick in his work. Nine eminent men of Ireland were engaged in that great revision of the laws of the land, three bishops, three kings, and three poets. But it was Dubtach who wound a thread of poetry around the whole.

Patrick is said to have performed many miracles before the men of Ireland, and this caused reverence and fear to fill their hearts. And his prophecies they also remembered when they came to be fulfilled.

At one time Patrick went to Ulster, to convert the people of Tyrone. He had a practice of converting the king of each district, so that the people would follow him in the faith. On this journey he said to his household, "Beware that you are not overtaken by that terrible lion, Eogan, son of Niall, for he is a fierce man, and a conflict between you would not be a pleasant one." But the companies of missionaries and warriors met. Before they could come to blows, Sechall, one of Patrick's bishops, held a conversation with the son of the king. Said Sechall to Muiredach, son of Eogan, "If thy father believes in God, thou shalt have a guerdon from me therefore." "What guerdon?" asked Muiredach. "Kingship shall descend from thee," said Sechall. "He shall do so, indeed," said the king's son. So Eogan believed in God and in Patrick.

Then Patrick went to Magh Bregh, in the province of Leinster, to the fort of Naas. The place of Patrick's tent was on the green to the east of the road. To the north of the fort was a well, wherein Patrick baptized the two sons of the house, and two daughters who had offered their virginity to God. And Patrick blessed the veils on their heads.

Then Patrick sent a messenger to the steward of Naas, to ask for food for his people. The steward feigned sleep, and the messenger returned to Patrick with that word. "By God's doom," cried Patrick in anger, "no wonder if it be a final sleep." Naas's household then went to waken the steward, and he was found dead because of the disrespect he had showed to Patrick.

Patrick founded churches and monasteries in plenty in Leinster, and left blessings on the Leinstermen. And he went to the Plain of Prostrations, where the great gold and silver idol Cromm Cruach stood, surrounded by twelve lesser idols covered with shining brass. Until Patrick's coming they had been the gods of every people who ever came to Ireland. Now they were overturned by Patrick, and he preached God in heaven in their place. But there was one in that province who had adopted Cromm Cruach as his special god, and this man, Failgre Berraide, boasted that he would kill Patrick in revenge for the overthrowing of the idol. But Patrick was not told of this by his people.

One day Odran, Patrick's charioteer, said to the saint, "Since for a long time I have been charioteering for thee, O master, let me today be in the chief seat, and do thou be the charioteer." Patrick did so on that journey. Soon they came to the district of Failgre, who ran to meet them at the sound of the chariot wheels on the stones. On seeing that it was Patrick's chariot he raised his spear to thrust it at the man who sat in the chief seat, thinking it to be his enemy. And Odran the charioteer died of that spear thrust.

Not long afterward Failgre died, and his soul went to hell. Then the devil entered Failgre's body, so that it dwelt among men as though it were alive. After some time Patrick came to Failgre's fortress, and tarried before the door, and asked one of the slaves where Failgre was biding. "I left him in his house," said the slave. "Tell him to come and speak with me," Patrick commanded.

The servant went to fetch his master, and found of him nothing but bare bones, bloodless and fleshless. In sorrow and grief the slave rushed to Patrick with the tale of what he had seen. Said Patrick, "From the day when Failgre slew my charioteer in my presence his soul went to hell for the deed he had done, and the devil entered his body." The fear of that happening, it is said, shook the hearts of many who did not already believe.

Patrick then went to Munster, where Oengus, king of the province, made him welcome. Oengus believed in God and in Patrick, and he was baptized, and a multitude of Munstermen with him. And Patrick said to them, "If Munstermen outrage me they shall have mutual slaughter amidst their land. Their realm shall be in disgrace."

Now while Patrick was blessing the head of Oengus the spike of the crozier went through the king's foot. At the end of the benediction Patrick saw the wound in Oengus's foot. Said Patrick, "Why didst thou not tell me?" "I deemed," Oengus replied "that it was a rite of the faith."

"Thou shalt have a reward for this," said Patrick. "From today to the Judgment thy successors shall not have death by slaying save one man only."

So Munster became strong in the faith, and Patrick left many churches there. And wherever he went he carried his household with him, so that they could build places of worship for the people and erect altars. Chalices and altars and bells he gave to each congregation, and the altars were not bare of linen embroidered with holy symbols. And his choristers taught the people hymns, so that their voices could be raised in praise of God.

Thereafter Patrick went to Armagh, to the place where Daire's fortress stood. This rich and honorable man gave him land on the Hill of Willows, and there Patrick built a church and started a monastery, and he filled both with relics brought from Rome. And from that church the Christian teaching spread out throughout the land.

This was Patrick's own rule of devotion, says the *Tripartite Life of St. Patrick*, the work which tells most of the legends of his life: "He used to sing all the psalms with their hymns and canticles and apocalypse and two hundred other prayers every day. He used to baptize and preach and celebrate the canonical hours according to due order. He used to celebrate Communion. He used to make the sign of the cross over his face every hour of the day. In the first watch of the night he used to sing a hundred psalms and make two hundred genuflections. In the second watch he used to lie in cold water, in the third he was in contemplation, in the fourth watch he lay on bare clay with a stone for a pillow, and a wet mantle over him.

"Now after founding churches in plenty, after consecrating monasteries, after baptizing the men of Ireland, after great patience and great labor, after destroying idols and images, and after rebuking many kings, who did not do his will, and after raising those who did his will, after ordaining three hundred and three score and ten bishops, and after ordaining three thousand priests and folk of every grade in the Church besides, after fasting and prayer, after mercy and clemency, after gentleness and mildness to the sons of life, after love of God and his neighbors, he received Christ's body from the bishop, from Tassach, and then he sent his spirit to heaven."

And when he was dead, this is what people said of him: "A fair garden with plants of virtue, a vine branch of fruitfulness, a fire flashing with fervor, a lion for strength and might, a dove for gentleness and simplicity, a serpent for prudence and cunning, a man mild, gentle, humble, and tender to the sons of life, but rough, ungentle, and harsh to the sons of death. And though great was Patrick's glory on earth, the faithful believe that it will be greater in heaven, that it will shine like a sun in heaven, and blaze brightly through eternity, that great honor will be his among the companies of the immortals."

Chapter VII

DOVE OF THE CHURCH

➜➤〉〈➤⟵

A N EXILE sat in his wooden hut and read a
letter from home. Around him stirred the
life of a great monastery. Monks chanted
in the chapel; scribes bent over the vellum
pages of their psalters. In the fields the
working brothers looked to the barley
which would make their winter's bread. Sheep grazed on
the hillsides, well tended not so much for their promise of
becoming mutton as for a source of wool for clothing and
sheepskin to make the scholars' parchment. Somewhere
about carbon was being compounded into ink, cockles were
crushed to scarlet splendor which would glow on the
ornamented pages of manuscripts.

Iona, the great monastery of St. Columba, in Scotland,
was thriving, growing, carrying Christianity to the pagan
Picts.

And Columba himself sat in his cell and sent his thought
across the sea to Ireland. He was a voluntary exile, this
thin, ascetic cleric, he who might have been Ireland's
high king. As descendant of Niall of the Nine Hostages
he was offered the kingship of the land, but he refused it
to become a cleric. A hundred years and more had passed

since Patrick had lighted that first paschal fire at Tara. They had been golden years for Ireland, and they had changed the temper of the land.

As though by a leisurely miracle the fierce fervor of the Irish, which had found its expression in warfare and fighting, had been transmuted by Christianity into love of God and of learning. The little churches of Patrick's planting grew and multiplied, and adapted themselves to the new spirit of the people. Church and school became almost synonymous, so closely entwined were learning and religion. In the church schools the Irish, always so thirsty for beauty and knowledge, learned not only of Christ, but of the magic that is locked in manuscripts, of Latin and Greek philosophers and poets, of the delights of exploring the byways of literature. So eagerly came the scholars to the schools of the churches, and in such large numbers, that soon the land was dotted with monasteries, each founded by some saint of the Church, and fostered by the rich princes of the land.

Columba, sitting at gray Iona, could count them in his mind: Bangor, on the shores of Belfast Bay, where seven alternate choirs, each three hundred voices strong, chanted the praises of God through night and day; Glendalough, in the valley of the lakes; Monastereven, on the banks of the Barrow; Monsterboyce in the Boyne valley; Clonmacnoise, St. Ciaran's Plain of Crosses. Lovely pictures rose in the saint's mind, and the lovely names of cloisters came from his lips as melodiously as though he were chanting— Aran and Armagh and Drumcliffe, Derry and Durrow and Killmore, Kells and Clonfert and Clogher. Their syllables touched his ear as sweetly as the sound of vesper bells drifting over quiet fields. Clonard, most famous of schools, where he had studied with St. Finian and where he himself had been tonsured, he thought of with affection; Magh Bile, where another Finian taught, and where Columba had copied the psalter which was the cause of his exile.

It was such a beautiful thing, that psalter of St. Finian's. Columba longed to own it, but psalters were precious things, not lightly owned or given. But parchment he could manage, and ink, and his fingers were eager at the work of copying. So every night he stole into the chapel, and worked by the light of burning rushes. It was not strange for him to spend his time at the chapel. Ever since he had been a boy he had been called Columcille, Dove of the Church, because so many of his hours were spent there.

Finian knew, in time, that his psalter was being copied, but he said no word till the work was finished. Then he claimed the copy.

A dispute arose then, which was taken to the high king for settlement. "To every cow belongs its calf," said the king, "and to every book its little book."

"That is an unjust decision," Columba protested, "and I will have revenge for it." So he called his clan together, and the battle of Cuildremne was fought. The book was recovered, to become the treasured relic of Columba's family, the Cinel Conaill, called O'Donnell in later times. Encased in a silver cover, which it was not lawful to open, the *Battle Book* was carried thrice sunwise around the army of the clan when they were about to engage in battle, that the host might return in safety and triumph. It was on the bosom of a cleric free from mortal sin that it was carried, and whether by its grace, or the might of the clan which possessed it, they remained, as they had been for centuries, strong princes of the north.

But the young Columba could know nothing of the later glory which his book would have. He rejoiced in its possession, but his heart was sad at thinking of the lives which had been lost because of it. He went to an old scholar who had been his friend, and asked what he should do in penance.

Now it was no small love which Columba bore for Ireland. He treasured the memory of the Little Field at Gartan, which had been his birthplace. He loved the wildness of Doire Ethne, where he had lived in fosterage, near the homes of ravens and eagles, badgers and pine martens. Dear to him were the oak woods which surrounded his first church in Derry. The sound of the axe on one of his beloved oaks was fearful to him. That first church had been built in the sight of the sea, and since then he had built a hundred others which the sea waters touched. He loved the cloisters of Magh Bile, and Clonfert, and Glasnevin. The sight of Irish people was sweet to him, and he loved to feel under his feet Irish stones and soil.

So the penance which was put on him was this: He should leave this land which he loved, and never see it again. Never again must he rest his eyes on his country's people, or his foot on Irish sod. And in exile he must bring to Christ as many souls as had been lost in the battle of Cuildremne.

So he set out for Scotland, his heart heavy within him.

"Plentiful in the east are tall fighting men," he lamented. "Plentiful trouble and illnesses, plentiful the hard, jealous hearts.

"Plentiful in the west are the apples, plentiful the kings and the making of kings, plentiful the wholesome sloes, plentiful the oaks with acorns. Sweet voiced her clerics, sweet voiced her birds, her young men gentle, her old men wise, her great men good to look upon, her women noble, of good rearing."

Truly could he utter that famous cry of his leave-taking: "A gray eye looks back on Erin, a gray eye filled with tears."

It was to Iona he went, a gray and rocky island off the west coast of Scotland. Sea gulls hovered about its cliffs, and their cries mingled with the washing of the waves.

On the eve of Pentecost he and his company of clerics grounded their little boat, and went ashore. Druids met them, and attempted to turn them back. They told Columba false tales of the island's conversion, that he was not needed there. Three things he had to overcome them: great size, great courage, and a mighty voice. He sent them scattering in fear. Then with care he marked an outline for his church.

Stone and wood and wattled huts would arise there, but first a sacrifice must be offered, that the buildings would be secure. So Columba offered heaven to any who would consent to die and be buried beneath the foundations of the church. It was Odran, one of Columba's bishops, who said, "I consent to die on that condition." And he accepted death, and was buried there.

Then Columba met the king of the land, and converted him to Christianity, and many others besides. The monastery of Iona became the vanguard of Christianity in Scotland, and a hive of scholars and clerics.

And now Columba, with thirty years of exile behind him, was reading that he was needed again in Ireland.

The tale has been told here of how Conor Mac Nessa listened to the controversy of the poets of his court, and was unable to understand the secret language which they spoke. He ordered then that a poet's training should no longer be a hereditary one, the privilege of certain families only. From that time on, any youth who wished could go to a bardic school and receive the twelve-year training. And since poets were so honored in the land, and were granted so many perquisites, their ranks had swelled to tremendous proportions. By the sixth century a third of the free men of Ireland were poets, and their entertainment and support was a heavy drain on the people.

"It is no easy thing to keep these poets," said Aed, the high king of the time. "Thirty young poets follow in the train of a chief poet, and twenty in the train of a junior poet. They make their demands with arrogance. I will call a convention to discuss their banishment."

Now Columba himself had a poet's training, and he felt that his land would be disgraced if it should banish this whole class of artists. So he planned to go to Ireland in their defense.

Over his eyes he bound three bandages, that he might not see Ireland, and thus break the bonds of his penance. Under his feet he bound Scotch grass. In this wise he came to the convention of Drimceatt.

The king rose up to make him welcome. "Let this be my welcome," said Columba, "to do my will."

"I will give you that welcome," promised the king.

"The poets must be retained," said Columba.

"I will not agree to that," Aed answered. "They are a great annoyance to us, and they eat bare the larders of princes and people. If things are not to their liking their satires fall sharply on the shoulders of their entertainers. The land can do without them."

"Do not say that," Columba pleaded, "for the praise which they will make for you will be enduring, even as the praise the poets made for Cormac Mac Art is enduring. Cormac's riches are withered, but his fame lives after him in the works of the poets. So your praise and your fame will remain after you, and after your riches have perished, if the poets are here to keep them alive."

"It is not I who will expel them, then," said the king, and the poets were allowed to remain, with some restrictions as to their number.

Then Columba turned to another matter. The son of the king of Ossory was held in hostage by Aed, and Columba had been surety that he would be released or exchanged in the space of a year. More time than that had passed, and still Scannlon was not released, and no captive was exchanged for him.

A hut of wattles was his prison, a hut set far apart in the wilderness, with no path to it. A little salt food was given the prisoner every day, and ale in such a scanty cup that he was tortured continually by thirst. Nine chains bound him, night and day, and fifty warriors outside his hut guarded him from escape.

"Scannlon must be released," said Columba to the king.

"He will die in his hut from thirst before I do that," Aed answered.

"We will say no more about it for a while," was the saint's promise. "God will be the one who sees to it that Scannlon unties my sandal tonight after nocturn, wheresoever he may be."

Then Columba rose and went out of the assembly to the Black Church of Derry. And after nocturn, when it was time for Columba to loose his sandals, there came to him Scannlon, released, so he said, by the hand of God.

So Columba returned with glory to Iona.

It was his custom to labor each day, and he divided this labor in three parts. The first part he preached the word of God to all, and bade them to love God and fear him. And he told his listeners to love their neighbors, and to pray earnestly for the dead. In the second part of the day he wove garments for the brothers, or worked at writing. Three hundred psalters he is said to have transcribed while he was at Iona, besides many hymns and holy works. In the third part of the day he did some work that should be of lasting profit to the monastery, and he did not cease in his task till the sweat came.

It was his wont to be alone in his oratory, or in some lonely place, after the hours and the mass were over, communing with God. And at the hour when Jesus was scourged he bared his body and scourged it. He shunned satiety and fat, and fought the battle of the full mouth. He never put a dainty bit into his body. The track of his ribs could be clearly seen through his skin. He never indulged desire.

And yet this man had not an unpleasant severity. Toward himself he practiced harshness. Toward others he was always gentle and kind. His writings have both wisdom and wit.

At one time a hermit who had been Columba's friend wrote him from his little hut in the desert. It was with sorrow that he wrote, for a great disaster had come upon him. Like all hermits he had no worldly wealth. His only possessions had been a cock, a little mouse, and a fly. The cock, he wrote Columba, had wakened him at midnight, that he might say his matins; the mouse had nibbled at his ear if he slept more than five hours thereafter, and when he should desire more sleep, wearied by much praying and many prostrations. And the use of the fly had been to walk upon every line he read in the psalter, and when he ceased chanting to remain upon the line where he had stopped.

But these treasures of the hermit soon died, and he wrote Columba complaining of his loss. The saint rebuked him in his answering letter. "My friend," he wrote solemnly, though his quill may have quivered with amusement, "you must not wonder at the deaths of the animals which have left you. Do you not know that trouble follows always in the wake of wealth?"

As the years lengthened, the saint looked longingly toward death. In the spring of his seventy-seventh year he went to visit the working monks on the western side of the island. "During the Easter festival in April," he told them, "I could have desired to depart to Christ, but lest a joyous festival for you be turned into mourning, my departure has been deferred." On hearing these words, the monks were greatly saddened. They bowed their heads as Columba turned his face to the east and blessed the island.

A short time after this, on an evening in June, he sat in his cell busy on still another psalter. He came to the words of the Thirty-fourth Psalm, "They that seek the Lord shall want no manner of thing that is good."

"I think I can write no more," he said. "Let Baithen write what follows."

He died with his monks about him and the sound of their lamentation in his ears.

And after he was dead, the chief poet of Ireland, Dallan Forgaill, composed an eulogy for Columba, Ireland's Dove of the Church. Stately and lovely are its phrases in Gaelic. Lovely and poetic is the rendering that Lady Gregory has given them in English. The poem is long, and this is not the place to record it in its entirety. But a few phrases, chosen with care and affection, will not libel the music of the lament.

"This is now the poem of praise and of lamentation that was made for Columcille, Speckled Salmon of the Boyne, High Saint of the Gael, by Forgaill, Chief Poet of Ireland.

"It is not a little story that this is, it is not a story about a fool it is, it is not one district that is keening, but every district, with a great sound that is not to be borne, hearing the story of Columcille, without life, without a church.

"It is not the trouble of one house, or the grief of one harp-string. All the plains are heavy, hearing the word that is a wound.

"What way will a simple man tell of him? He that used to keep us living is dead, he that was our right hand has died from us, he has died from us, that was God's messenger.

"A shelter to the naked, a comforter to the poor, he was eager, he was noble, it is high his death is. We hope great honor will be given to him on the head of these deeds."

Chapter VIII

QUIET GARDENS

->>)<((-

THERE IS never a quiet garden without its birds. Though it is set in the midst of noise and ugliness, if it is large, and cool, and leafy, birds will come to it from afar. Thrushes will find refuge in its treetops, finches and robins and wrens will contend for downy trifles to make their nests. Even humming-birds will hang on throbbing wings before sun-touched columbine.

Now Ireland was for three centuries a lovely garden of learning, and birds came to it from distant lands. The Huns, terrible and devastating, were roaming Central Europe. From the Rhine to the Pyrenees they burned, destroyed, and ravaged. Every city, every town, every monument of civilization and time they ravaged and left desolate. Scholars fled before them, and found refuge in the green island to the northwest. There culture and learning were nurtured while terror reigned outside. And when the storm was over, from Ireland there spread out again Christianity and the love of letters.

"The classic tradition," says M. Darmesteter, one of the many scholars who have made this period in Irish history the subject of research, "to all appearances dead in Europe, burst into full bloom in the island of the saints, and the Renaissance began in Ireland seven hundred years before it was known in Italy. During three centuries Ireland was the asylum of higher learning which took sanctuary there from the unsettled state of Europe. At one time Armagh, the religious capital of Christian Ireland, was the metropolis of civilization."

The Venerable Bede, speaking of Ireland of the seventh century, describes the welcome the Irish gave to the foreigners. "Many of the nobles of the English nation and lesser men had set out thither, forsaking their native island either for the grace of sacred learning, or a more austere life. And some of them, indeed, soon dedicated themselves faithfully to the monastic life, others rejoiced rather to give themselves to learning, going about from one master's cell to another. All these the Irish willingly received, and saw to it to supply them with food day by day without cost, and books for their studies, and teaching, free of charge."

Each monastery was generally related to one particular clan, and the clan leader set apart land and tribute for its upkeep. By custom and right the first-born male child of every marriage went to the monastic church. By custom every first calf and every first lamb went to it, and every tenth birth afterward, human or animal. Tithes of cattle and crops, and the first gathering of the produce of the fields were dedicated to it, and every seventh day of the week.

With this patronage, and the enthusiasm of the people for learning, it is no wonder that these institutions flourished and grew famous.

The school that Patrick had founded on the Hill of Willows at Armagh had seven thousand scholars by the middle of the sixth century, and Monsterboyce was well started on its five-hundred-year career as a seat of Irish art and culture. Dagobert, Prince of Austrasia, studied at Slane, and Sigebert, another royal child from the Continent, also sat under Irish teachers.

It was a pleasant life these scholars led, austere and yet poetic. No worry assailed them, and if their bodies were not indulged with material luxuries, their minds at least fed on rich fare. Their huts were generally grouped about a central chapel, and their souls were exalted by frequent services. Classes were held out of doors in summer, and the voice of the lecturer often mingled with a blackbird's note.

As for the clerics, this was their chosen vocation. They dedicated their souls to God, and combined spiritual ecstasy with a life of service. After the devotions of the day were over their occupations varied. The untonsured youths sat under instruction. The working brothers of the monasteries tilled the fields, tended cattle, and contrived to supply all the various articles used by their community. Their needs were simple, and their vows were strict. Still, wool must be woven for the monks' robes, leather tanned to make the rude sandals. Barley for bread must be sown, and tended, and reaped at harvest time. Someone must cook, and fish, and gather eggs. Someone must shear the sheep, and card the wool. Someone must prepare the parchment which the elder brothers inscribed with such loving industry. Ink must be made from carbon, and colors found for the illuminated manuscripts. Some of them at best were thin and transparent, but the scarlet they used, made from cockles, was thick and vivid. A most beautiful color, the

Venerable Bede relates, which never faded with the heat of the sun, nor with the washing of the rain, but the older it grew, the more beautiful it became.

The seniors, the brothers brittle with age, read the Scriptures and copied psalters. That was for them achievement and honor. "Scribe" seems a modest title now, but in an age when printing was unknown, and every book was a transcription, it was a distinction dearly cherished.

And many a monk, busy at his task of copying the Gospels or recording events in the annals of the times, has interrupted his serious work for a moment to note some detail of the life around him in words that are both loving and poetic. On the margin of one of the St. Gall manuscripts the scribe has set down a little poem in Gaelic to tell of the happiness in his heart.

A hedge of trees surrounds me,
A blackbird's lay entrances me,
Is it praise for my labors?
From the top of the bushes a gray-mantled cuckoo chants to me.
May the Lord protect me from doom!
Happily do I work under the green-wood.

And somewhere another monk stopped his work to listen to a robin's song. Perhaps he whittled his quill to a finer point to cramp these words on the margin of his page: "Wondrous is the robin there, singing to us, and our cat has escaped from us."

That not all the Irish had turned to the scholarly life is shown by the grumbling aside of one scribe. "It is a great shame of you to demand scrivening of me today," he complains, "when you made a raid in Ossory yesterday, and got great spoil."

Other marginal notes on other manuscripts tell of ink that is bad, of vellum rough and full of holes, of hands that are tired, and eyes that cannot see longer in the dusk. One monk at least had intimations of mortality. "Alas, O hand," he lamented, "how much white vellum hast thou written. Thou wilt make famous the vellum while thou thyself wilt be the bare top of a faggot of bones."

But the usual marginal note was one asking the prayers of future readers, either for the scribe himself or for the brothers of the monastery. "A prayer here for the students," pleads one, "and this is a difficult little story, and let me not be blamed for the script, for the ink is bad, and the vellum defective, and the day is dark."

It is not strange that in this atmosphere of ecstasy and devotion some of the brothers would feel the need to draw apart from others and commune more intimately with God. Sometimes singly, sometimes in small groups, they would withdraw into the wilderness to contemplate their Master, and search their own souls. Culdees they were called in time, the name meaning Friends of God.

The poetry they have left behind tells of their simple wants: a little hidden hut in the wilderness to be their dwelling, an all-gray lithe little lark to be by its side, a clear pool to wash away sins, a beautiful, enfolding wood to nurse many-voiced birds hiding in its shelter. A southern aspect for warmth they asked, a little brook across the floor, a pleasant church, with linen altar cloth, and shining candles above the pure-white Scriptures. Twelve brothers to be in the house, sons of God, enraptured with his praise, Salmon to feed them, and trout, and leeks, and the bees' bland honey. Silence and fervor, tranquillity without guile, without contention. And the sweet sound of the little bell. At its voice their ready hearts lifted up in praise and thanksgiving.

Ah, yes, a quiet garden of learning and devotion in many ways. But every garden has its Eve, and every Eve her serpent. Patrick is credited with driving the snakes from Ireland, a baseless tale of modern times. To the contrary, Patrick named as a serpent something which had been no serpent before. The Christian idea of morality which Patrick introduced into the island was at odds with the old customs, which accepted sex as a natural hunger.

Before his coming the pagan ways of the people had not glorified chastity. Marriage was simple, and not regarded as a sacrament. There is no mention of a marriage ceremony in the pagan tales. Only consent and the payment of a bride price were ordinarily required. "Is this a time when our coming together would be easy?" asks a warrior of a chance-met maid. Monogamy was not always practiced, and marriages were not necessarily lifelong. Maeve of Connaught seems to have had at least three husbands, with no remaining record or legend of her departure from them. And lovers were something about which she saw no reason for reticence.

"There was never a time," she said to her husband Ailill, during the famous pillow-talk which resulted in the Cattle Raid of Cualnge, "when I had not one man in the shadow of another." Fergus Mac Roy, with whom she "mingled in love," was the father of three of her children. The poets and historians who have handed down the tales of her career have added no note of condemnation. She was a pagan queen, following the pagan customs of the time.

Patrick's coming did not immediately change these customs, but at least a new ideal was set up. Marriage became a sacrament. Virginity and chastity were honored. "She loved the lot of virginity" and "She dedicated her virginity to God" are phrases found with increasing frequency. But the renouncing of love was not always easy.

A manuscript in the possession of the Royal Irish Academy, describing the monastic life as practiced at Tallaght, tells how some of the clergy dealt with the problem. Some nameless scribe has set down the dictates and usages of Abbot Maelmain, a saintly man who closed his ears to earthly music that they might be lent to the music of heaven.

Seven years of penance he dealt to those who were given to lust and to frequent and various mates—the same punishment meted out to killers and shedders of blood. If one of the laity accepted spiritual direction, he was to keep himself chaste on three nights of the week, and on Sunday if possible. The groat, that was given to a lad or a young man for accompanying someone in the sin of lust or to a woman, if the lad or woman did penance thereafter, must be given to the poor. It was not held meet that it should be returned to the giver.

If at the end of a meal the body happened to be roused to lust, slightly or strongly, it was not held amiss that the meal be cast back on the Lord in displeasure at him, as if one should say, "There, keep thy meal for thyself." A trial of this kind would not be often made, the abbot promised. Or one should subtract a part of the meal, and pray God thereafter. Persons whose desires were excited, either through hearing confession or merely through meditating, or through youth, to them strict abstinence to subdue them, "because it is excess of blood in their body that is the cause. Afterward, when the blood fails, lust and desire fail.''

The story is told of a saint who had a sister. Now desire lay heavy on the girl, ''for it is a third part as strong in woman as in man.'' The saint regulated the girl's portion and pittance for a year. On that day year she came to him, and confessed that her desire still persisted. The saint was busy sewing. He thrust his needle into her palm, and three streams of blood flowed from her hand. Said he, ''No wonder if it is hard for the body, wherein are these strong currents, to contain itself.'' He thereupon diminished her food for a second time. She was on that ration for a year, and her desire still persisted. Again the saint thrust the needle, and again three red streams poured out. That year her food was even less, and when the girl went again to her brother not a drop of blood came out of her. ''In future,'' said the cleric with satisfaction, ''keep on this pittance till death.''

If a man constantly kept to the pittance prescribed by the Rule of Tallaght, even though human weakness stirred desire, the abbot counted it no great matter, provided there was no yielding to desire.

The monks thrust temptation from them by having no women about. But in some of the schools girls must have been admitted as scholars. It is told that St. Ciaran, the future abbot of Clonmacnoise, when studying at Clonard, had as his fellow pupil the daughter of a king. Taking as a rule of his conduct the words of the Book of Job, ''I made a convenant with mine eyes, how then shall I look upon a maid,'' he never allowed himself to gaze upon the young princess, and he said he ''saw nought of her body, so long as they were together, save her feet only.''

But all young clerics had not his strength of mind. There is the story of the young nun who was handmaid to St. Molaisse. She was loved by a clerk of the church, and when her time drew near, she sent him away, in fear that the anger of the saint would harm him. "It is enough that I should be ruined," she said, and her lover left her. She died in childbirth, and St. Molaisse, instead of choosing a grave in holy ground, let her be buried in the Bog of Leighlin.

After a time anxiety and devotion drove the young cleric back. When he heard of the nun's death he was filled with remorse, and he built a hut of wattles beside her grave. For a year he prayed beside it, every day reciting the *Beatus* and the psalms seven times, and making a hundred prostrations. Then one day Fursa the Pious came to the church.

"What holy person lies buried in the bog?" he asked of St. Molaisse.

"That is no holy person, but a devil of a nun," answered the saint.

"But I see a service of angels, steadily passing from the grave to heaven," Fursa insisted, and when Molaisse looked, he, too, saw the angels. So the nun was carried to the churchyard, and buried in sanctified ground. The young clerk went away with Fursa the Pious, and became a holy man.

"Shame on my thoughts, how they stray from me," confesses one young monk, sore tempted by his flesh. "I fear great danger from it on the day of eternal doom. During the psalms they wander on a path that is not right. They flash, they fret, they misbehave before the eyes of great God. Through crowds, through companies of wanton women, through woods, through cities . . . swifter are they than the wind. Now through paths of loveliness, anon of riotous shame, they run a race of folly anear and afar. After a course of giddiness they return to their home. Though one should try to bind them, or put shackles on their feet, they are neither constant nor mindful to take a spell of rest. Neither sword-edge nor crack of whip will keep them down strongly. As slippery as an eel's tail they glide out of my grasp. Neither lock nor firm-vaulted dungeon nor any fetter on earth, stronghold, nor sea, nor bleak fastness restrains them from their course."

The first of her three great struggles had begun in Ireland, a struggle which, like the third, continues to this day.

Chapter IX

AND THEN THE VIKINGS CAME

HE SUN was shining on a more or less peaceful Ireland at the end of the eighth century. England was no longer dependent on Irish teaching and monasteries. The schools of Canterbury now gave English scholars the learning that so many of them had crossed the Channel to find. On the Continent, Charlemagne was practicing penmanship with a hand that was more facile in wielding his good sword Joyeuse. His Palace School was a place of scholarship and learning, and his was the satisfaction of carrying on the work that Irish missionaries had started, that of bringing back to a Europe devastated by the Huns the culture of the past, and of converting it to Christianity.

But away to the north was a land black with forests, rockbound, unfertile. Only in a few sun-touched valleys could crops be raised. The fierce, brave people who held this land were pirates and marauders by necessity and by choice. They loved the sea, and their long, many-oared ships could carry them far on the whale's path. As their land became more and more crowded, their dragon-prowed fleets were often abroad. Bands of young men, chosen by lot, would set out to plunder neighboring coasts. Their ships would be ready on the shore, the rowers at the oars. Then the leader would cast into the air a feather or a spear. Where its finger pointed as it fell, there they would go. There was so much land to pillage that they could leave it all to chance. Sometimes it was the coasts of France they plundered, sometimes England was their prey.

In 793 a Viking fleet landed at Lindisfarne, a monastic settlement in Northumbria. As the shallow boats landed on the shore, each warrior took from the boatside his shield, found battle-axe and spear, leaped ready-armed to the beach. While guards stood by the ships the raiders ran to their bloody work. They burnt the monastery and its shrine, killed its monks, plundered its treasure. Alcuin, the most cosmopolitan scholar of the time, friend of kings and clerics, wrote despairingly of that raid: "Three centuries and a half have we and our forefathers been here in this fair Britain, and never before has such a horror fallen upon the land as now has come upon us at the hands of the heathen. Nor has anything like their mode of navigation been heard of before. See the Church of St. Cuthbert, drenched with the blood of the priests of God, reft of all its treasures, the noblest spot in all Britain given over to be a prey of the heathen. There, whereafter the departure of Paulinus from York Christianity took a new beginning among our people, it seems as if a beginning were to be made of misery and war. Who would not be afeared? Who would not weep for the enslavement of his people?"

The next year two other English monasteries were raided, but storms wrecked the Viking ships and the invaders were captured and put to the torture. For a generation England was free from the Northmen's ships.

They had found their way to Ireland. In 795 a Viking fleet of a hundred and twenty ships raided the Island of Rechru, on the eastern Irish coast, where a monastery founded by Columcille himself still flourished. In 822 they swooped on seven-choired Bangor, "and the relics of Comgall were shaken from their shrine."

Land, and ravage, and kill, and burn, was the Viking program. Then away to the ships, and back to their distant homes, laden with spoil. So suddenly they came. So soon they went. But when they had gone the work of centuries was ruined. Every treasure was stolen, all the books and manuscripts the monks had labored on for years were burned or thrown into sea or river, the brothers were lifeless, and the country was laid waste. And that story was to be repeated in Ireland time after time for two hundred years.

At first, it was only offshore islands and settlements close to the coast which knew this quickly striking terror. Then the raiders, learning the geography of the country, began to build strongholds on the shore, and from them to venture inland on their raids. Fleets of Norse ships floated far upstream on Irish rivers, and the flames that their oarsmen kindled lighted all the Irish sky.

But soon even that was not enough. When they had plundered now, what need of going home? Why sail back to the barren north, when sword-land could be won on this green isle? By the middle of the ninth century the strangers began to settle the country and live on the spoils.

They did not win the land easily. The *Annals* tell of fleets of foreign ships on the Shannon and the Boyne, of bloody raids, of monasteries plundered. They tell, too, of great slaughter of the invaders by the Ulstermen, of

Danish defeats at Killarney, of fierce battles gained by the men of Erin, of victories when scores of enemy heads were collected by the Irish king.

But there is no denying that it was not a united Ireland that opposed the men from the north. That was Ireland's undoing then. It was Ireland's undoing when Strongbow came, it is her undoing now. The threat of danger does not ordinarily unite her. The high king, nominally head of the country, actually could count on only those lesser kings whom he had conquered and whose hostages he held. There was no central army, no national defense. The days of the Fianna were long since over, and there was no Finn Mac Cool to weld the tall warriors of Ireland into formidable phalanxes. For two centuries women had been freed from battle service. Clerics could no longer be called on to carry a sword, though there were a few king-abbots and warrior-saints to leave a lusty fame behind them. Though there was never a time when fighting was completely unknown to the land, and never a time when an Irishman would not reach gladly for a sword, still it was not a militaristic country that the invaders found. The opposition that the invaders met might be fierce, but it was the fierceness of a clan, of a community, at the most of a province called to arms by its prince.

In 838 the Norse tyrant Turgesius brought a royal fleet to Lough Ree. For thirteen years he harried the northern half of Ireland, and assumed sovereignty of all the foreigners there. He aspired to conquer the land, make it all his, and plant, in the place of Christianity, his own pagan beliefs. He assailed Armagh three times in a single month, and drove out its abbot and monks. For four years he held the church, and practiced his heathen rites where the bell of the mass had once been heard. The altar of Clonmacnoise was desecrated by his wild queen Ota, who shrieked forth her prophecies from its violated height.

After this, even more foreigners came to Ireland. Fingal—fair foreigners—the Irish had called the first invaders, who probably came from the Scandinavian peninsula. Dubhgal—dark foreigners—they called these even fiercer newcomers. Vikings, men of the bays, the Irish named them both, and later generations mistakenly and indiscriminately called them Danes. The two foreign forces battled against each other and against the Irish, and always they were reinforced by new shiploads of warriors from northern lands. Futile as sweeping back the sea was the task of withstanding them. In time, there was not a cove or a river-mouth without a fleet of strangers, and the greater part of Ireland was plundered by them. There was not a cave underground that they did not explore, there was nothing that they did not ravage.

Irishwomen were often their victims. "The plundering of Edar by the foreigners, who carried off a great prey of women," the *Annals of the Four Masters* record for the year 819, and other annalists repeat that entry time after time. The invaders were always susceptible to the charms of Irishwomen, and this was in time a great factor in the assimilation of the foreigners. It may also have been the cause of the downfall of the tyrant Turgesius.

Geoffrey Keating, the priest who wrote his history of Ireland while a fugitive when James I was trying to wipe out Irish learning, tells the tale of Turgesius' death. No other authority mentions it, and it cannot be taken for actual history. Still, Keating often ventured forth from his cave near Tipperary and traveled in disguise over the country in search of ancient vellum books still preserved in the families of scholars and historians. He had access to materials and manuscripts which other historians had not, and he may have had authority for the tale.

At the time when Turgesius was claiming authority over every stranger in Ireland, says Keating, there was a provincial king, Malachy of Meath, who had a lovely daughter. Turgesius made demand on the king for the girl, but Malachy demurred. "I do not think that it is as your wife that you want my daughter," he said, "and if it is known that she has been with you it will not be easy for her to find a husband. Let me send her to you quietly in the night."

Turgesius agreed to that. "But she has maidens about her," continued the king, "of such beauty that you may prefer one of them to her. I will choose fifteen of the loveliest to accompany her, and from them you may make your choice."

The Northman found no fault with that plan, and he and Malachy parted. But a plan had been formed in the mind of each man. The Viking invited fifteen of his chosen captains to be with him that night, and promised them entertainment. Malachy went to his young warriors, and selected fifteen with the smoothest faces and the comeliest bodies. These he dressed as women, beneath whose garments were concealed sharp knives and daggers.

That evening at Turgesius' order his captains stacked their weapons in one central pile, and went each to his own room. When Malachy's daughter and her companions came to the fort, the king kept the princess by his side, and sent to his captains all her attendants. Soon that fort was a place of slaughter and turmoil. Malachy, who had been waiting outside with an army, rushed in and captured Turgesius. A great defeat was given the invaders, and Turgesius was drowned in a lake. For a while the foreigners' power in the land was lessened.

But after forty years of peace, Earl Ottar the Black swept into Waterford harbor with his fleet of a hundred ships. The Irish seas foamed again with the eddies of hostile oars. Ten thousand men came in that fleet, and all Munster and Leinster were plundered and put under tribute to the foreigners. Look to an ancient tale, an almost contemporary work, for the picture of that oppression. The *Wars of the Gael and Gall* was written soon after the battle of Clontarf, when Brian Boru crushed the power of the Danes, and it was probably the work of Brian's chief poet.

"The whole of Munster," says the Todd translation of this work, "became filled with immense floods and countless sea-vomitings of ships, and boats and fleets, that there was not a harbor, nor a landing port, nor a dun, nor a fortress, nor a fastness in all Munster without fleets of Danes and pirates . . . and the evil which Erin had hitherto suffered was as nothing compared to the evil inflicted by these parties. The entire of Munster was without distinction plundered by them on all sides, and devastated. They spread over Munster, and built duns and fortresses and landing ports over all Erin, so that there was no place in Erin without numerous fleets of Danes and pirates. They made spoil-land, and sword-land, and conquered land of her throughout her breadth. They ravaged her chieftainries, and her privileged churches and her sanctuaries and they rent her shrines and her reliquaries and her books. They demolished her beautiful ornamented temples, for neither veneration, nor honor, nor mercy, nor sanctuary, nor protection for church or for sanctuary, for God or for man was felt by these furious, ferocious pagans, these ruthless, wrathful people. They killed the kings and the chieftains, the heirs to the crown, the royal princes of Erin. They killed the brave and the valiant, and the stout knights, champions and soldiers and young lords. They brought them under tribute and servitude. They reduced them to bondage and slavery." Many were the maidens they forced into slavery, many the pleasant youths they carried away over the broad green sea.

And when the land was stricken and helpless, there came still another fleet, more numerous than all other fleets before it, headed by Imar, chief king of the foreigners, and his three sons. They landed at Limerick harbor, and all Munster again knew plunder and pillage. The enemy chiefs levied pledges and hostages, and brought the country to indescribable oppression and servitude.

Imar ordained kings and chiefs and stewards and bailiffs in every territory, and in every chieftainry, and levied royal rent. "And such was the oppressiveness of the tribute," continues the tale, "that none of the men of Erin had power to give away the milk of his cow, or as much as the clutch of eggs of one hen in succor or in kindness to an aged man, or to a friend, but was forced to preserve them, for the foreigner's steward and bailiff, or soldier. And though there was but one milk-giving cow in the house, she durst not be milked for an infant of one night, nor for a sick person, but must be kept for the steward of the foreigners. And however long he might be absent from the house, his share and supply durst not be lessened. Although there was in the house but one cow, it must be killed for the meal of one night if the means of a supply could not otherwise be procured. And an ounce of silver for every nose, besides the royal tribute afterward every year, and he who had not the means of paying it had himself to go into slavery for it."

It was at this time that the people of Erin dared not wear silk or satin, or any new garment, but must deliver them to the invaders. And while the oppressors were resplendent with new finery, and many jewels and ornaments of gold, the Irish themselves wore only poor worn shifts and castoff clothes.

There was, however, a noble, highborn tribe who never submitted to tyranny, the Dalcassions of Munster. "This was a tribe," says the *Wars of the Gael and Gall*, "from whom it was never lawful to levy tribute, or hostages, or foster-ship fees." To them belonged the lead in entering an enemy country and the rear in returning, and they had the right to an alternate king in Cashel.

"There were governing and ruling this tribe two stout, able, valiant pillars, two gates of battle, two poles of combat, two spreading trees of shelter, the two sons of Kennedy, Mahon and Brian. Now, when they saw the bondage and oppression that was inflicted on the men of Munster and Erin, the advice they acted on was to avoid it, and not to submit to it at all. . . . They afterward carried off their people westward, and dispersed themselves among the forests and woods of the tribes there. They began to plunder and kill the foreigners immediately after that. It was woe to either party to meet the other because of the conflicts and battles and skirmishes."

But after a time the elder brother Mahon wearied of the conflict and made a truce. But Brian was not willing to follow him in this, because no matter how small the injury he might do to the foreign foes, he preferred it to peace, and though all others were silent on that head, he could not be. His warriors upheld him in that. "Death is hereditary with our people," they said, "but dishonor is not." So they continued the fight, and great was the slaughter they made against the Danes.

Great, on the other hand, were the hardships the enemy inflicted on Brian and his people: bad food and bad bedding and wild huts in the forests to live in. Mahon sent to inquire of his brother as to his condition, and was called a coward for his pains.

Mahon then called before him in one great place all the people of his tribe, and asked them what decision they wished to come to—whether they should make peace with the foreigners or should war upon them. They all answered, both old and young, that they preferred death and destruction to the oppression of the pirates. And it was the voice of hundreds as the voice of one man.

After that the foreigners hosted, and went against the Irish at Sulcoit. "A fierce, crimson battle was fought there from sunrise to midday. The foreigners were at length routed, and they fled to the ditches and the valleys, and to the solitudes of that great sweet-flowering place afterward. They were followed and killed and beheaded till evening."

The foreigners fled till they entered the fort of Limerick, but the Irish followed and killed them in the fort. Two thousand was the number of the slain.

That was the turning of the tide for the men of Erin. They were the ones who plundered now. They carried off from the foreigners their jewels and their best property, their saddles, beautiful and foreign, their gold and silver, their beautifully woven cloth of all colors and all

kinds, their silks and satins, scarlet and green and all pleasing colors. They carried away their soft, youthful girls,
their blooming, silk-clad young women, their active, well-
formed boys. The fort and the town they reduced to a cloud
of smoke and red fire. Then the whole of the captives were
collected on the near-by hills. Everyone fit for war was
killed, and everyone fit for a slave was enslaved.

It was Mahon, son of Kennedy, who was king of Munster
at this time. He took pledges and hostages of all the men
of Munster, and he killed the billeted soldiers of the foreigners in every territory. Seven defeats he gave to the foreigners. He burned Limerick twice, and banished Imar over
the sea to Wales for a year.

It was not the foreigners who brought about the death of
Mahon, but the people of a rival Irish tribe. The clan of
Cairbre united against him, and the great warrior was
killed by their leader. When news of this fact reached Brian,
he lamented greatly. He undertook the redress of the
Dalcassions for the killing of their chief, and assumed the
headship of the clan. He was not a wisp in the place of a
club, the people said, or a stone in the place of an egg, but
he was a hero in place of a hero, and valor after valor. He
made a ruthless, untiring war in revenge for his brother's
death. His reign, says the record, was full of battles, wars,
combats, plundering and conquest at first, but it became
bright, placid, happy, peaceful, prosperous, and wealthy.
Some of his adventures are here related.

Imar and his two sons were killed by Brian. Three years
before the tenth century ended he plundered the Islands of
the Shannon, which the Vikings had long held. He disturbed every place where the wives and children of the
foreigners were. He found gold and silver in abundance,

much of wealth and various goods in those islands of the fortress.

For eight years Brian was plundering and burning. All of southern Ireland came into his hands. He built a maritime fleet, in the manner of the Vikings, and stirred the waters of Brefne and Connaught. Then Leinster revolted from him and joined its force with the Danes. But Brian battled with them at Glenmama, and many were slain on both sides. The foreigners and the Leinstermen of Dublin were defeated. The castle of Dublin was plundered and burned by Brian, and he remained in the town from Great Christmas to Little Christmas.

Dublin had been the chief fort of the foreigners, and there Brian found great stores of wealth. Gold and silver and bronze and precious stones and beautiful goblets were hoarded there. All the plunder which the foreigners had taken from churches and sacred places was now recovered. Their good luck and fortune turned against the foreigners, and all the evils they had inflicted were fully avenged upon them. Brian killed and destroyed and exterminated and enslaved, says the story, "so that there was not a winnowing sheet from Benn Edair to the coast of Kerry in Western Erin that had not a foreigner in bondage in it. Nor was there a quern without a foreign woman. No son of a soldier or an officer deigned to put his hand to a flail, or any other labor on earth; nor did an Irishwoman deign to put her hand to the grinding of a quern, or to knead a cake, or to wash her clothes, but had a foreign man or foreign woman to work for them."

In the five weeks that Brian was at Dublin he fought five and twenty battles, besides sundry small skirmishes. All of Leinster was then ravaged by him, and its king captured. The king of the foreigners, too, submitted to Brian's power.

Then Brian returned home in triumph to Kincora. Men of learning say there was not a yeoman of the men of Munster who had not received enough plunder to furnish his home with gold and silver and cloth of gold, and all kinds of property.

Brian was now well nourished by success. He made demands on the High King of Ireland for hostages or battle, and when the high king found he could not rally enough allies to his side, he relinquished the throne to Brian and gave him men in hostage. Brian took hostages also from Ulster and all the north except the Cinel Conaill, the Clan of Columcille. But three years later when he made his circuit of Ireland there was not a chief who did not place men in submission to the new ruler, the only high king who really held the whole island under his rule.

That was a time of peace and glory for Brian and all Ireland. The king caused the foreigners to fly. He enslaved and reduced to bondage the foreign stewards and collectors, their swordsmen and mercenaries, their comely, large, handsome youths, their smooth, graceful girls.

After the banishment of the foreigners out of Erin and after the country was restored to a state of peace, it was said that a lone woman came from Torach in the north to Cloidhna in the south, carrying a ring of gold on a horse rod, and she was neither robbed nor insulted the whole of her journey.

Brian now undertook to repair the ravages that the Danes had inflicted on the country. He erected churches and sanctuaries. He paid professors and masters to teach wisdom and knowledge. He sent messengers over the seas to buy books and writings to replace the ones the pagans had burned and thrown into water. "By him were erected churches and bell-towers and many other works in like manner. By him were made bridges and causeways and highroads. By him were strengthened the duns, and the fastnesses and the islands, and the celebrated royal forts of Munster. He built the fortifications of Cashel of the Kings, and many others. He continued on this way prosperously, peacefully, giving banquets, hospitable, just-judging, venerated, chastely, and with devotion for fifteen years."

Revolt finally ended this peaceful and prosperous time, revolt which started within Brian's own family. The King of Leinster, who was brother to Brian's wife Gormley, a beautiful stormy petrel of a princess, was called on to pay tribute to the high king. Three straight pine masts cut from the woods of Leinster, he was bringing to Brian. The Irish were now following the example of the Danes, and building up fleets and commerce. It may have been for one of these ships that this tribute was levied.

At any rate, the masts had been cut, and the King of Leinster was himself in the company which was bringing them to Kincora. As they were ascending a rough mountain road the King of Leinster put out his hand to help with one of the trees, and thereby loosened a silver button from his silken tunic.

When the company arrived at Kincora the King of Leinster went to his sister and asked her to sew on the button.

She took the garment from him, and cast it in the fire, and began to reproach him for being in submission to Brian. A quarrel between Brian and the lesser king started soon after that, and the King of Leinster went away angry.

His people, when he told them of the quarrel, decided to rebel against Brian, and they gathered allies to help them. Leinster and the foreigners opposed Brian, and they were helped, too, by the Earl of Orkney, and allies from the Continent, and Britain.

Brian gathered to him all the men over whom he had power, the men of Munster and Connaught and Meath. They marched on Dublin, and all the plain to the north of the city was plundered by them.

It was with a proud eye that the old warrior, Brian Boru, looked back on his battle phalanx, huge, compact, moving haughtily and in silence. Three score and ten banners fluttered over them, of red and yellow and green, and all other colors, together with the lucky gold-spangled standard of the King of Brefne. That banner had brought victory to every battle in every conflict up to this time.

Hot for combat were these troops, armed for battle with glittering spears, terrible sharp darts, broad axes for cutting and maiming, swords for hewing and hacking. Their bright bossed shields covered handsome tunics, glossy, neat, white shirts. Precious jewels glittered in their crested golden helmets.

All the Danes and their allies had strong, polished armor encasing their bodies from head to foot. Their arrows were terrible and sharp-piercing, and had been anointed and browned, says the account of the *Wars*, "with the blood of dragons and toads and water-snakes of all kinds, to be cast and shot at the valiant captains of the enemy. They had hideous, barbarous quivers, and polished, yellow-shining bows, and strong dark spears. They had polished triple-plated corselets of refined iron, and warm-gleaming brass. They had valorous, hard-striking swords."

Over them floated the raven banner of the Valkyries, "woof-woven with entrials of men, warp hard-weighted with heads of the slain," says the account of the battle given in the *Orkney Saga*. Victory it brought to its own side, but death to the man who bore it.

These two great forces swept into battle as though a stern, terrific judgment day had come, and they to take vengeance on it. "Such thrusting," says the *Wars*, "such clashing and hewing there ensued that the foreigners and their women who watched from the battlement of Dublin declared that they saw flashes of fire in the air on all sides."

From one of the lesser kings who fought there under Brian we have a story of the battle which is incorporated in the *Wars*. "When the forces first came together each began to pierce the other. There was a field and a ditch between us and them, and the sharp wind of spring coming over them toward us, and it was not longer than the time a cow could be milked, or two cows, that we continued there, when not one person of the two hosts could recognize each other, though it might be his son or his brother who was nearest him, unless he should know his voice, we were so covered, as well our heads as our faces, and our clothes, with drops of gory blood, carried by the force of the cold, sharp wind.

"And even if we attempted to perform any deed of valor we were unable to do it, because our spears over our heads had become clogged and bound with long locks of hair, which the wind forced upon us, so that it was half occupation to disentangle them and cast them off. And it is one of the problems of Erin whether the valor of those who sustained that crushing assault was greater than those who bore the sight of it without running distracted before the winds, or fainting.

"They continued in battle array and in fighting from sunrise to evening. This is the same length of time which the tide takes to go, to flood and to fill. It was at the full-tide that the foreigners came out to fight in the morning, and the tide had come to the same place again at the close of day when the foreigners were defeated. The tide had carried their ships away from them, so that they had no place to fly but the sea. An awful rout was made of the foreigners, and of the Leinstermen, so that they fled simultaneously, and they shouted their cries for mercy and their whoops of rout and retreat. They fled to the sea like a herd of cows in heat, and from gad-flies and from insects, and they were pursued closely by the Dalcassions."

Many were the sword-dead after that battle, and many the sea-dead, too.

Brian himself was not engaged in the conflict. Some say that his age prevented him from fighting, a great age no matter which disputed figure one accepts. Others say that as the battle fell on Good Friday it was his vows of devotion which kept him from bearing a sword on that day.

This is the story of the battle as it relates to Brian: "When the forces met in combat, his cushion was placed under him, and he opened his psalter, and he began to clasp his hands and pray after the battle had commenced, and there was no one with him but his attendant Latenn.

"Brian said to him, 'Watch thou the battles and the combats, while I sing the psalms.' He sang fifty psalms and fifty prayers, and fifty paternosters, and he asked the attendant after that what the condition of the battle was.

" 'Mixed and closely confounded are the battalions, and each of them has come within grasp of the other, and not louder in my ears would be the echoes of blows from Tomar's Wood, if seven battalions were cutting it down, than are the resounding blows upon heads and bones and skulls, on both sides.'

" 'What is the condition of my son's standard?'

" 'It is standing, and many of the banners of the Dalcassions are around it, and many heads are falling around it, and a multitude of trophies and spoils, with heads of the foreigners are along with it.'

" 'That is good news indeed,' said Brian.

"His cushion was readjusted under him, and he sang the psalms and the prayers and the paters in the same manner as before.

" 'What now is the condition of the battle?' he asked his attendant.

" 'There is not living on earth one who could distinguish one from the other. For the greater part of the hosts on either side are fallen, and those who are alive are so covered with spatterings of crimson blood, head, body and vesture, that a father could not know his son among them, so confounded are they.'

" 'What is the condition of my son's standard?'

" 'It is still standing,' said Latenn.''

So again the cushion was readjusted while the old king repeated his paternosters and his psalms, and the fighting continued all the time.

" 'What of the forces now?' Brian asked.

" 'They appear to me as if Tomar's Wood was on fire, and the seven battalions had been cutting away its underwood, and its young shoots for a month, leaving its stately trees and immense oaks standing. In such manner are the armies on either side, after the greater part of them are fallen, leaving a few brave men and gallant heroes only standing. Their further condition is that they are wounded, and pierced through, and dismembered, and they are disorganized all around like the grindings of a mill turning the wrong way, and the foreigners are now defeated, and the standard of Murrough your son has fallen.'

" 'That is sad news,' said Brian. 'On my word the honor and valor of Erin fell when that standard fell, and Erin has fallen now indeed, and never shall there appear henceforth a champion comparable to that champion. And what avails it to me to survive this, or that I should obtain the sovereignty of the world, after the fall of my son?'

" 'Woe is me,' said the attendant, 'if thou wouldst take my advice, thou wouldst mount thy horse, and we would go to the camp, and remain there amongst the servants, and everyone who escapes this battle will come to us, and around us they will rally.'

"While the two were engaged in conversation the attendant perceived a party of the foreigners approaching them. The Earl Brodar it was, with two attendants.

" 'There are people coming toward us here,' said Brian's attendant.

" 'Woe is me, what manner of people are they?'

" 'A blue, stark-naked people.'

" 'Alac, they are the foreigners of the armies, and it is not to do good that they come.'

"He arose and stepped off his cushion, and unsheathed his sword. Brodar passed him by, and noticed him not. One of the three who were there, and who had been in Brian's service said, 'King king, this is the king.'

" 'It is not he, but a noble priest,' said Brodar.

" 'By no means,' said the soldier. 'That is the great King Brian.'

"Brodar then turned around and appeared with a bright, gleaming, trusty, battle-axe in his hand, with the handle set in the middle of it. When Brian saw him he gazed at him, and gave him a stroke with his sword and cut off his left leg at the knee and his right leg at the foot. The foreigner dealt Brian a stroke which cleft his head utterly, and Brian killed the second man that was with Brodar, and they fell mutually by each other."

So died Brian Boru, named by his enemies Best-Natured of Kings. As for his countrymen, they quarreled among themselves as to whether his fame outshone Conn of the Hundred Battles, and Conaire the Great, and Niall of the Nine Hostages. It is the author of the *Annals of Clonmacnoise* who records the controversy, and there is no doubt about the casting of his ballot. He held, without qualification, that Brian bore the bell away from them all. Simply he records his convictions:

"He was a meet salve to cure the festered sores of Ireland. All the physick of the world could not cure it else, wherein a short time he banished the Danes, made up the churches and religious houses, restored the nobility to the ancient patrimonies and possessions, and in fine brought all to a notable reformation."

Chapter X

"WE HAVE FOUND A GOLDEN CUP"

So the Danes were subdued, and the light of their pillage fires faded from the Irish sky. Now on a calm and moonlight night the monks no longer quaked in their monasteries, fearing attack by the vandals. The Danes were still in Ireland, secure in their seaport towns. Their high-prowed ships still rode the waves. Flashing oars carried them to France and England, and the homeland to the north. Roving and trading always, they were building up a commerce which would have a large part in the later development of the country. But the fierce hatred they had had for the Irish was cooled. Their ambitions were bridled by defeat, so that they were content to be colonists in the land they had hoped to conquer. They were even beginning to embrace the religion they had so vigorously abhorred.

When the English arrived, a century and a half after the battle of Clontarf, they found Hasculf the Dane governor of Dublin, and no Irishman more fierce in defense of the country. But those days of English invasion are so dark, so much unhappiness filled their hours. We do not need to face them yet. Let us turn from them for a while to speak of pleasanter things.

127

Not many years after St. Columba, his gray eyes filled with tears, had looked back on Ireland for the last time, another cleric sailed from an Irish port. It was the time of chanting choirs, of little bells struck at midnight in desert places, of voices of scholars from many lands blending in recital. The Irish people had welcomed the new learning and the new religion with something approaching romantic fervor. They were enchanted, enraptured with the new way of life. It was not enough for them to enjoy it themselves. The ardor that filled their hearts directed their feet to other lands, and moved their tongues to preach. Columba was the first of countless exiles in this cause, and the monastery he founded on the gray rocks of Iona marked the beginning of the great period of Irish missionary work abroad.

The second was like him even in name, Columbanus, Prince of Druids, famous equally as the greatest poet of his time and as the Irishman who helped carry Christianity back to Europe after the devastation of the Continent by Germanic hordes.

It is so like the Irish, fervent in their devotion to the new ideal of chastity, that they ascribe fear of fleshly temptation as the reason why Columbanus fled from Ireland. As a youth he was beautiful, and many maidens would have dallied with him. Was it love he wanted, or purity? With one breath he ached for love, and with the next he worshiped purity. What was he to do? A legend of his early life says that he sought counsel of a holy recluse in her near-by cell. She looked on him compassionately.

"Twelve years ago," she said, "I myself left my own house to enter into the war with sin. Inflamed by the fires of youth, you will attempt in vain to escape from your frailty while you remain on your native soil. Have you forgotten Adam and Samson, David and Solomon, all lost by the seduction of beauty and love? To save yourself, young man, you must flee."

His mother tried to stop him, and threw herself down in the doorway. He stepped over her body, and left his home forever. It was to the north that he turned at first, and on an island in Lough Erne found sanctuary with the scholar Sinnell. The older man put him to work on a commentary of Psalms, thinking that holy work would drive away unholy thoughts. It was hardly the choice of wisdom. "All thy garments smell of myrrh, and aloes, and cassia, whereby they have made thee glad. . . . The king's daughter is all glorious within: her clothing is of wrought gold. She shall be brought unto the king in raiment of needlework: the virgins her companions that follow her shall be brought unto thee." He was not yet thirty years old, and his blood was hot within him.

Bangor knew him next, and for twelve years of study the music of the perpetual chanting of the choirs fell sweetly on his ears. But still he could not rest. Something within goaded him. There were twelve companions with him when he set sail from Bangor for the Loire, and the countries which still lay beneath the Hun-made ruins of the old Roman civilization.

Attila used to boast that where his horses had trod grass never grew again. Dark forests now covered the land which had once been the scene of happy cultivation. Wild beasts prowled the thickets, and made their lairs in the crumbling stone ruins of Roman temples. The fallen marbles that had once been statues of gods and famous men were now overgrown with brambles and briars. The people who still remained lived miserably in the woods, stripped of all comfort, culture, art, and religion. The scattered courts of the princes were pale and distorted pictures of what the old life had been under the emperors. Laymen could scarcely read or write, and virtue and learning seemed about to perish together.

His little bell in his hand, his cross before him, book-satchel on his back, Columbanus led his little band through this wild country. Wherever he found listeners he preached to them. Wherever night overtook the company they slept, shelterless and without comfort. Their sandals wore thin, their robes became tattered. Wild and uncouth they must have seemed, but they carried with them the seeds of learning and religion.

So they came after several years to the court of Grunthan, least dissolute of all Clovis's grandsons. It was the prince's wish that Columbanus stay with him, and convert the people of Burgundy to Christianity. The ancient Roman castle of Annegray was near by, and from its ruins Columbanus built the monastery which was to mean so much to the country, and to Christianity. Soon the noble Franks and Burgundians were bringing their sons to him to be educated, and even asking him to cut their own long hair, the sign of their nobility and freedom, and admit them as brothers. After a few years their numbers were sufficient for him to organize a perpetual service of song, and the voices of the monks rose night and day, "unwearied as those of the angels."

Rich gifts were brought to the abbot, but any who came to Columbanus, rich or poor, was bound by bonds of poverty and labor. They cleared away the tangled growths, felled trees, planted fields and gardens. A man worked till

he slept on his feet. He fasted often, and eight times a day
the chapel bell rang to call the monks to prayers.

In the strict Rule of Columbanus the abbot found, perhaps, his own answer to the question he had asked the
aged recluse so many years before. There is no more mention
of temptation. Now he had peace, and peace gave him
gentleness. "The birds came to receive his caress, and the
wild creatures of the wood showed no fear of him. Squirrels
ran in and out of his cowl, and perched happily on his
shoulders. Once in the forest a wolf sniffed at his garment,
and left him unharmed."

In time the growing monastic family taxed the halls of
old Annegray. Near them were the ruins of the Roman
castle of Luxeuil, one of the places which had suffered
most from Attila and his Huns. They had filled the moat
of the old castle, scaled its walls, and once inside, had
massacred all the inhabitants. Long deserted, the old idols
formerly worshiped by the Gauls toppling in the woods,
the stones of the Roman baths moss-covered and cracked,
it was still a place of dignity and beauty. From these ruins
of an old civilization grew the abbey of Luxeuil, to be for
centuries a stronghold of the new civilization, and the
monastic metropolis of Burgundy. Two years later, Columbanus was able to found not far away the monastery of
Fontaines.

Those years in the foothills of the Vosges Mountains
must have been filled with much gratification for the old
abbot. Three monasteries already knew his rule, and their
schools were filled with the children of the noble Burgundians. Order and learning now existed where he had found
only ruins. His life had been hard, but he had achieved
much. In his rare leisure he turned happily to the writing

of exquisite prose, and to devising quaint metrical variations of Greek verse. His devoted disciple Valerie had made him a garden that produced flowers of unequaled fragrance. A mark of divine favor, Columbanus held it, and once when the young monk entered the hall where the abbot was lecturing, he carried with him so strong a perfume of these flowers that the air of the hall was filled with it.

The lecturer paused, his nostrils appraised the perfume. "It is thou, Valerie, my beloved," he exclaimed with delight, "it is thou who should be the lord and abbot of this monastery, and not I."

But the haven of the old castle walls was invaded by the anger of the young king's grandmother. She had been a beautiful young princess of Spain, Brunehalt, but in her old age her ambition to rule had made her forget virtue and kindness. She encouraged the young king in a life of dissipation that she herself might rule the country. When Columbanus tried to reform the court, she turned against him and had him banished. It would have pleased her to send him back to Ireland, and he was conducted to a seaport town. When he was seated in the boat that was to carry him back to his country the wind failed. Three times a start was made, and three times the boat was becalmed. The superstitious sailors became convinced that the Lord was against the journey, and allowed their passenger to land.

Once again he was without a home. Once again the world was before him. With one companion who had come with him from Ireland he journeyed perilously through many lands. In Switzerland, on the shores of Lake Constance, he found a fierce and cruel people who worshiped the god

Wodin. He undertook to convert them to Christianity, but a religion which preached gentleness and love had no appeal for these savage people. Then Columbanus tried harsher methods. He broke the people's idols, burned their pagan temples of worship, and threw their gilded images into the icy Alpine waters of the lake. The boilers in which they had prepared beer as a sacrifice to Wodin were hacked and ruined.

In revenge the people warred upon the strangers, and refused them food. They drove them from their rude shelters. The two Irishmen were forced to live on wild birds and woodland fruits. But, as always, they cleared what land they could, and soon had a garden of fruit trees and vegetables. The waters of the lake afforded them fish, which they caught in nets of Columbanus' making.

After three years the hopelessness of their task became apparent. "We had found a golden cup," mourned Columbanus, "but it is full of serpents."

The time had come for Columbanus to part with his favorite disciple. St. Gall was ill of a fever, and could not travel far. He lingered in the neighborhood, and from that lingering came the monastery of St. Gall. Columbanus left the Alps behind him, and traveled to Lombardy. In a secluded gorge of the Apennines, under the patronage of the Lombard king, he founded the last of his monasteries, Bobbio. There the story of clearing and building and planting and teaching was once again repeated, and there Columbanus spent the last years of his life. He was weakening now, and his exertions were limited. But his fervor never failed, and his delight in composing verses in Greek lasted his lifetime. "Frivolous trifles," he called them deprecatingly to a friend to whom some were sent.

There was nothing frivolous about his influence on the Continent. His monasteries, always strongholds of learning and piety, were fruitful parent stock, and from them countless others branched out. The companions he had brought with him from Ireland, the monks he had trained and taught at Luxeuil, the brothers and cousins of his disciples, fired by the example of the exile from Bangor, founded daughter abbeys throughout the land, and put them under the Rule of Columbanus. A hundred years after his coming the map of Central Europe is dotted with them. Their names are a musical roll call: Fleury and Cusance, and Besançon, Bèze, Jouarre, Reuil. The list stretches out to nearly a hundred. They filled the valley of the Marne, climbed to the Alps, sought the sea to the west. St. Valerie of the lovely gardens at Luxeuil founded one at the mouth of the river Somme, near the shore of the English Channel. One cannot help wondering if the flowers there were as fragrant as those of the old castle garden which Columbanus had so deeply loved.

It was hardly a pattern which the old abbot set, for none who came after him accomplished so much. But he was the first of countless Irishmen who for centuries went to France and Germany as missionaries, so that an Irish pilgrim, "walking the world," as they said, would not have to travel many miles to find a shelter where the brothers were his countrymen, and where the manuscripts of the monastery library were inscribed not only in Latin but also in the familiar Gaelic characters.

At the end of the eighth century, when Charlemagne, master of all France, was doing his best to build up scholarship and learning, the Irish influence was strong. Charlemagne himself was no great scholar. His hand was more facile with his good sword Joyeuse than when cramped around a pencil, though he kept under his pillow a slate so as to practice penmanship in the night. Nevertheless, he was determined to have the greatest school in the world at his court, and bring to it the best scholars in every department of learning.

It is true that the head of the famous Palace School was an Englishman, Alcuin, but he was in all probability trained in an Irish school. At any rate, his correspondence with Colchu, greatest scholar in Ireland, and headmaster of Clonmacnoise, was affectionate and deferential. He addressed him as "dear master," and sent him gifts of silver and consecrated oil. The Church increased in all quarters of Europe, he reported. The ancient Saxons and all the Frisian tribes, yielding under the pressure of King Charles, some to bribes, some to threats, had all accepted the Christian faith. He feared he might have committed some offense, since his eyes had not been rewarded for so long with a sight of the master's delightful letters. He wrote that all Colchu's men who were at court served God prosperously.

Who were they, these Irishmen at Charlemagne's court? Some of their names are known: Joseph, and Dungal the astronomer, and Dicuil, who wrote in 825 a complete geography of the world as it was known then. Clement, another Irishman, took the chair of chief teacher soon after Alcuin's retirement to Touraine. The stream of exiles seems unending.

In the time of Charlemagne's grandson, Charles the Bald, "all Hibernia, scorning the perils of the sea," had landed on French soil, "a herd of philosophers." Their reputation for scholarship remained untarnished, though Ireland was no longer the center of learning of the world.

John Scotus Erigena, greatest philosopher of his time, and some say greatest scholar of the Middle Ages, was one of the Irish exiles, as one can see from his name. The weight of his learning did not smother his wit. It evidently did not crowd out his affection for what was poetically called "the heavenly dew."

"What is there between Sottum and Scottum?" the king once asked Erigena, when the two were drinking together. "The width of the table, sire," the Irishman answered.

The exiles did not come empty-handed to the Continent. Their book-satchels were fat with manuscripts which had been inscribed at Kells, and Clonmacnoise, and Bangor. The libraries of Liége, and Bobbio, and Vienna, and many another European monastery, hold them to this day. Sheepskin which became vellum in the valley of the Boyne may lie now on shelves of abbeys whose windows look out on the Loire or the Rhine.

It was not only books that some exiles brought, but gold. More than one Irish king provided the money which founded abbeys in far lands. Conor O'Brien, King of Munster in the early part of the twelfth century, was the patron of St. James of Ratisbon, one of a dozen or more Irish monasteries in Germany. "Now be it known," says the chronicle of the abbey, "that neither before or since was there a monastery equal to this in the beauty of its towers, columns and vaultings erected and completed in so short a time, because the plenteousness of riches and money bestowed by the kings and princes of Ireland was almost unbounded."

Far away and long ago were the towers of St. James builded. The monks who were present at their consecration have been dust these eight hundred years and more. But the story of their lives is testimony which does not perish.

Let us speak of Marianus Scotus, scholar and scribe of St. James. "So great a grace of writing did Divine Providence bestow on him," says his biographer, "that he wrote many and tedious volumes with a rapid pen. With his own hand he wrote the Old and the New Testaments, with explanatory commentaries of the same books, not once or twice, but many times, in poor habit, and on slender food. At the same place he wrote many little books and many manuals and psalters for indigent widows, and poor clerics of the same city, for the health of his soul, without any hope of earthly gain. Moreover, many converts of the monastic order, who in faith and charity, and in imitation of the holy Marianus, coming from the territories of Hibernia, dwelt in Bavaria and Franconia, on a pilgrimage, were for the greater part supported by the writings of Marianus."

The old cleric worked not only by day but also by night. So numerous were the volumes which he inscribed that a legend grew up about his labors. The darkness of the sunless hours, so it was said, was illuminated by the radiance of his shining fingers.

Another Marianus came to St. James later in that century, to enrich further the tradition of its scholarship. He had left Ireland in his early manhood, and had taught for a while the liberal and other arts in Paris. "In those first days when youth in me was happy, and life was swift in doing, and I wandering in the divers cities of sweet France, gave all my might to letters." It was not Marianus who wrote those words, but a countryman of his, who spoke for many.

What magic was in Paris in those old days! It was the city so beloved by scholars that they lived gladly in crowded garret rooms, and shared among many one gown for lectures. It was the Paris of Pierre Abélard, famed scholar and tragic lover, whose name, even here, for pity and love must be linked with his beautiful Héloïse. It was the city of John of Salisbury, and Giraldus Cambrensis, and Nicholas Breakspear, minor actors, all of them, in the great drama which is to come.

Marianus had this Nicholas Breakspear for a pupil, and then went on to Ratisbon. The shabby Englishman's travels did not end till he was in Rome, and had become Pope Adrian IV.

When Gregory, Abbot of Ratisbon, was admitted to the Pope's presence in Rome the latter asked about his old teacher in Paris. "Master Marianus is well," replied Gregory, " and is living with us as a monk at Ratisbon."

"God be praised," exclaimed the Pope. "I know not in the Catholic Church an abbot who has under him a man as excellent in wisdom, discretion, genius, eloquence, good morals, benevolence, judgment, and other divine gifts as my Master Marianus."

But Ratisbon is far from Ireland, and the struggle we must speak of is at hand. Let us go back there, back to the land which Marianus in Paris called "Island of Saints and Scholars," and see for ourselves what sort of place it had become.

There is no denying that forty years after the Danes were subdued Ireland was in a sorry state. No king as strong as Brian Boru had come after him, and the country he had ruled as supreme monarch had fallen into disunity, with each part quarreling with every other. The morals of the people, undermined by long years of warfare and unsettled conditions, had reached their lowest ebb. Hear the confession of the annalists, in recording the happenings of the year 1050. "Much inclement weather happened in the land of Ireland, which carried away corn, milk, fruit and fish from the people, so that there grew up dishonesty among all, that no protection was extended to church or fortress, gossipred or mutual oath, until the clergy and laity of Munster assembled with the chieftains under Donogh, son of Brian, and Cele, son of Donnecan, the head of the piety of Ireland, at Kildulua, where they enacted a law and a restraint upon every injustice against great and small. God gave peace and favorable weather in consequence of this law."

The scribe who made that entry doubtless thought he was writing the truth. To a certain extent he was. The shores of the island were free of the ships of invaders. There was no great struggle over the high kingship going on. But the annals of succeeding years are not devoid of mention of blindings, sometimes of brother by brother, of murders caused by malice and envy, of a king killed in a church steeple after only three days' reign. But English and Welsh annals of the same time are recording instances so similar that one realizes that they were part of the violent and vindictive life of the time. One must remember that in Ireland, as elsewhere, peace is always comparative.

So "peaceful" Ireland repaired the ravages of two centuries of invasion. Learning blossomed anew in the land, and scholars from across the seas once more came to Irish schools. Artists in metalwork were modeling those chalices and crosses whose lovely and intricate designs have delighted the eyes of all succeeding generations. Somewhere in the island the *Book of Hymns* was being written, and so was the *Book of Leinster*, and the *Book of the Dun Cow*, the three most important relics of Celtic literature in the world today. At Clonmacnoise, looking out on St. Ciaran's Plain of Crosses, Abbot Tigernach was compiling the annals which bear his name. From Scotland and England were coming harpers to be instructed in the playing of the quaintly named harp-strings, "the two sisters," "servant to the sisters," "lying together," "string of the half note," and all their melodious comrades.

St. Dunstan in England was as entranced with the sweetness of the music played by his Irish teachers as he was with the brilliance of their minds. "If he himself should at any time forsake the cithera for letters they would take it up, and strike the humming strings with sweet sound." So wrote William of Malmsbury in the twelfth century, and he adds an admiring comment on the continued excellence of Irish scholarship. It is high praise. William of Malmsbury was not one to speak lightly, and a better judge of scholarship never existed.

The Church itself was undergoing reforms. It had never followed closely the Roman pattern, but now renewed contact with the Continent was making the Irish variations obvious, and changes were being made in services and constitution. The old order was essentially monastic. Abbots were the supreme rulers, and bishops executed their special functions at their command. The bishops had no jurisdiction, and sometimes several of them lived together in one group.

When Malachy of Armagh became bishop, early in the twelfth century, he was filled with eagerness to "root out barbarous rites, and to plant the rights of the Church. . . . He instituted anew Confession, Confirmation, and the marriage contract, of all of which those over whom he was placed were either ignorant or negligent." Malachy was not a person to be defeated in his purpose. When faced with the necessity of going to Rome to receive the pallium from the Pope, he set out bravely on the long journey and would have walked much of the way, since there were few horses for his many companions. In York, however, he was presented with a pack horse, "rough to ride, at first, but afterwards, by wonderful change, he found that it suited him well, and ambled pleasantly."

While this adaptable beast was plodding toward Rome, burdened with Malachy, "a man who could not but be dear to those who knew him," an Irishman of quite another feather was disturbing the homeland. The prologue now is finished. The stage is set. The characters are waiting in the wings. We cannot hold the curtain longer. It rises, and the great tragedy of the English Invasion of Ireland begins.

Chapter XI

"TREMBLING SOD"

→»)«←

I T HAS long been the popular belief among outsiders that Ireland was invaded for love of a beautiful woman. A princess seized by an ardent lover, flight, capture, and parting: all these romantic ingredients have wound mistily about the name of the Irish Dervorgilla, and made her a figure of fabulous charm. And in this gay phantasmagoria her lover, Dermot Mac Murrough, King of Leinster, has been a hero worthy of her glamour, a sturdy figment clothed in the virtues of strength and passion. Tradition has made him an impetuous Romeo, sacrificing a country on the altar of young love, a bright and shining suitor who would not halt at any means which would help him to win back his heart's desire.

But to the Irish, and all who read their annals, he is the Villain of all history. He brought the English to Ireland in 1169, not for love of a princess—that affair was seventeen years past and of small moment to him—but to help him win back the province from which he had been banished because of his long-continued tyranny and cruelty.

Glance at the entries concerning him which appear in the various chronicles of the times. In the year 1133, according to the *Annals of Clonmacnoise*, he exercised great cruelties and tyranny upon the Leinster nobility. He killed two princes of the province, and "did excrably put out the eyes of another." A little later he forced the Abbess of Kildare out of her cloister, and compelled her to marry one of his own people. Her ravishing accompanied the death of a hundred and seventy of her townsmen and kin. Waterford, where resident Danes had a fleet of two hundred ships in the harbor, was besieged by Dermot in 1137, and hostages taken from the city. For a time there is no mention of him, but it can hardly be assumed that he spent the years peaceably. That was not his nature. In 1152 he was embroiled with O'Rourke, King of Meath. It was his usual story of battle, and plunder, and seize. "Dermot Mac Murrough, King of Leinster," say the *Annals of Clonmacnoise*, "took the lady Dervorgilla, wife of O'Rourke, with her cattle with her, and kept her for a long space to satisfy his insatiable, carnal, and adulturous lust."

The Four Masters give the abduction only brief mention. The great synod of Drogheda, with three hundred Irish ecclesiastics meeting with the papal envoy, dazzled their eyes, and blinded them to matters which seemed of less importance.

Dervorgilla is thought to have gone gladly, having told her lover that her husband, the one-eyed O'Rourke, King of Meath, would be away. Still, it is no picture of a youthful romance. Dervorgilla was forty-five at the time of the elopement, and Dermont over sixty. In less than a year, Dervorgilla had been taken from Dermot by a raiding party led by an O'Connor, and was back with her husband. She did not stay with him long. Within a year she entered the convent of Mellifont to spend in penitence her long old age. She is seen no more in the world of men, and the only word that comes of her is when she lays an offering of gold, and a golden chalice, on the altar of the abbey, and later when she founds the church of nuns at Clonmacnoise.

But Dermot was very much of the world. His hand was against all men, and his great body often in combat. His voice became hoarse with much shouting of his battle cry. Cruelty, tyranny, injustice, he practiced them all. Finally even his own Leinstermen turned against him. They joined with the men of Meath and Brefne, and the Danes of Dublin, to burn his camp, demolish his stone castle at Ferns, and banish the tyrant overseas.

The oppressor gone, the princes and clergy and laymen of Ireland met peaceably at the Yellow Ford of Tlachtgha. Many good resolutions were passed at this meeting, say the Four Masters, respecting veneration for churches and clerics, and control of tribes and territories, so that women used to traverse Ireland in safety alone.

Meanwhile the exiled Dermot cast about for ways to recover his kingdom. He knew Henry II of England to be an ambitious king, and one not afraid of battle. But Henry, while he listened courteously to Dermot's invitation to invade Ireland, and help him recover his lost kingdom, was busily engaged in fighting in France. He had long ago cast his eyes toward Ireland, but had been hindered by his mother from attacking the island. Now Aquitaine seemed more important to him than Ireland, and he refused to be drawn into Dermot's quarrel.

But wait. Wales was full of turbulent knights, richer in courage than in worldly goods. Henry had had more than one skirmish with them. Why not give them license to fight in Ireland? If they were engaged abroad they would not be disturbing the doubtful security of Henry's rule in Wales. And if they should fall by Irish swords—

So Henry, King of England, Duke of Normandy and Aquitaine, and Count of Anjou, to all his liegemen, English, Norman, Welsh, and Scots, sent greeting. He let it be known that he had received into his grace and favor Dermot, Prince of Leinster. Whosoever of his vassals should give aid to him in recovering his territories was assured of the king's license and favor on that behalf.

Armed with these letters patent, Dermot made his way to Wales. Had he more definite directions from the king? One cannot be sure. It may have been chance alone that took him to the Earl of Pembroke and his myriad kinsmen. But consider who these people were.

Eighty years before, while Henry I was still a prince, and William the Red was king of a newly Normandized England, there had been a fierce old prince of South Wales, Rhys ap Tudor. While fighting him, the young Prince Henry had taken as hostage, and mistress, Rhys's lovely young daughter Nesta. "The Helen of Wales," she was called, not only for her beauty.

This princess had had, in her eventful life, two lovers, two husbands, and many sons and daughters. Her children, and their descendants, constituted a menace to the English rule. Royal Welsh blood mingled with the blood of the reigning house of England in the veins of Robert, Earl of Gloucester, and Henry, Nesta's sons by Henry I. Royal Welsh blood mingled with noble blood of Normandy in the veins of all his half-brothers, sons of Gerald of Windsor and Stephen of Abertivy. Legitimate or not, they were princes in an unpeaceful land. Also, as cousins of the unconquered Prince of Wales, Nesta's brother Griffin for whose head the king had offered "mountaines of gold," they were potential allies for him in the intermittent struggles of the Welsh against the English. Though they were reft of their possessions by succeeding kings, though they were often imprisoned, and pitted, when possible, one against the other, they were still a threat to the English rule. Richard, Earl of Pembroke, was their leader.

It was this Richard, called Strongbow, grandson of Nesta's son by Henry I, who promised aid to Dermot of Leinster. Lately dispossessed of his castle of Pembroke, impoverished, restless, and ambitious, he welcomed the chance to build his fortunes in Ireland. Dermot promised him the hand of his daughter Eva in marriage, and the succession of his kingdom at his death. The bargain concluded, Dermot sailed quietly back to Ireland, and spent the winter in hiding, not as a prince, but as a private person.

But when, in the spring, there came to him the news of the landing of two of Richard's knights, with attendant archers and men-at-arms, off went his poor mantle, and on went his princely attire again. His hoarse voice once more shouted his battle cry, and such is the nature of the Irish people that some of them, hearing again that strident summons, rallied to the prince, and joined his army.

So with great joy, at the head of five hundred men, he marched to Bannow, and joined the English.

The great jovial Robert FitzStephen, son of the Princess Nesta, on instructions from his kinsman Strongbow, had mustered thirty men-at-arms from his own kindred in Wales, sixty men in half-armor, and three hundred archers and foot soldiers. Just released from three years' captivity at home, his fortunes low, his spirits high, Ireland looked a land of promise to this soldier of fortune, who was as fond of battle as he was of wine and women. With him, the earl had sent one Hervey de Mountmaurice, his uncle, a luckless, wily man, without armor or money, whose business it was to spy out the resources of the land.

With these adventurers were joined Maurice de Prendergast, with ten men-at-arms, and a large body of archers. Since they were all met to replenish their fortunes, in return for aid in arms, many oaths and promises passed between them and Dermot. Then the combined forces, their banners high, marched toward the town of Wexford.

The townsmen, fierce descendants of the old Danes, sallied forth to meet them. But when they heard the strange voice of the English trumpets, the rattling of swords against mail, and the horses' neighing, and saw with fresh eyes the glittering armor of horses and men, the like of which they had never seen before, fear altered their minds, and they retired into the town.

The English lost no time in preparing for an attack; with loud cries and desperate vigor they attacked the walls. The townsmen repulsed the sally, casting down from the battlements large stones and beams. Next day the English renewed the attack with more cunning and deliberation. The defenders of the town, distrustful of this new manner of warfare, lacking men and munitions and provisions for a siege, and recalling that Dermot was their rightful king, sent messengers to entreat for peace. It was restored by submission of the town, and the delivering of hostages to Dermot.

As spoils of war, the town of Wexford, and all the adjoining territory, was given the English commanders.

The Wexford success brought increase to Dermot's army. With English and Irish to the number of three thousand they set out for Ossory, where Dermot had an enemy. Neither dastard nor coward was Duvenald, Prince of Ossory and when the invading army came into his land they found the bogs and woods trenched and plashed, and valiant men against them. So long as the fight was in the woody places success went to the defenders, but when they pursued the enemy to open country, where horseman with spears could ride against them, the tide of fortune turned. The Irish were defeated with great slaughter. Three hundred heads of Ossory men were heaped in one gory pile, and Dermot, with ghoulish delight, turned them over one by one in order to recognize his dead enemies.

Meanwhile, news of the English invaders and their success with their Irish ally had come to the ears of Roderick O'Connor, King of Connaught. High King of Ireland, he also claimed to be, but his deeds do not justify the title. It is little less than irony to name him that, and place him with Conn of the Hundred Battles, and Niall of the Nine Hostages, and fiery old Brian Boru. For Roderick was not valor after valor, and stout heart after courage, but he was a wisp of straw in place of a club, and a word in place of a blow. Dreading battle as he did, it was not hard for Dermot to buy off his opposition with promise of submission when Leinster should be rewon. Dermot even gave hostages to the Connaughtman, for he held another man's safety as lightly as he did a promise.

These matters being settled, and the English forces being strengthened by the coming of Maurice FitzGerald, another of Nesta's sons, and his followers, it was not long before all the neighboring districts of Dublin were laid waste, and ravaged by fire and sword.

Now Dermot was seized with an appetite to have all Ireland in his power. The whole island in place of a province for them to divide was not sad news for Dermot's allies, and they encouraged him in his ambition. Letters were sent to the Earl of Pembroke, urging him to join them with all haste. Success is a pungent bait. The prize was now richer than it had been before. The earl applied to the king for permission to invade Ireland, and received the royal license.

So more ships sailed for Irish ports, and more invaders landed. The little princes along the coast met them as they could. They raised their troops, they ranged the shores. Their cry was kill, kill, kill. But still the English came, hungry for gain and eager to risk life for fortune.

It was fall before Richard himself landed. He had marched through Wales, gathering recruits as he came. Two hundred men-at-arms he had when he sailed from Milford Haven, and other troops to the number of a thousand. A fair wind carried him to Waterford, where he landed September 10.

Raymond le Gros, whom Richard had sent before him, had already displayed his banners against the walls of the town. The next day the combined forces advanced to make the attack. Twice they were repulsed by the townsmen. Then Raymond, making a breach in the walls, rushed in with his men, and gained a bloody victory.

Waterford and Wexford had now been won. The earl tarried only long enough to claim in marriage the daughter of Dermot Mac Murrough, as he had been promised. A garrison was placed in the town, and the whole English force, led by Richard, Earl of Pembroke, and all of Nesta's adventurous brood, with banners displayed, marched toward Dublin.

Where is the sword of Ireland now? Where is her valor? Where is her might? Erin's evil is on her. Is there none to warn her of it? Is there none to cast it off? Bitter, bitter is the answer. Ireland's sword is in a feeble hand. Ireland's might is divided. Valor? Yes. Valor always. Valor to last through hundreds of years of misery and oppression. But what good is valor unless it has a leader? What profits courage if it makes the fight alone? Bound together, the forces of Ireland might have thrown off this grievous yoke. Led by such a king as Brian Boru, the Irish would have swept the English into the sea. But Brian is dead. There is no one great enough to wear his mantle.

The English came to the walls of Dublin. They had come by devious ways, avoiding the strong tribes which might have disputed their passage. They found Dublin warned against them, and ready in defense. A truce was agreed upon by both sides, that the terms of a treaty of peace might be discussed. But when the Irish had put down their swords, and withdrawn from the walls, two bands of English, on opposite sides of the city, rushed to the barriers, and took possession of the place. A great slaughter of the citizens followed. But many of them, under the Danish ruler Hasculf, escaped in their ships and boats, and sailed to the northern islands to secure reinforcements.

A few days sufficed the earl for putting the city in order under his rule. Then leaving Miles de Cogan as constable, he marched with Mac Murrough to Meath, and the whole of that province was plundered and laid waste by fire and

sword. Clonard was ransacked, and the churches of Kells
and Telltown and Slane and many others were burned and
robbed.

Did the high king come to defend his people? "You have
strayed out of your province," was the word he sent to
Dermot. "You have broken the bounds agreed between us.
Restrain your foreign allies to the limits of your own province, or I will have your son's head cut off, and sent to
you."

But Dermot was now determined to have the monarchy
of all Ireland, if it cost him his son's head and many another's. He sent that message to Roderick, and received in
due time the head of the son he had given in hostage.

What was an enemy's head to the English? Things were
now going well with them. They swept their swords over
the camp of southern Ireland, and carried off armor, horses,
and enough provisions to keep them for a year.

In time, news of this success of the English forces flew
abroad, and came to the ears of Henry. He was not pleased.
His little scheme had failed him. Instead of being overwhelmed by the Irish, his troublesome knights were whirl-
ing high on the wheel of fortune. Overwhelmed with
jealous rage, he sent them word to return to England before
the ensuing Easter, under pain of banishment from his
kingdom forever.

Here Richard showed himself a diplomat and a politician.
Of all his comrades he chose the amiable, curly-haired
Raymond to act as courier to the king. The chubby man
knew as well how to win a heart as a fortress. His charms
were augmented by a letter from the earl. "I came into this
land by your Majesty's leave and favor (as farre as I remember) to aid your servant Dermot Mac Murrough. What I

have wonne, was with the sword. What is given me, I give you, and hold under your favor."

These gentle words not proving effective, the earl sent another messenger, this time his uncle, Hervey de Mountmaurice.

Now Hasculf the Dane, late governor of Dublin, who had fled from the city as it was captured by the English, came down from the northern islands with three score ships. Filled with fighting men they were, all well appointed in the Danish manner, being harnessed with good brigandines, jacks, and shirts of mail. Their shields, buckles, and targets were round, and colored red, and bound around with iron. In battle array, with hearts as firm as their armor, they marched to the east gate of the city, and prepared to assault it.

Miles de Cogan came out to give them battle, and both sides lost many a tall man. But Richard de Cogan, brother of Miles, having secretly issued out from another gate, fell upon the Danes from the rear, and the two brothers had the killing of them before and behind. But even in defeat and capture old Hasculf was defiant, and boasted that the English victory would not endure for long. Off came his head at the word of de Cogan.

The Irish, during all this time, were plotting among themselves the overthrow of the English. Mac Murrough, who had brought them to the island and made, as the Four Masters said, of all Ireland a trembling sod, had died an unmourned death at Ferns. If the English could be expelled, the troubles of the Irish would be lightened. Lacking a leader in Roderick of Connaught, they trusted themselves to the wisdom of Lawrence O'Toole, Archbishop of Dublin. He sent messages to all the princes of Ireland and the kings of the neighboring islands, imploring them to join forces and lay siege to the city of Dublin by land and by sea.

Godfrey, King of the Isle of Man, mustered a fleet of thirty sails in answer to the summons, and the Irish princes encircled the city by land. The Plains of Fingal to the north were clouded with their coming.

Within the town the downhearted English were further discouraged by news that Robert FitzStephen, in his fort near Wexford, was beseiged by the Prince of Limerick and all his men, and, instead of being able to send aid to the English at Dublin, was in need of help himself. In this dark hour the captains laid open their soldiers' bag of tricks, and selected two of the surest. Surprise was the first, and knowledge of the enemy's weakness the second. Roderick O'Connor was encamped with the Irish, an open invitation to any discerning general to aim his attack at that point. Disaster fell on the unready Irish, and the English had the killing of them all that day. Dusk found the victors returning to the city not only with the honor of the field, but with rich booties and preys of victuals, armor, and other pillage, as much as man and beast could carry.

To the south the earl went then, having left Miles de Cogan in charge of Dublin. Wexford warned him not to enter, lest it behead FitzStephen. At Waterford he met Hervey de Mountmaurice, just returned from his errand to the king. An angry message was in his hand, and the angry words of the king still sounded in his ears. The earl was to come to England at once.

The first wind from the west carried Strongbow to the king, whom he found at Gloucester assembling an army to invade Ireland. Peace was not established between them till the earl had renewed his oath of allegiance to the king, and yielded to him the city of Dublin, with all the cantreds adjoining, and all towns and forts bordering the sea which had been won by the adventurers. What remained, the earl and his comrades were to retain, holding them from the king.

If the king seemed irritable, and if his gray, bloodshot eyes flashed more readily in anger than was their wont, the cause was not hard to find. Thomas à Becket was dead. Both Louis of France and Pope Alexander were raising loud cries at his murder. The king had no desire to be questioned about the matter. He had placed an embargo on messages from France, but that was no guarantee that some papal legate would not manage to reach him. Ireland must have seemed a haven to him then, particularly when he had ordered that no vessels were to sail after him to the island.

On October 18, 1171, Henry's fleet of four hundred ships sailed into Waterford harbor. Strongbow was in the king's company, as well as William FitzAldelm, Humphrey de Bohun, Hugh de Lacy, Robert FitzBarnard, and other knights to the number of five hundred. Four thousand men-at-arms trooped after them.

The king did no fighting in Ireland. That was not necessary after the success of the earl's men. He came, in rich apparel, his bright banners fluttering over an army encased in armor and mail. The Irish had learned how impregnable the shining steel made their foes. To fight against them was out of the question, unless the Irish were united by a call to arms, and there had been none. One by one the princes of the south came to Henry and submitted themselves.

To understand why they did so, one must remember that for ages the Irish had been accustomed to having their high king make a circuit of the island to receive the homage and hostages of the lesser kings and chieftains. Their submissions affected the chiefs personally, but did not affect the territorial rights of their tribes, which continued undisturbed from generation to generation.

Certainly the Irish had no idea that this monarch had come to take their land from them, to place strangers over them, and to rob them of their treasures. They probably felt that in doing homage to Henry they were but yielding to a temporary emergency, and that the ceremony which they had performed would have no lasting consequence.

By the time Henry came to Dublin all but Roderick O'Connor and the princes of Ulster had paid homage to him. The High King of Ireland, though he was for once a coward, did not kneel to anyone, and the princes of the north were born and bred to haughtiness and independence.

Henry stayed in Ireland till the following spring. While he was there he did not fail to strengthen his own position and to weaken the earl's, by alluring to his side such men as Raymond le Gros, the best soldier among the English, Miles de Cogan, and many others. The bickering and jealousy among the English, as much a part of the invasion as the destruction of the Irish, had its first blossoming from royal seed.

About the middle of Lent an ill wind from the east brought news to Henry. Not only were two legates from Pope Alexander in Normandy to question him about the murder of Thomas à Becket, and threatening to put all England under an interdict unless he came to meet them, but Henry's sons, abetted by many of the nobles of England,

Aquitaine, and Anjou, were conspiring against the king. Since he could linger in Ireland only at the expense of his kingdom, Henry met the dawn of Easter Monday at Wexford harbor, and with a strong wind at his back sailed for home.

Before he left, he took thought for the security of his rule in Ireland. Over the cities he placed his best and most loyal soldiers as governors: Hugh de Lacy, FitzStephen, and Maurice FitzGerald over Dublin, Humphrey de Bohun and two others over Waterford, FitzAldelm and two comrades over Wexford. They were all supported by men-at-arms and common archers.

And Richard, Earl of Pembroke, the man who had really conquered Ireland and made Henry's conquest possible, what position of trust has he? What province has he been granted in fee? Dublin? Limerick? Cork? No. These have been given to others. Not Meath. Hugh de Lacy has been given that. Not Munster. Robert FitzStephen has that. Not Connaught. Connaught is too wild and rocky to have figured in the royal considerations. No. The earl was safely tucked in Henry's pocket, where his ambitions would not be embarrassing to the king.

But while the king was bargaining with the papal legates, fighting English earls, and French and Scottish kings, and taking prisoner on both sides of the French sea so many nobles, knights, and officers that there could hardly be found fetters and dungeons enough to hold them, Ireland stirred to revolt. The king was put to it to decide whether to lose Ireland altogether, or to risk it under Strongbow's rule. So back to Ireland as chief governor came the earl, and found most of the princes of the country rebelling against the English. O'Rourke, King of Meath, contesting for his province against Hugh de Lacy, had stirred all the island against foreign rule. Worse still, the English troops, being without their wages and without the plunder to which they were accustomed, were talking return to England or desertion to the enemy.

The earl at once appointed Raymond le Gros as captain. Under his energetic command a raid was soon made upon Offaly, and great preys of horses and armor were taken. Lismore was spoiled next, and then the enriched and encouraged English returned to Waterford by the seaside route. Part of the way they traveled by boats, and the men of Cork came out to meet them. The sharp fighting did the Irish no good. The English went on their way with increased booty. Raymond himself, traveling the coast road, collected four thousand head of cattle, and brought them into Waterford.

Raymond was the man of Ireland now. Raymond was the one who came to the aid of cities besieged by the Irish. Raymond was the one who plundered successfully and planned cunningly. When the death of his father took him for a time to Wales, the earl enticed him back with the promise of his sister Basilia in marriage. So Hervey de Mountmaurice, who had come to Ireland as a spy for Strongbow, and had transferred his service to the king, now wrote his lord in England that Raymond entertained ambitions which the king would do well to crush. Raymond was levying troops, he said. Raymond was making his men bring all their plunder to a common stock, and reserving for himself a prince's share before dividing it among the soldiers.

The king ordered Raymond back to England. The year was 1176. But before he could sail Strongbow died suddenly in Dublin. So word of his death went to Henry, and Raymond waited new orders before crossing the sea. When the king's new governor, William FitzAldelm, arrived, flanked by John de Courcy, Raymond loyally enough surrendered all the cities, towns, and castles of Ireland which had been in his custody.

It was from the gates of Dublin that Raymond came out to meet the new commander. All his available kinsmen, to the number of thirty, mounted on noble steeds, bright in forbidding armor, and all having on their shields the same device, supported him as he rode out to make the surrender.

"I will speedily put an end to all this bravery," muttered FitzAldelm to a comrade. "These shields will soon be scattered." From that hour, says his cousin, Giraldus Cambrensis, in his story of the invasion, FitzAldelm and all the other governors of Ireland were so moved by envy of Raymond, the FitzMaurices and FitzStephens, and all their blood, that they took every opportunity of injuring them. Finally nothing was left to these pioneer adventurers but remote and barren territories, dangerously bordering enemy country.

As for FitzAldelm, he did not forget to collect all the gold he could lay hands on. But he was a timid man, and in his raiding stuck cautiously to the towns and garrisons of the coast. Seeing this, John de Courcy, who had come to Ireland with him, made plans of his own to invade Ulster. Riding a white horse, with twenty-two men-at-arms and three hundred archers following him, this white knight set out for the north. Giraldus Cambrensis says he did so in fulfillment of a prophecy of the Scottish Merlin that " a white knight, sitting on a white horse, and having birds on his shield, shall be the first to enter the province of Ulster with force of arms." It is more likely that he did so in fulfillment of a desire to possess the riches of the northern princes.

His coming was so unexpected that he entered the city of Down without opposition. There his troops, who had been before "in great need, and half starved, were refreshed with the plunder and booty they took."

Roderick Mac Dunlevy, King of Ulster, quickly gathered his forces to expel the foreigners, and Ulster became a battleground. Twice the knight on the white horse had the victory. Then the fortunes of war turned, and the Irish, overtaking de Courcy in a narrow pass as he was carrying off a herd of cattle, inflicted such defeat upon the English forces that only eleven men-at-arms were left to stand by the leader.

But fight as the Irish would, English castles kept going up. From them the foreigners would sally forth to fight and pillage, then retreat with their plunder behind stone walls. The towers and turrets which had risen so success-fully first in Normandy, then in England and Wales, now threw their silhouettes against the Irish sky. As stone was laid on stone the English power strengthened. As raid followed raid Irish towns were burned, Irish treasures carried away. The English captain who could not conquer the country he had been granted was soon replaced by another with a sharper sword. The governor who added no new possessions to the crown lands found himself recalled. So Ireland was slowly conquered.

But what of the Papal Bull, that much-publicized document which usually monopolizes every account of the English invasion of Ireland? What of the license by letter which the English claim gave Henry the right to enter and possess Ireland "for the reforming of manners, the planting of virtue, punishment of sin, and the increasing of the Christian religion"? One thing, and one only, can be said of the Papal Bull with any certainty. It was the most successful red herring known to history. Diverted by this doubtful document, historians have argued over its authenticity for ages. Led astray by the righteous tone of a paper which probably had no official existence, few have thought to ask the real reason why the English came to Ireland.

Actually, the Bull was an afterthought by the English. When Ireland had been entered, and robbed, and subdued, when the land had been taken from its rightful owners, and "granted" to Henry's followers, then the king sought for justification of the invasion on the grounds that Ireland needed reform. Henry not only sought the approval of Pope Alexander III, but claimed that his predecessor, Pope Adrian IV, had given him authority to enter the island for the purpose of reforming the Irish people. The Irish, the English have always claimed when justifying the rape of the island, were a base rabble of naked savages.

The Irish civilization, it is true, differed from the English. It has been the ill fortune of the English that they have never been able to see good in anything that did not follow English patterns. It has been their good fortune that they have been dominant enough to have this taste accepted in many quarters. But the country which for centuries had blossomed with monasteries and schools, which had cradled the Christian Church and civilization when they had no home elsewhere, and which had sent countless teachers and missionaries to England and the Continent, which still boasted great scholars, and artists, and musicians, and clerics, could hardly be called uncivilized and unchristian. Even had it been so, it is questionable whether the king who had just stained the altar of Canterbury with the blood of Thomas à Becket was the proper person to speak of "beautifying the Church of God."

No. It is only too evident that the English came to Ireland solely for their own material gain. Every chapter of Giraldus Cambrensis' book, that nearly contemporary work, and one meant, primarily, to laud the English, tacitly admits that. What does Maurice FitzGerald say to his comrades in a moment of discouragement? Does he remind them that they are doing God's work, and that the Lord will help them? Not at all. "We came not to this land to be idle," he cries, "or to live deliciously, but to try fortune, and seek adventure." Henry's son John, whom the king sent to the island in 1185, came, Giraldus admits, "for his own aggrandizement, not for the cause of Jesus Christ." Other reasons Giraldus enumerates to explain why Ireland was always so troublesome to the English: "Besides, the care and custody of all the towns and castles of the sea-coast, with the lands, revenues, and tributes appertaining to them, which ought to have been administered for the public good, and for the defense of the enemy, were assigned to persons who thought only of hunting out money: and keeping themselves carefully within town walls, they spent their time and all that they had in drunkenness and surfeiting, to the loss and damage of the good citizens, instead of the annoyance of the enemy."

"The enemy" was sufficiently annoyed. Beginning with the years when the first of the adventurers made their appearance, the Irish annals are pitiful with recordings of plunderings, burnings, battles. Churches and monasteries were not spared. On the contrary, because of the treasures they contained, they seem to have suffered most. "Clonard was plundered by the foreigners," say the *Annals of Tigernach* for 1175. "Columcille's Durrow, and the whole of Meath from Athlone to Drogheda was laid waste by the foreigners." That entry, varying only in details, is repeated endlessly through the years in the different annals. The Four Masters, in the entry of 1185, call Hugh de Lacy, "the profaner and destroyer of many churches, Lord of the English of Meath, Breffne and Oriel, he to whom the tribute of Connaught was paid, he who had conquered the greater part of Ireland for the English, and of whose English castles all Meath, from the Shannon to the sea was full . . . " Meyler FitzHenry, descendant of Nesta and Henry I, came to Clonmacnoise in 1200, and "took the spoyles of the town and churches."

One's imagination might fall short of what really happened during a spoiling were not an entry in the *Annals of Clonmacnoise* for 1202 obligingly explicit as to the exploits of the English de Burgh and his followers. "They took from out the church [of Clonmacnoise] the holy vestments, books, chalices, cloth, linen and corn, and all other things they could finger, so that they left the crofts, gardens and houses of the town vast and void, like an empty chaos without any manner of thing but their empty and foottrodden grounds."

The *Annals of Loch Cé* confirm this. "They left neither church nor territory . . . that they did not pillage and destroy, so that neither church nor altar, nor priest nor monk nor canon nor abbot nor bishop afforded protection against this demoniacal host, and they used to strip the priests in the churches, and carry off the women and every kind of property and stock found in the churches, without regard to saint or sanctuary, or to any power on earth, so that never before was there inflicted on the Connachtmen any punishment of famine, nakedness, and plundering like this punishment. . . . They were there three days, so that they polluted and defiled the whole monastery, and such was the extent of the defilement that the mercenaries of the armies had the women in the hospitals of the monks, and in the houses of the cloisters, and in every place in the entire monastery beside. No structure in the monastery was left without breaking and burning, except the roofs of the houses alone, and even of these a great portion was burned and broken."

Chapter XII

"WARME NESTE"

>>><<<

I T WAS an English scholar of the sixteenth century who inspired the title of this chapter. "The English," wrote Stanihurst, "griping with their talants so firmlie that warme neste, that from the Conquest to this daie the Irish enemie could never rouse them from thence."

Nor could the marauding English completely dislodge the Irish from that warm nest, nor tame them to submission. A playful deity, concocting a struggle that would last for centuries, where success would fall first on one side and then on the other, could not have matched his adversaries more evenly. Irish swords would always be bared against the English. But the pride of each great Irish prince in his own power and grandeur would keep them from uniting their banners in battle to drive out the invaders. Greed and ambition would continually spur the English to further violence against the Irish, "taking from them, whenever opportunity offered, their blood and thei. land." But jealousy flourished as rankly among them as it did among the Irish, and kept them, too, from a complete victory. It would be four hundred years before Elizabeth would conquer the Irish, and even then there would still be smoldering in the Celtic heart the quenchless fire of revolt.

Henry assumed that the battle had been won. He and his son John, who succeeded him, provided Ireland with the framework of a government, and granted Irish lands on loyalty for service. Land was the basis of the English feudal system of government. Theoretically, it belonged to the king, and he granted it at his pleasure. The rewards he exacted in return had begun prettily with garlands, gilliflowers, and damsels to wait upon the queen, had turned playful with gifts of coursing dogs, and the feeding of the royal hunting pack, then practical with horses to bear the king's scullery and treasures. By the time of the Irish invasion the furnishing of armed men to fight the ruler's wars was the usual price of land, though money rents were not unknown.

Now Ireland was portioned out to English knights, who held the land in the English manner. Ireland, like England, had its great officers of government, its justiciar, treasurer and chancellor, its council or parliament, its court of laws. But Ireland, unlike England, was filled with Irish people. How did the new government regard them? Except for five princely families, called the Five Bloods, the new rulers ignored the native people, or regarded them as enemies. Their lands, which had been family possessions for countless centuries, were granted away as though they were tenantless holdings. English laws were only for English colonists, and those of the Irish who acquiesced to the foreign rule.

Primarily, it was treasure the English wanted from Ireland. The Earl of Pembroke, that pioneer adventurer, had not set foot on the island till he had the report of his spy

on the country's wealth. Henry II had not been tempted
to cross the Channel till the success of the earl and his
kinsmen had aroused the kingly jealousy. With the establishment of a government over Ireland, the English mon-
archs began draining away its treasure. By the end of the
thirteenth century Ireland was yielding Edward I six
thousand pounds a year in revenue, and their shilling
equaled today's pound. Besides this, the king did not
hesitate to requisition from the island various stores to
help him in his foreign wars. In 1297, Edward wrote Richard
de Burgh, Earl of Ulster, and a dozen other English nobles
ensconced in Ireland, entreating them, on their fealty and
affection to the king, to provide themselves with horses
and arms, that they might be prepared to go to the king
in France, and attend him "in the king's own proper person" wherever the king might command.

The same day he ordered that ships then loading with
corn at Irish ports should sail to Gascony to provision the
English troops fighting there. Money levied out of corn
and issues of Ireland, "and other matters from which it
can be levied," was to be deposited in Dublin Castle awaiting the king's orders.

The next year the king's Scottish campaign compelled
him to order his officers in Ireland to provide him with
eight thousand quarters of wheat, ten thousand of oats,
two thousand of ground malt, a thousand hogsheads of
wine, five hundred carcasses of salt beef, a thousand fat
pigs, twenty thousand salt fish, "and cause them to be
dispatched to the port of Skinburness, near Carlisle."

Nothing was too much to be asked of Ireland, nothing
was too little. The State Documents which record great
levies of gold and provisions also tell the story of the king's

servant. John de Bentley, the king's valet, having faithfully served the king as well in Ireland as elsewhere, Edward I commanded John Wogan, Justiciar of Ireland, to commit him, in the king's name, to some competent office or bailiwick.

Then it was ships Edward called for, sixteen well-equipped ships to be provided by Irish seaport towns, to be sent to the king at Berwick on Tweed "on the feast of St. John next ensuing."

This looks, indeed, like conquest. But rents and revenues and service came from those who acknowledged the king's force, and all Ireland did not do so. Practically every Norman "county" contained tracts which remained in the hands of the native Irish, and whole districts knew no lord but an Irish one. State papers like the foregoing tell the English tale, but the native chronicles and histories mirror an Ireland hardly touched by English influences, or resolutely at war against them.

Hostings and hatred of the English fill the pages of *The Triumphs of Turlough*, the Gaelic history which recounts the wars of the O'Briens of Thomond against the de Clares. Never were villains so black as these English. Never were fighters more brave than the grandsons of Brian Boru. It is only natural to question the accuracy of such a biased story, but historical evidence, and other writers, bear the author out. The treachery of the English was only too true. But though Sean McGraith, the fourteenth-century author, meant nothing but praise for the warlike O'Briens, the pages of his book unconsciously show that, brave though the O'Briens were, there were members of the family who would side with the English if it was to their advantage. As for Irish pride, it stalks haughtily across every printed page. Not quite at random are the extracts quoted. The moral that they carry is obvious to all.

About 1258 the Gaels, wearying of the oppression of the foreign adventurers, "desired by election of one supreme king (to whom they should all submit) to be freed from this iniquity of the English, and as was their right, to vindicate Ireland for themselves. All together, then, they took counsel, and were resolved to appoint on the banks of island-studded Erne a place of meeting to which Ireland's chiefs and nobles in general should repair.

"Then, with well-nigh all the gentlemen of the southern half and of Connaught, Conor O'Brien's good son Teigue sets out to keep that tryst. Under O'Neill, all Ulster's gentlemen came to meet them.

"Now in time of old it was the custom that whoso, being ruler, whether of a cantred or a province, accepted another chief's gift or wage (for in this matter they are the same) did actually by such acceptance submit to the giver as his chief paramount, and in virtue of the same take on himself to do suit and service, to pay him rent and tribute. Therefore, or ever they took their seats in order to this conference, northwards across the river O'Brien sent to O'Neill a hundred horses by way of stipend.

"O'Neill, when he saw this, in violent anger commanded his people to send back over said river two hundred horses wearing gold-adorned white bridles which (with an eye to this congress) he had himself provided for bestowal on the men of Erin, so great he deemed both his right to have, and his might to hold Ireland before ever another Gael. Also, because that previous to this occasion, not his own country of Tyrowen only, but the whole of Ulster was agreed to have him.

"But at sight of those horses with their bridles Teigue returned them, along with their due complement of armed men that, whether by fair means or by forcible, should compel acceptance of the stipend. Whereat O'Neill, marking O'Brien's pride and haughty temper, in dudgeon returned homeward. From which dissension it resulted that the men of Erin broke up without concert of measures to keep Ireland against the English, saving this alone, that after a while they would a second time assemble anent this same question . . .

"A good choice was this that they would have made [of Teigue], seeing that from the date when first he was of strength to handle warlike arms he never was day nor hour but he pondered and kept unremitting watch how he might cast off oppression from the Gael; for under heaven was no animal nor other created thing that he hated and loathed more than he did an Englishman's progeny, neither throughout length nor breadth of that country did he ever suffer one of the breed to occupy so much as a nutshell of a pauper's bothie. Proof of which he furnished by his deeds at Limerick, where [in 1257] he inflicted on them sore loss of knights and captains, besides all other affairs in which he had to do with them . . .

"De Clare within himself had mused that, Turlough being chief, it would be all to no profit that from the King of England he had obtained a chartered right to the lands of Thomond. The resolve at which he stood was to nourish this same schism between the noble scions [of the O'Brien family] until such a time as they and their followers being mutually enfeebled, he might step in and filch the country from them."

But Turlough was not one to be outmaneuvered, and in

the end, after warfare so constant that chieftains often
made bedfellows of their naked swords and slept with
hand grasping spear, the de Clares were defeated, and
Turlough had his triumph. For twenty-nine bright years
he ruled Thomond in happiness and plenty. "During that
time, from knave to noble none was docked of any tittle
appertaining to his condition: poets were not straightened
for land, with chieftains wine never ran low. The captains'
herds were not thinned. Neither for fat hogs nor for other
provision did hospitallers want, penury and poverty were
not, but every man was able to attend to and to perform
the office of his station."

But Thomond, where O'Brien ruled, was not all Ireland.
As the thirteenth century vanished and the fourteenth
began, the hold of the English on many parts of the island
seemed secure. But England's foreign complications were
producing a situation favorable to the Irish. In Scotland
Robert Bruce was making himself one of the romantic
figures of history, and a menace to the English. In fighting
him, Edward of England was using Irish corn and Irish
ships. Even a man less clever than Bruce could see that
now was the time to stir up the Irish against their old
enemies, and so hamper the English. Donal O'Neill, King
of Ulster, was Bruce's ally in Ireland.

Whether O'Neill, humbling for a time that famous
northern pride, first suggested the Scottish alliance, with
the hope that Ireland under Bruce's rule would be happier
than it was under the English, none can be sure. A contemporary account of Bruce's invasion, by an unknown writer,
says that he did. It is certain, from one of O'Neill's letters,
that he did his best to enlist other Irish princes in a struggle
to drive out the English, and make the Scotsman king.

It was in 1317 that O'Neill sent his greeting to Fineen McCarthy, King of Desmond, and accompanied it, evidently, with a letter from "the most noble prince, the Earl of Carrick [Robert Bruce's brother Edward] now to be our king. You may see for yourself," says O'Neill, "with what eagerness he has embraced the honor we have offered him, and what a fresh army he is preparing to send across here, in which his brother, too, a most valiant king, and the whole Scottish nation promises to assist him, from which certain destruction threatens the sacrilegious and accursed English, who, worse than the inhuman Danes themselves, are busy heaping injuries of every kind on the inhabitants of this country, not bravely and openly, as becomes brave men, but by foxlike fraud and deceit promote their own interests by disseminating quarrels and intestine feuds among us, so that we, being weakened by wounding one another, may easily yield ourselves a prey to them."

The Irish dream of expelling the English remained a dream. For a time the new invaders triumphed, partly because of the quarrels between the English who were opposing them, and were as divided among themselves as the Irish. O'Neill could muster some of the Irish princes to help the Scots, but not all. O'Brien in the south would not be brought in, but opposed the invasion, and he was not the only Irishman to do so. It was not relief from the English that the Irish gained, but more destruction, more warfare, more misery.

"This year," says Camden's annals for 1317, "corn and other provisions were exceeding dear. Wheat was sold at three and twenty shillings the crannock, and wine for eight pence, and the whole country was in a manner laid waste by the Scots and those of Ulster. Many housekeepers, and those formerly able to relieve others, went a-begging, and great numbers died of hunger. The pestilence and famine were so severe that many of the poor died."

Other annals speak of the destruction the war brought, of Ulster harried and spoiled, of churches consumed to mere ashes, chapels unspared, children killed without remorse, towns ransacked, and corn destroyed.

One year more, and Bruce's adventure in Ireland was over. The Scots were overcome by the English at the Battle of Faughart where Edward Bruce met an unmourned death. Even the Four Masters, forgetting that he had come at an Irish invitation, call him "the destroyer of all Ireland in general."

But if the Irish did not win their freedom, at least the balance of power turned to their favor. Now the playful deity put its finger on the Irish side, and the temporary supremacy of the English was over. For a while now, partly because of weak kings and unworthy officials, the English government would gradually lose the ground it had gained.

Out came Irish swords again, to strike at the nearest English. The Mac Murroughs of Leinster, the O'Briens of Munster, then O'Neill and O'Donnell won back lands that the English had taken, till finally only Dublin with its surroundings was left to foreign law. There the invaders entrenched themselves within the Pale, and tried, by rampart and by writ. to maintain themselves unmodified by Irish influence.

By the famous Statute of Kilkenny no alliance "by marriage, gossipred, fostering of children, concubinage, or by amour" was to be made between the English and the Irish. English customs were to be followed, English fashions worn, the English language and laws used, to the exclusion of the Irish. Even the Irish method of riding was taboo, and Englishmen of a certain wealth were required to ride on saddles.

Because the colonists had abandoned the use of the bow, it was required that every person "do not use the plays which men call hurlings, with great sticks, and a ball, upon the ground, from which great evils and maims have arisen, to the weakening of the defense of said land, and other plays men call quoitings; but that they do apply and accustom themselves to use and draw bows, and throw lances, and other gentlemanlike games, whereby the Irish enemy may be better checked by the liege people and commons of these parts."

"Outside the Pale," an English historian has said, "the Irish were living in misery and discomfort." All too often that is the picture that is painted of the island where Columcille built his churches, where Colchu wrote to foreign kings, where musicians touched soft strings to the beguilement of all the world. It will be well, perhaps, to look for a while at Ireland beyond the Pale as it was in the Middle Ages.

Even after two hundred years of warfare with the English, Ireland, though ravaged, was still a place of industry and charm. Its harbors, where in these days only a shabby fishing boat shows a sail, then knew ships from France and Spain and Italy, and other countries of the Continent. From their holds came wine of Gascony, satins and silk, salt, spices, figs, and saffron, iron for guns, and painted glass for church and chapel windows. Home they would sail with cargoes of Irish cloaks, linens, and serges—fabrics loved by the ladies of Italy and Spain, Irish stone and marble, Irish timber, Irish salted fish, sometimes Irish works of art wrought from fine gold.

The harbor towns were goodly, with houses of hewed stone, some built in the Spanish fashion. For roofs all thatch and straw was forbidden. In the streets merchants from other lands mingled with citizens dressed in the Irish fashion, with great cloaks swinging about them, tunics rich with silk embroideries, and peaked shoes of fine leather. Nearly ninety "chief haven towns" could be counted in Elizabeth's reign, before the Irish trade was throttled: Limerick, "wonderful prosperous city," Sligo and Waterford, "harbor of the sun," Bantry and Baltimore and Kinsale, Cork with its paved streets and bridges, Galway set in loveliness. With one view, an Italian traveler related, he saw "boats passing up and down the river, a ship entering the harbor in full sail, a salmon killed with a spear, and hunters and hounds pursuing a deer." The visitor had been in many lands, but never before, he said, had he witnessed a sight that combined so much variety and beauty.

Had he traveled north, to the country of the Maguires, Lords of Fermanagh, in Ulster, he might have seen a picture of still greater charm. Less powerful than the neighboring O'Donnells and O'Neills, the Maguires were still great chieftains of the land. Splendid horsemen they were always, and patrons of learning, and scholars, and travelers and traders known to far lands. At Enniskillen they kept a flotilla of ships whose masts stood up like a grove along the shores of Lough Erne.

A poet who visited the Maguires' court when it was at the height of its glory told of the life he saw there. Blithe uproar of the chase greeted him while he was yet afar off.

In wood and field wolf dogs and greyhounds were at work. The horses that their masters rode so superbly were at exercise, and the speed of their slender brown legs was being tried.

In the courtyard charity was dispensed by gentlemen of the clan. Minstrels and poets crowded the great hall. In their sunrooms the ladies of the family and their women embroidered with golden threads fine tissues they had woven. Fighting men sat in their quarters, and over the head of each man hung his shield and arms, as they had hung in Conor Mac Nessa's Speckled House at the time of Cuchulain and the Red Branch Knights.

Artisans by the regiment were at work: masons and carpenters, artificers in gold who worked at lovely beakers, smiths who forged weapons. In huge dyeing vats mantles and rugs took crimson stain, swords were tempered to the steely blue that delights a soldier's eye, spearheads were riveted to shafts, swords were sharpened.

At dinner they sat in due order, Maguire in the central seat, the poet placed in honor at his right. Song and story and harp music entertained the company. The hall was rich with sparkling wine and golden cups.

When bedtime came the ladies retired to their own quarters. Couches with coverlets of down rested the gentlemen in their short sleep. Then Maguire and his men took on their fighting harness. Javelins and spears were brought, horses saddled. By the time dawn lighted the blue hills they had ridden to a day of pillage or battle.

Those of the nobility and gentry who loved hawking and hunting repaired when they could to the great open Plain of the Curragh of Kildare, it being a place naturally adapted to pleasure, "for in this clearer, fairer, aire the falcon goes to a higher pitch, or mounts so high as to be scarce visible, the hounds enjoy the scent more freely, and the courser, in his swift careere, is less sensible of pressure or opposition than other where.''

These were the people that it profited the English to speak of as living in ''more than Indian barbarity.'' Invective and abuse against the countless English libels are worse than useless. They do not remedy and they do antagonize. Fortunately, the old libels against the Irish fall of their own weight when one takes the trouble to inquire into their past. The pages of ancient books are bright with pictures such as these, of poets' gatherings, of artists recompensed, or generosity that flourished richly.

All the Irish poets, brehons, bards, harpers, gamesters, jesters, and others of their kind were invited by an O'Kelly to his house one Christmas time, where everyone was well used during the holidays, and given gifts at parting.

Margaret, wife of O'Connor Faly, in one year held two general feasts of bestowing, of both meats and money, and ''all manner of gifts.'' Two thousand and seven hundred persons came to her first feast, besides gamesters and poor men, as was recorded in a roll of her guests.

Margaret stood by the church's door, clad in cloth of gold, her dearest friends about her, her clergy and judges near. Her husband, on horseback ''by the church's outward side,'' saw that all things were done in a seemly manner, and each guest served successively.

An offering of gold Margaret made that day, and took two young orphans in fosterage. The highways and bridges that she built, the mass books she had copied, all were remembered after her death. She did all manner of things profitable to serve God and her soul, say the Four Masters, and denied no living creature what he asked, "saving her body alone."

Somewhere in a corridor of time fifteen centuries long, the trappings and regalia of Irish poets and bards had been altered, but they were not lowered in dignity. The musical branches of golden bells which the chief poets of Christ's time had carried no longer tinkled over their shoulders. No more were they warmed with soft mantles of birdskin. But they, with kings and judges, were still the most highly honored of men. It was still their due to claim "the king's shoulder," the place next him at table, and their right to be rewarded with gold and hawks and horses and land.

Each great family had its great scholars. A Maguire compiled the *Annals of Ulster*, an O'Donnell was the author of a life of Columcille. There was seldom a generation of the O'Neills without its poet. And the chieftains of these clans cherished above gold the vellum manuscripts that even then were dark and brittle with age.

Is it any wonder that a stranger, coming among these people, should fall a victim to their charms, "give up their foreignness for a pure mind, their surliness for good manners," and become in time as Irish as the Irish themselves? "The English blood of the conquest is in manner worn out of this land," says a State Paper of the time, "and at all seasons in manner, without any restorations is diminished and enfeebled. And contrary-wise, the Irish blood ever more and more, without such decay, encreaseth." To English officials of the Pale such transfer of allegiance from one culture to another seemed very strange. To give up English dress, to follow new customs, to take more delight to speak the Irish language than their own! They should, thought one critic, "rather take scorn to acquaint their tongues with the language of the conquered." It was a great mistake, he was afraid, this lowering of the barriers between the two people, "for the speech being Irish, the heart must needs be Irish too." And truly Irish many an English heart became.

The long years which followed on Strongbow's coming saw more than one Norman family in Ireland gradually succumb to the charm and propinquity of the Irish culture. And why not? In Ireland they had made their fortunes, here they were great people. However noble their blood, they had brought no riches with them, but had won them here. They lived now in magnificence, and the years of the conquest became centuries. It would have been strange, indeed, if their minds and lives had not been altered to Irish ways.

Of all the great Anglo-Irish families none reached greater glories than the Geraldines, descendants of the Maurice FitzGerald who had come to Ireland with Strongbow. Within a century the family had divided into two branches, the Desmonds and the Kildares. Equal in valor and tenacity and pride the two lines flourished, their heads took titles. Year after year their members became more Irish. When the Earl of Desmond died in 1398 the *Annals of Clonmacnoise* call him "a witty and ingenious composer of Irish poetry, a learned and profound chronicler, and in fine one of the English nobility that had Irish learning and professors thereof in greatest reverence of all the English in Ireland."

"Some of the English," wrote Spenser in Elizabeth's time, "are degenerated and grown more Irish, yea, and more malicious to the English than the Irish themselves. The English Pale hath preserved itself through nearness of the state in reasonable civility, but the rest that dwell in Connaught and Munster, which is the sweetest soil in Ireland, and some in Leinster and Ulster, are degenerate, yea, and some of them have quite shaken off their English names and put on Irish, that they might be altogether Irish. The like is reported of the old followers of the Earl of Desmond, who for some offense by the queen against him conceived was brought to his death most unjustly at Drogheda in 1467, notwithstanding he was a very good subject of the king. Thereupon all his kinsmen of the Geraldines, which was then a mighty family in Munster, in revenge of that huge wrong, rose into arms against the king, and utterly renounced and forsook all obedience to the crown of England. And with them all the people of Munster went out, and many others of them that were English thenceforth joined with the Irish against the king, and turned themselves very Irish, taking on them Irish habits and customs, which could never be clean wiped away."

Forty years later, Gerald, Earl of Kildare, head of the other branch of the Geraldines, in pride picked up his pen and wrote to all the family of the Gherardinis, his claimed kinsmen, dwelling in Florence, to acquaint them with the good fortunes of his house.

"Know then," he wrote after a pompous salutation, "that my predecessors and ancestors passed from France into England, and having remained there for some time, they in the year 1170 arrived in this island of Ireland, and by their swords obtained great possessions and achieved great feats of arms, and up to the present day have increased and multiplied into many branches and families, insomuch that I, by the grace of God, possess by heredity right the

Earldom and am Earl of Kildare, holding divers castles and manors, and by the liberality of our most serene Lord the King of England I am now his Deputy in the whole of Ireland during the pleasure of his majesty, an honor frequently obtained heretofore by my fathers and predecessors.

"There is also a relation of ours in these parts called the Earl of Desmond, under whose lordship there are one hundred miles in length of country.

"Our honor has increased beyond measure, in a multitude of barons, knights, and noble persons, holding many possessions, and having under their command many persons . . .

"If there is anything we can procure for you through our labor and industry, or anything you have not got, such as hawks, falcons, or dogs for the chase, I beg you will inform me of it, as I shall, in every possible way, endeavor to obey your wishes. God be with you, and do you love us in return.

"From our Castle of Castledermot, the twenty-seventh day of May in the year one thousand five hundred and seven."

No modest letter, surely, but one which spoke only truth. Many things the earl did not mention which would have made plain the power held by his house. King's officers the earls might be, in succeeding generations, but they used their power selfishly. "Crom-a-boo," was their battle cry, and when it sounded the liegemen and nobles who rallied to it fought for the glory of the Kildares, and not for the English king. Their own great holdings they ruled by Irish laws, and did not try to impose English justice or English customs on their Gaelic followers. Knowing and loving Irish culture, they did not treat the Irish as an inferior race, but as their equals. By intermarriage

and fosterage the O'Donnells and O'Neills were their allies.
No wonder, then, that they were suspected of hoping for
a crown. No wonder that other lords with equal ambitions
should be their enemies, and "labor with tooth and nail
to overcrow and consequently to overthrow the other."

It was from Castledermot that the great earl happened
to write. Many another ancient fortalice was under his
command, and guarded his Leinster holdings. Had he chosen
to write from Maynooth he could with truth have told of
its store of beds, its goodly hangings, its rich wardrobes,
and brave furniture, which made it counted "for household
stuff and utensils one of the richest earls' houses under the
crown of England." He could have told of his library of
books in English, Latin, French, and Gaelic, of the three
hundred brood mares in his great stables, of his private
army of four hundred spearmen. The earl had been the first
to import cannon into the land, and his guard, when they
stood sentry before his habitation, bore six hand-guns out
of Germany. His name, it was said, had greater terror to
the Irish than other men's armies.

Everthing dark and flashing and passionate is not necessarily Italian. These qualities belong to some Irishmen, too.
For all that their Italian blood was far away, the two
branches of this great family were much alike. They had
the same ambition, the same tenacity of purpose, the same
fierce intensity. Pride was part of their make-up, and boast-
fulness. The Gherardinis of Florence and the Kildares and
Desmonds of Ireland were alike in their assumption of
superiority. They were of the nobility and they knew it.
They were meant for ruling and they ruled.

So Henry VIII, coming to his long reign, knew the English power in Ireland at its lowest ebb. Not only was he

opposed by the Irish princes, but also by the Anglo-Irish. The only land left to English rule was the district of the Pale, out of which the English "durst not peep."

But Henry, fat and amorous though he was, was a statesman born. His counselors in Ireland might send him plan after plan for the reformation of Ireland. It was the crafty schemes of the monarch himself which restored to some extent English rule to the island.

If men of English blood had been seduced to the Irish way of life by proximity, he would seduce great Irish princes in the same way. He would invite them to England, he would give them English honors. He would take their sons as hostages, and educate them in the English manner, bending their loyalty to his favor. To his lord lieutenant, the Earl of Surrey, in letters dated 1520, he advised politic practices more than exploit of war, "till such time as the strength of the Irish enemy shall be enfeebled and diminished, as well by getting their captains from them as by putting division among them, so that they join not together."

This should be done, he pointed out, not only to restore English pride and power, but to furnish revenue as well. "For to be plain to you," he admitted to Surrey, "to spend so much money for the reduction of that land, to bring the Irishry in appearance only of obedience, without that they should observe our laws, and resort to our courts for justice, and restore such dominions as they unlawfully detain from us, it were a thing of little policy, less advantage, and least effect . . .

"We think right expedient . . . that you declare [at assemblies and common councils] the great decay, ruin, and desolation of that fertile land, for lack of politic government and good justice, which can never be brought in good order unless the unbridled sensualities of insolent folks be brought under the rules of laws . . . Show them that of necessity it is requisite that every reasonable creature be governed by a law."

All this must be so politicly and secretly handled, he warned the earl, that the Irish would conceive no jealousy or suspicion that they would be put from their lands. He gave Surrey authority to punish criminals (except those of high names) and to knight worthy persons. It would be better though, he thought, for the earl to send O'Neill with other of the greatest personages to him in England.

"We trust," he stated modestly, "so to entreat them that they shall not only the better love and obey us hereafter, but also change their old Irish manners, and fall to more curial, discreet, and cleanly order than ever they used before."

Against Kildare, the present earl, son of the great earl who had written so pridefully to his Italian cousins, he admitted that he had no evidence, and so could do nothing to check his power.

It was great, the power of Kildare; even greater than his father's had been. There was a story, unverified but plausible, that once when Wolsey in jealousy and anger had blurted to the king, "Sire, there is none in all Ireland who can rule this man," the king had laughed and answered, "Then in truth this man shall rule all Ireland." Whether true or not, the story is important. This was the method the weak English government in Ireland always used to curb its unruly princes.

It was always the lot of the FitzGerald family to be suspected of treason. Even in Holinshed's day, later in the century, such slanders were raised, such malicious inventions forged against them, "that such as are in authority cannot but of force suspect them, unless they were able, like gods, to prey in the bottom of each man's conscience."

But the time had not yet come for the overthrow of the Kildares. For fourteen years the earl would be alternately honored with office, then suspected and imprisoned, but if he planned treason it was never proved against him. His foes worked hard enough to accomplish that, and his foes were many, both in Ireland and at court. There was always the jealous Earl of Ormonde in Ireland, and Wolsey in England, warning the king against Kildare. Perhaps Henry's own affairs of the moment were occupying too much of his thought for him to take seriously the ambition of the Geraldines.

For Henry, in London, was in love. Anne Boleyn, aunt of Henry's illegitimate son, was his good sweetheart, he wrote, and he wished himself, especially of an evening, in her arms. And Anne wished herself married. But there was Catherine of Aragon, wife to Henry for twenty years. So a bishop's seal was forged, and a cardinal offered gold, and the Pope heard the king's plea for a divorce. And when the bishop disclosed the forgery, and the cardinal would not be bribed, and the divorce was not granted, Henry, urged by Anne and his own passion, threw off his allegiance to the Pope, and declared himself supreme head of the Church in England. A complaisant Parliament upheld him, and backed by their authority the Archbishop of Canterbury gave Henry the divorce the Pope withheld. So was born the Church of England, and the English Reformation began.

At the outset there was no change in doctrine. Luther was a heretic, so far as Henry was concerned, and death from burning fagots, or worse, awaited any who expressed a belief to the contrary.

If Henry had not been so fatuous, if Anne had been less imperious, less determined to be a wife, then there would have been no break with Rome, no divorce, no marriage for Anne, no Elizabeth as queen. And without Elizabeth's statesmanship (from Henry) and imperiousness (from Anne), how different would have been the history of England and Ireland, and perhaps of all the world. They were little things to work such mighty changes. Henry's love did not last for long. Anne's pride was purely selfish.

But Elizabeth, if she was born too soon after the secret marriage, was at least born in wedlock. A superstitious man, looking carefully at the history of Ireland after her birth, might have cause to think that the destinies of the island were entwined with those of the Tudor princess. The news of her death came to Dublin the day the last rebel Irish prince went on his knees in submission. She was not yet a year old when young Lord Thomas FitzGerald threw down the sword of state in Dublin, and declared himself no longer Henry's minister, but his foe.

It was June 11, 1534. Gerald FitzGerald, the Earl of Kildare about whom Henry had written fourteen years earlier, was in the Tower of London, finally charged with treason. He had, said his enemies, taken guns and ammunition from Dublin Castle to fortify his own strong Maynooth. Those were charges no king could overlook. Summoned to England, the earl left his sword of office with his son, and went to defend himself before a king only too alarmed at the Kildare power.

In Dublin there came to his son a false rumor that his father had been made shorter by a head, and that the same fate awaited him. The boy was only twenty, and hotheaded. He burst into the Council Chamber and shouted his defiance of England. He hurled from him the sword of state which his father had entrusted to him, and went into rebellion. He declared himself not only the champion of Ireland, but of the Catholic Church, then being assailed by Henry in England.

He was too young, and no general. He could rage undefeated for a few months while England gathered forces to destroy him, but when the English troops landed his day was done. Maynooth, where he had sent a garrison, was battered by heavy artillery. Not being able to snare Thomas himself from the woods and bogs into which he disappeared, the English took him by treachery, and sent him to the Tower. "We beseech you," the Council of Ireland wrote to Henry, "according to the comfort of our words spoken to the same Thomas to allure him to yield, to be merciful to him, especially concerning his life."

Not Henry. Coldly he thanked the officers who had made Thomas's capture possible. He intimated plainly that the boy's death would have been more welcome than his body. The king had spent forty thousand pounds in crushing the rebellion, and he was well frightened. Now was the time to crush these Geraldines, who might so easily lose him Ireland.

Thomas's five uncles were seized, and lost their heads and bowels at Tyburn. Thomas himself had two years of misery in the Tower before he lost his. "I have never had any money since I came into prison but a noble," he wrote a friend, "nor have I had neither hosen, nor shoes, nor shirt but one; nor any other garment but a frieze gown, for a velvet furred with budge, so I have gone wolward, and bare-foot and bare-legged divers times (when it hath not been very warm) and so I should have done still and now, but that poor prisoners, of their gentleness, hath sometime given me old hosen and shoes, and old shirts." This was the end of the boy who, for his rich raiment, had been known as Silken Thomas.

But the power of the Kildares did not perish as easily as the king might wish. Though six Kildare heads dropped into the baskets of Tyburn, though the old earl died of grief in prison, though estates were seized and titles attainted, and only two young boys left of the ancient line, the Kildare name was to be a rallying cry for the Irish for years to come. The cause of the Church and the Geraldines would unite the Irish people as no ruler had been able to unite them for years.

The English realized the danger. Everything possible was done to capture the young Gerald who was now the heir, but he was harbored among the faithful Irish till he could escape to the Continent. In 1538, Cowley wrote to Cromwell: "I assure your lordship that this English Pale, except the towns and some few of the possessioners, be so affectionate of the Geraldines, that for kindred, marriage, fostering, and adhering as followers, they covet more to see a Geraldine to reign and triumph than to see God come among them, and if they might see this young Gerald's banner displayed, if they should lose half their substance, they would rejoice more at the same, than otherwise to gain great goods."

A year later another officer warned that "by some manner of means the boy might be had, though he should be bought of some of the traitors about him." "Would God he were in our hold," prayed another, "or else right out of the world." But these were merely precautions. The English power was now greater in Ireland than it had been for two hundred years.

The executions, both in England and in Ireland, which had followed Silken Thomas's rebellion had put the country in fear of the king. It was not conquered, but it quaked. "Irishmen were never in such fear as now." Lord Leonard Grey, the new deputy, struck skillfully at the strongest chiefs. O'Connor submitted. Desmond castles were taken, and the great bridge-fortress of O'Brien was demolished. Athlone, castle and garrison, was retrieved from the Irish. All these English victories had their effect. The Irish chiefs began to listen to the urgings of the king, and to accept earldoms from him.

In the Queen's Chapel at Greenwich, richly hung with cloth of arras, and well strewn with rushes, Conn O'Neill was created Earl of Tyrone in 1543. In like manner, Murrough O'Brien became Earl of Thomond. William Burgh was created Earl of Clanrichard, and Donough O'Brien became Baron of Ibranan.

While the king was, as he thought, "alluring" the nobles to him by English titles and honors, he was putting through Parliament acts which would sever him from the great mass of the Irish people and unite them against him in time to come, as they had never been united before. By Act he became supreme head of the Church. By Act he claimed the money which hitherto had gone to Rome. By Act he seized the monasteries and abbeys of Ireland, and all their wealth, jewels, and ornaments. He celebrated his parting from the Pope with phrases as insulting as possible to the old Church.

As if to make more certain the unpopularity of the new

Church he sent to Ireland as archbishop a man who made enemies of everyone he met, including his own bishops. Irate letters concerning him were soon crossing the Channel to Cromwell and the king. Edward Basnet, Dean of St. Peter's, complained that the archbishop would not confirm his election without payment of two hundred pounds. The king heard such stories that he himself wrote the archbishop a terrifying letter. "The good opinion we had of you is in manner utterly frustrate," he admonished the Reverend Mr. Brown. "Nor neither do you give yourself to the instruction of our people there in the word of God, ne frame yourself to stand us in any stead for the furtherance of our affairs. Such is your lightness in behavior, and such is the elation of your mind in pride, that glorying in foolish ceremonies and delighting in 'we' and 'us,' in your dream comparing yourself so near a prince in honor and estimation, that all virtue and honesty is almost banished from you."

Quaking from the royal reprimand, the archbishop attempted to force the Irish clergy to preach the king's supremacy, and to remove relics and images from the churches. He only made matters worse. Not even in Dublin could he induce any "either religious or secular, to preach the word of God, or the just title of our most illustrious prince."

He asked further power from England to make his prior and dean remove the "Romish reliques" which they found so sweet, and for "a chide to them and their canons."

But if poor Mr. Brown was childishly querulous in his impotence, he could read a sign that would be written ever larger as time went on. "It is observed," he wrote the next year, "that ever since his Highness' ancestors had this nation in possession, the old natives have been craving foreign powers to assist and rule them. And now both English race and Irish begin to oppose your Lordship's orders, and do lay aside their old national quarrels, which I fear will, if anything will, cause a foreigner to invade this nation."

Henry ruled against old relics. The Sacred Staff of St. Patrick was publicly burned in Dublin, the Holy Rood of Ballybogan turned to smoke and ashes, all images and relics were torn down. "There was not in Erin a holy cross, or a figure of Mary, or an illustrious image, over which the Saxon's power reached, that was not burned," mourned the *Annals of Loch Cé*. The people were ordered to deface the Bishop of Rome from their primers and other books, and to have henceforth no confidence or trust in him, to have no further fear of his great thunderclaps of excommunication or interdiction. Parliament had decided that this was so, they were told, and they were expected to believe it. They were to say a Pater Noster and an Ave for the souls of the dead.

One is not surprised to learn that by 1553 the Chancellor of Ireland would write "as for preaching we have none, which is our most lack, while the ignorant can have no knowledge, which were very needful to be redressed. Irishmen were never so weak, and the English subjects never so strong as now."

When Mary, daughter of Henry and Catherine of Aragon, succeeded her Protestant brother Edward on the throne, the old religion was restored. With joy the Irish people greeted the news. The disgruntled Protestant Bishop Bale recorded their enthusiasm. "They rung all the bells in the cathedral minster and parish churches, they flung up their

hats to the battlement of the great temple, with smilings
and laughings most dissolutely—the Justice himself being
therewith offended—they brought forth their copes, candle-
sticks, holy water, stock, cross and censers; they marched
forth in general procession most gorgeously all the town
over, with Sancta Maria, ora pro nobis, and the rest of the
Latin litany. They chattered it, they chaunted it with
great noise and devotion; they banquetted all day after,
for that they were delivered from the grace of God into a
warm sun."

Their religion was restored to them, but the Irish people
were to find that even a Catholic sovereign does not easily
give up prerogatives of earthly power. The monasteries
were not restored, nor the treasures which had come from
them. With complete lack of consistency Mary called herself "Queen of England, France and Ireland, Defender of
the Faith, and on earth the supreme head of the churches
of England and Ireland."

She ruled Ireland as harshly as her family had before her,
and her deputies used methods as cruel; tribes were raided,
villages burned, rebels shot down. Old Richard Cox observed that "Though Mary was a very zealous Papist, yet
the Irish were not quieter during her reign than they were
under her brother; but on the contrary, their antipathy
against Englishmen and Government induced them to be
as troublesome then as at other times."

Chapter XIII

NEMESIS

➤➤➤≪≪≪

IRELAND'S RED-HAIRED Nemesis, known in England as "Good Queen Bess," came to the throne in 1558. Twenty-five, she was then. Aquiline, arrogant, greedy, and untrustworthy, she was one of the world's most fascinating women, then and for all time. Men were like moths to her flaming hair. From the gallant Sir Thomas Wyatt, who died in an attempt to put her on the throne while her sister Mary was still alive, to the Earl of Essex, who fluttered about her in her old age, they gave her everything from flattery to devotion. Some she banished, some knelt to the headsman's axe, some merely disappeared, but on all their hearts was etched her name. And scholars today, turning over old letters and documents which reveal all her duplicity, all her intrigue, her villainy even, fall victim to that ineffable quality that was hers, and write of her books that all but throb with passion.

Of all the men she knew, perhaps her ministers in Ireland were least susceptible to her charms. They had to read her state letters, and they were tart, and never tender. Ireland was such a bother. Those stubborn people over the sea would not succumb to England. They would not give up their Irish ways for gentlemanlike manners, and accept the English rule. They were always rebelling, and trying to be free. Three main rebellions Elizabeth put down in Ireland in her long reign, and countless small broils and uprisings. She took the lives of the greatest men in Ireland. As trophy of her first victory, the head of Shane O'Neill, Earl of Tyrone, was raised on a pike over Dublin Castle. Twenty years later, London Bridge showed the blood-drained face of the Earl of Desmond, to prove that Munster was at last subdued. When Elizabeth's life was near its end Hugh O'Donnell died in Spain, and Spanish candles lighted his requiem, but State Papers in London show that English poison caused his death.

Now, so soon after her crowning, there was the fear that Ireland might be made the basis of an attack by her enemies. Double reason now why Ireland must not be free. With France and Spain against her, the island was too close a steppingstone to England. "The danger is in my sight so fearful," warned her deputy, the Earl of Sussex, in 1560, "the matter, if it be attempted by foreign power, and aided by civil faction, so easy to be compassed, and the resisting thereof so difficult, as I am forced by duty to give advice that it should be in time prevented, not so much for the care I have of Ireland, which I have often wished sunk in the sea, as for that if the French should set foot therein, they should not only have such a entry into Scotland as her Majesty could not resist, but also by the commodity of the havens here, and Calais now in their possession, they should take entirely from England all kinds of traffic by sea, whereby would ensue such a ruin to England as I am afeared to think on."

Elizabeth was afeared to think on it, too, and on the

state of Ireland itself. The names she feared had been frightful to her father, and to other Englishmen before that, O'Neill and O'Donnell, O'Byrne, O'Connor, the Earl of Desmond. The young Kildare who had fled from Henry when his brother Thomas was hanged was now in part reinstated on his lands, and there was cause to think that he entertained his family's old pretensions. A spy of the English said there was communication between Kildare and his cousin the Earl of Desmond, to the end that the English might be expelled.

"Procure the Earl of Kildare to come to England," Elizabeth secretly instructed Sussex. "Avoiding sinister suspicion the deputy shall arrest the earl and also at one instant cause the chiefest of his counselors that are to be the most distrusted to be taken. Procure, too, the Earl of Desmond."

"Bring them to England, entice them to Dublin," she would instruct her officers throughout her reign. And the men she feared would find themselves in the Tower of London, or shivering in the clammy rooms of the keeps of Dublin Castle.

A year later she was writing Sussex concerning Shane O'Neill, who remained in great power in the north, "and in all his deeds showed himself a rebel and a traitor." She was prepared to spare no charge, she told the deputy, "to scourge and subdue him and his accomplices to the very extremity. . . . Our pleasure is that you shall do the best that in you lieth, using our authority and force, either by taking and subduing said Shane and the country by him occupied, and his accomplices, or else by utter expulsion of him and his. For the better exploit thereof, you shall do well, before this your enterprise, to solicit and provoke James O'Neill and his brother Sorley Boy to make war upon said Shane, at the same time that you shall determine your attempt, and the like you shall seek to be done by O'Donnell and his followers and all others soever you think meet, using such good reason and persuasion to each of them as you see expedient and more probable to allure them further to our service." It was the old story of dividing the Irish among themselves. It still worked.

Elizabeth did well to fear O'Neill. He was the strongest man in Ireland. "The Lion of Ulster," lusty, vigorous, and well named Shane the Proud. He fought his rivals, he ruled his subordinates, and loved many women. His amours seem to have annoyed the English greatly, though they had taken their own Henry Tudor complacently enough, and Shane's women made no objection. He carried off the sister of the Earl of Argyle, and from an enemy she turned to a strong ally.

Son of the Conn O'Neill who had been granted the title of Earl of Tyrone by Henry VIII, and who had died cursing the English for their treachery, and all who sowed corn to nourish them or spoke their foreign tongue, Shane carried on his father's hatred, and surrounded himself with gallow-glass and kerne. When he was in the field sixty grim and redoubtable warriors, with sharp, keen axes, terrible and ready for action, guarded his tent. All night the light of the thick king-torch by his doorway flickered on swords and head-pieces and shirts of mail.

When he went into battle he used the same kind of troops that St. Leger had praised to Henry VIII, horseman, and gallow-glass and kerne. "No properer horsemen in Christian ground," St. Leger had said, entranced, as all men were, by the sight of an Irishman on a horse, "nor more hardy, nor yet that can better endure hardness. . . .

As for the footmen, named gallow-glass, who be harnessed in mail and skull-caps of metal, every one of them has his weapon, called a 'sparre,' a long-handled axe, much like the axe of the Tower. And for the most part their boys bear for them three darts apiece, which darts they throw, or they come to the handstrife; these sort of men be those that do not lightly abandon the field, but bide the brunt of death. The other sort, called kerne, are naked men, but only their shirts and small-coats, and those have darts and short bows; which sort of people be both hardy and active to search woods and morasses.''

English soldiers, used to easier battlefields than the mountains and fastnesses of Ulster, had hard going against these men. The deputy, from the bitter past, knew this quite well. He had other means of dealing with dangerous men. Soon he was reporting to the queen on a proposition he had made to Shane's senechal, Neal Gray, to poison the earl, the deputy adding, "If he will not do what he may in our service, there will be done to him what others can."

But that attempt to kill the earl, like the other two which State Papers indicate, had no success. It was the queen's diplomacy which brought Shane to London at last, and kept him there, long after he would have returned. On a day in 1562, people on London streets beheld a company of Shane's axe-bearing gallow-glass. "Bare-headed, with curled hair hanging down," says Camden, "yellow surpluses died with saffron, long sleeves, short coates and having mantles," at whom the English gazed with wonder.

The cause of dispute between Elizabeth and O'Neill concerned the descent of the title of Earl of Tyrone. Shane claimed it as oldest legitimate son. Because of Shane's personal strength, the English thought it best to give the title to a man of doubtful parentage, who had been brought up to the age of sixteen as the son of a Dundalk blacksmith. Elizabeth found Shane as keen a diplomat as herself. She proclaimed in his favor, and finally let him return to Ireland.

He met there with stories that did no credit to Elizabeth's word. In spite of the queen's promises that Ulster would not be molested in the earl's absence, her men had raided Ulster cattle and castles while Shane had been in England. Out of four thousand kine taken, but forty had been returned, and goods to the value of two thousand marks. The earl complained of this to the queen, with no result.

Shane broke his word then. In disregard of his treaty with the queen he invaded the O'Donnell's country of Tyrconnell. Sussex sought to lure him within grasp, but Shane was wary of English invitations now, and he refused to go to Dundalk, where he would have been taken. He refused to go to Dublin, though the lord lieutenant offered his sister as bait. "Word was sent out of the English Pale," Sussex confessed to the queen, "that my sister was brought over only to trap him, and that if he came to any government he would never return."

When Shane went into revolt, and subdued the Ulster clans who had been intrigued into going against him, the English could do nothing. They patched up a peace with Shane, a peace suspiciously generous. Sussex was again depending on other means than force. But though the poisoned wine this time actually came to Shane's table, and was drunk, to the mortal agony of many people, Shane still lived, never to trust the English again. He threw off the title of Earl of Tyrone for the Irish one of The O'Neill, and went into active rebellion.

Not only Ulster was his objective now, but all Ireland. He invaded Connaught, and tried to collect the old tribute of Irish kings. He constantly guarded himself with four hundred armed men, and held in readiness to bring into the field a thousand horse, and four times as many foot soldiers. The peasants and husbandmen of his country he furnished with armor and weapons, and trained them up in knowledge of war. He held large lands. He made a bond with Scotland. From England Elizabeth watched, and she saw in him a likeness to the Earl of Kildare. Shane had outwitted Sussex; she tried another deputy, Sir Henry Sydney. But when he arrived, Shane would not meet him, but sent a letter outlining his grievances against the government. Sydney could not reply, for they were all well grounded.

It was some time before the deputy could contrive a meeting, and when he did, he was alarmed at Shane's ambition. "I care not to be made an earl," Shane said, "unless I may be better and higher than an earl; for I am in blood and power better than the best of them, and I will give place to none but my cousin of Kildare, for he is of my house. You have made a wise earl of Mac Carty More; I keep as good a man as he. For the queen, I confess she is my sovereign; but I never made a peace with her but at her own seeking. Whom am I to trust? When I came unto the Earl of Sussex upon safe-keeping, he offered me the courtesy of a hand-lock. When I was with the queen, she said to me herself that I had, it was true, safe-conduct to come and go; but it was not said when I might go; and they kept me there until I had agreed to things so far against my honor and profit, that I would never perform them while I live. They made me make war, and if it were to do again, I would do it. My ancestors were kings of Ulster, and Ulster is mine, and shall be mine. O'Donnell shall never come into his country, nor Bagenal into Newry, nor Kildare into Dundrum or Lecale. They are now mine. With the sword I won them, and with this sword I will keep them.''

Elizabeth sent more troops to Ireland, who spent more days in garrison than they did in fighting. O'Neill hovered and ranged the field, and showed himself ready to try combat. But at the first skirmish the fury of O'Neill's charge scattered the English and killed their captain. He besieged Derry for a whole winter, and then blew up the town. The retreating English forces were harried all the way to Dublin by the pursuing victors. The Pale knew Shane's fire and sword that summer, and so did the English-held town of Dundalk.

The lord deputy, with four regiments at his command, determined to make a new raid upon O'Neill. In the meantime, instructed by Elizabeth, he so handled matters that Shane was unfeathered of all his best friends, aids, and allies, and put at war with his strongest foe. Most important of all, the lord deputy made a treaty with two chieftains with whom O'Neill had lately been embroiled, that they and their Scots would help the English in the subduing of Shane.

On June 22, 1567, Shane entered the Scottish camp, hoping to make an alliance with his late enemies. And they after greeting him with dishonest heartiness, and offering him wine, falsely promised the aid that Shane had come to ask. Then one of the traitors, issuing out of the tent, gathered his Scots in a throng, and suddenly reappearing in force before O'Neill, with swords hewed in pieces the

earl and all his companions except a few who escaped by
flight. "Very nimbly did they mangle him," is the way
the Four Masters put it.

Then Captain Pierce, the author of this scheme, cut
Shane's head from his body, and wrapped it in a kerne's
shirt. Four days later he sent it to the lord deputy in Dublin,
who caused it to be set upon a stake above the castle wall.

And so, for a reward of a thousand marks, this revolt
was quieted, a valiant Irishman slain, and English rule
made more secure.

And for its further security the letter bags which Elizabeth's couriers carried between Dublin and London bulged
fat and heavy. The phrasing and the messages might differ,
but always the edicts had one aim: the elevation of the
English to power, and the weakening of the Irish. "Consideration to be had of the counties of Leix and Offaly, how
they may be re-inhabited with good subjects, and the rebel
O'Connors and O'Mores expelled." . . . "No lords or
or any others shall keep more horseman or footman than
they are able to maintain at their own costs." . . . "No
man not being in a captain's book to wear any weapon."
. . . "Marrying or fostering with the Irish is treason,
which is to be qualified with loss of goods and lands during
life . . ."

Elizabeth, like other English rulers before her, had listened to the battle cries of strong Irish nobles, and had
been afraid. "The Strong Hand to Victory," rallied
O'Brien's men to him at the threat of war. "Crom a boo,"
the Kildares cried. "The Red Hand to Victory," the O'Neills
shouted as they rushed to combat. One by one the fighters
were put down, and their voices for a time were hushed.
A new voice was rising now, rising higher and stronger,

and gaining in insistence. It was the voice of the Irish poets; it was the voice of Ireland itself. It chanted a warning to the people: "Beware of England, beware of English honors; do not be divided among yourselves by this enemy. Part not with your patrimony for foreign titles. Fooboon on the foreign-gray guns, fooboon on the golden chains our nobles wear in token to submission. Foreigners are dividing our territory, and there is none to nick them out."

Henry had heard that voice, and so had his frail son Edward. It would keep alive, forever, the very Irish spirit that the English wished to kill. So laws were made to still it. No poet could write in praise of any but the king. No poet could speak against England, or anything that was English. Now Elizabeth went further. She would root out all Irish learning, all Irish schools, all Irish patriotism. And since Ireland and Catholicism were now linked, she would root out the old religion, too.

She sent commissioners to suppress the schools, to destroy books and manuscripts, to harry all scholars, teachers, and poets, to take all learning from the people. Ignorant, obedient subjects she wanted, rather than learned rebels. Poets had been honored before. Now she would make them outcasts.

For all that they had lived in luxury and known rich rewards, the poets were a hardy race. If Elizabeth thought she could starve them into submission, she soon knew her mistake. "To be in threadbare mantles is no disgrace to sons of learning," the poets chanted. "To be somewhat run to decay is not a shame to any so long as his science is progressive." They had had the king's shoulder, and the king's meat and wine. Now they slept under hedges, in fear of their lives, but their voices were not stilled.

They sang the lack of an Irish champion. Too many Irish nobles had gone to England, and in the "queen's closet" of Greenwich or Hampton had taken titles and golden chains from the English ruler. Some of them learned how hollow was the honor. Some of them lived to renounce it, and to return their allegiance to the land of their ancestors. Now a man with Norman blood arose to renounce the English, and to draw his sword in the cause of Irish freedom. It was Desmond's turn to make a try against the queen.

Doubtless the effort was inevitable. With all their pride and all their possessions and all their power, it was only strange that the Desmonds put off the contest for so long. More than three hundred castles acknowledged the Desmond lordship when Elizabeth became queen, and the earl could call six hundred nobles of his race to his banner. They led clansmen and kerne by the thousand to his aid.

As always, the Geraldines' power was envied by the Ormondes. There was a handsome young Earl of Ormonde now, who spent much time at court. "My black husband," Elizabeth playfully called him, and took his part in all the quarrels his house had with the Desmonds.

In 1567 the Earl of Desmond and his brother were imprisoned in Dublin Castle. From there they were taken to the Tower of London. It was a long banishment, and an uncomfortable one. They had not, they wrote pitifully, as young Thomas of Kildare had written, so much of their own as to buy a pair of shoes, and they despaired to have anything out of their own country. In Munster a kinsman, Sir James FitzMaurice, was guarding the Desmond interests, but he could do nothing to procure their release.

When Elizabeth was excommunicated by the Pope in

1569, Sir James asked aid of France and Spain, but Elizabeth was dangling the hope of a marriage with her before the royal houses of these two countries, and they would not move against her. Sir John Perrot went to Munster to put it in order, and in his eyes FitzMaurice was a fox he must hunt out of his hole before that could be accomplished. But the fox kept to the fastnesses of Aherlow Wood, and it was three years before he wearied of being chased by Perrot, and submitted. Desmond and his brother were brought back to Ireland then, and from Dublin the earl escaped to his own country. He took back from FitzMaurice his lands and his castles, and FitzMaurice went to France.

The English spies who followed him there had ill news for the queen. FitzMaurice went to the Pope to get his blessing on a Catholic rising, and from then on there was constant rumor of the aid he was promised by foreign kings. Six tall ships and twelve hundred Frenchmen at one time; three ships from Spain at another. In March of 1579 it was reported that FitzMaurice was at Biscay with seven shallops, and that the Pope bore all the charges.

Doubtless FitzMaurice was in communication with his kinsman, and expected Desmond's aid when the foreign troops would be landed in Ireland. But when, on a July afternoon, the six Spanish ships sailed into the narrow harbor of Dingle in Kerry, Desmond did not join them, but proclaimed himself on the queen's side. The deserted FitzMaurice set off to recruit new aid in Munster, and was killed in a skirmish on the way.

The Earl of Desmond has been much condemned for his tardiness in going to war, as his cousin, Silken Thomas, was condemned for his haste in defying Henry VIII. This Gerald, Earl of Desmond, had been impetuous, too, in his youth. Like so many of his family, he had been held the handsomest man of his time. He had had the rashness which the Irish define as "courage out of its wits." But that was many years ago, and the time between had been filled with hardship. Read Elizabeth's letters to see how she had persecuted him, how she had scolded her ministers for their "slender dealings" with him. Read of his many arrests, of his years in prison. The dampness of Tower rooms had robbed his joints of their elasticity. The long procession of prison days had dulled the spontaneity of his enthusiasm. He knew Elizabeth's power, and how she punished rebels. Is it strange that he hesitated to defy her?

Eventually he did. Pressed for pledges of peace by the lord deputy he refused to supply them, and went into rebellion. For Ireland? For the Church? No, not primarily. They were abstract questions to a weary, aging man. But his honor. That was different. He had a fine conception of himself, and of his obligations. It is probable that the sixteenth Earl of Desmond went to war with Elizabeth because he was a gentleman, because his family name was so enmeshed with the plans that James FitzMaurice had made on the Continent, that he could not withdraw his support of them without tarnishing the reputation of the Desmonds, and of all the Geraldines.

He asked aid of other Irish princes. "It is so that I and my brother are entered into the defense of the Catholic faith, and the overthrow of our country by Englishmen, which had overthrown the Holy Church, and go about to overrun our country and make it their own, and to make us their bondsmen, wherein we are to desire you to take part with us, according as you are bound by conscience and by nature to defend your country; and if you be afraid, we should shrink from you. After you should enter this cause you shall understand that we took this matter in hand with great authority, both from the Pope's holiness and from King Philip, who do undertake to further us in our affairs as we shall need, wherefore you shall not need to fear to take one part of it; and be assured we will never agree with none of your adversaries without your consent."

The Earl of Clancare and other smaller chieftains joined Desmond, and they faced Ormonde's troops, who distinguished themselves from the Irish with red silken crosses upon their breasts and backs.

"The Earl of Desmond has burned Youghal," wrote "that painful gentleman," Lord Justice Pelham, to the queen. "Clancare has done the same to Kinsale. All obstinate Papists wish well to the rebels in respect that the Pope's banner is displayed and a government expected that will settle them in their religion. It is generally given in all parts that a wonderful navy is prepared in Italy."

Elizabeth was not too pleased with Pelham, and he knew it. "Your Majesty's letter of the twenty-eighth of November showeth several causes of your disliking me since I entered your service. The proceeding against Desmond was a necessity. Neither the Viscount Barrie, Roche, nor any of their quality in Munster would in any way show themselves enemies to this action till they were sure by that public act that your Majesty would deal thoroughly for his extermination." That was what he wrote to the queen.

To Sussex he explained: "Her Majesty takes offense at the proceeding against Desmond. I could better have liked that her Majesty should have converted her forces to the north [where the first Earl of Essex was transplanting

Englishmen] or to the reducing of Leix and Offaly to the perfection which your Lordship left it, than to make war on any of the English nation. Nevertheless the earl had so far waded in the foreign practice of James FitzMaurice and Dr. Saunders as he thought it impossible to be reconciled to her Majesty's favor."

In February of the next year Ormonde and the Earl of Desmond were fighting west of Tipperary. Then the skirmish shifted to Aherlow Wood. Pelham wrote imploring the queen to aid the royal force with all things necessary, especially "victuals and munitions, as the powder wasteth apace. I mean on the next Monday to begin my journey through the county of Cork."

By that time, every man in Munster was persuaded of foreign aid. "Many gentlemen and free-holders of Limerick," the lord justice wrote the Council in London, "are fled to the rebels. A general revolt is to be feared as soon as any foreign aid shall come." A week later he repeated his alarm. "I do assure your Lordships that there is no corporation nor almost any kerne in Munster that doth not look expressly for a navy of Spain to arrive shortly, and therefore the bruit cannot be suppressed, but is clearly dispersed throughout the whole realm, and such captains of countries as have not already entered the confederacy have their friars and renegade priests ready to solicit for them at their landing. . . . We propose to destroy all Dingle. We doubt not but to make as bare a country as ever Spain set foot in."

So the lord justice and the Earl of Ormonde, dividing their forces, marched through the rebel's country, scourging it with fire and sword. "We entered Connelough in two companies," Pelham records, "Ormonde toward the

Shannon side, and I upwards toward Newcastle, and marched all day without offense of any enemy, wasting and spoiling the country to the foot of the mountain of Sleulougher. The people and cattle, flying before us in the mountain, were followed by some horsemen and light footmen. We encamped in two places, not far distant one from the other, near Desmond's first and most ancient house of Castle Shenet. Finding the country plentiful, and the people but newly fled, we left our camps guarded the next day, and searched some part of the mountain. There were slain that day, by the fury of the soldiers, above four hundred people found in the wood, and wheresoever any corn or house was found it was consumed by fire.''

They took three castles from the Burkes, and the castle of Carrigofoil, whose plate the lord justice sent to the queen. A company of men about a mile from Adare encountered with the Earl of Desmond "in most brave manner, with eighty horsemen, and five hundred footmen marvelously well appointed, who came to the very push of the English pikes, but were forced to retire with loss of sixty of their company."

So through the spring the scourge lasted. The invaders showed mercy neither to the strong nor to the weak. They killed blind and feeble men, boys and girls, sick persons, idiots, and old people.

Sir Henry Stafford related that English soldiers entered an Irish camp, "found none but hurt and sick men, whose pains and lives they soon determined." And again, having burnt the houses and corn and taken great prey, he diverted his forces to another place, and harrowing the country, "killed all mankind that were found there for a terror to those who would give relief to renegade traitors." He entered Aherlow Wood, where he "did the like, not leaving behind man or beast, or corn or cattle." A fellow officer reported that he had left "neither corn nor horn, nor house unburnt," from one end of Munster to the other.

The Earl of Desmond and his wife were fugitives now, their castles and lands taken from them. They found what shelter they could under forest boughs, or in damp mountain huts. Very hardly they escaped the English soldiers, whose service in the province never abated. The earl's brother was wounded in a skirmish which lost the Irish a hundred and fifty men. Still living, the Geraldine was handed over to Captain Walter Raleigh, who caused him to be hanged and quartered, and his remains made a prey of fowls over the gate of Cork.

In this dark time the longed-for Spanish aid arrived. The bay of St. Marie of Smerwick on the Kerry coast was the landing place of the foreigners, who numbered about seven hundred men, with pikes and munitions and all kinds of artillery sufficient for five thousand men.

The castle of the Golden Rock, which the strangers took and held, was soon besieged by the English on two sides. Three ships of the queen's navy under Sir William Winter menaced it by sea. The Earl of Ormonde, who was joined by the lord justice, Captain Walter Raleigh, and other English officers, encamped their combined forces as near the fort as might be. With artillery landed from Sir William Winter's ships the fort was continually battered. The Four Masters affirm that there was no solitude or wilderness from the Carn of Brea to Knockmaa in which the sound and roar of the English cannon were not heard.

At the end of four days the Spaniards, despairing of aid from the Earl of Desmond, and not being able to withstand the battering of the cannon, offered to surrender with certain conditions, but the lord justice required an absolute yielding or none at all. At length the Spaniards, seeing no help at hand, and with winter approaching, offered to yield themselves and the fort without any condition at all. As a symbol of their defeat they hung out a white flag, while the sad cry of "Misericordia, misericordia" rose as from one great throat.

The lord justice sent in orders for the entire company to disarm themselves. The men brought all the armor of the fort to one place, and laid their pikes across it. Then Captain Raleigh and another Englishman entered the castle and made a great slaughter, the most part of the men being put to the sword, "it not being thought good to show them mercy."

But notwithstanding the overthrow of the Spanish, and the blow to Irish hopes of freedom, Munster, Leinster, and a great part of Connaught were in actual rebellion, so that new bands of men had to be sent out of England to destroy the rebels, and these were kept busy in the province for a year.

Again Adare woods had a human quarry, this time the Earl of Desmond. "He slept but upon couches of stone or earth; he drank but of the pure, cold streams, and that from the palms of his hands, or his shoes, and his only cooking utensils were the long twigs of the forest for dressing the flesh meat carried away from his enemies." So the Four Masters tell of the man whose chain of castles had stretched across Munster.

Wherever he fled, or sought protection, there the English followed, and the Irish people were in as sore straits as their leader. Munster was brought to such wretchedness, wrote Spenser later, "as that any stony heart would have rued the same. Out of every corner of the woods and glens they came creeping forth upon their hands, for their legs could not bear them; they looked like anatomies of death; they spoke like ghosts crying out of their graves; they did eat the dead carrions, happy where they could find them, yea, and one another soon after . . . and if they found a plot of watercresses or shamrocks, there they thronged as to a feast for the time, yet not able long to continue there withal; that in a short space there were almost none left, and a most populous and plentiful country suddenly left void of man and beast."

In the month of August of 1583 it was advertised to the garrison at Kilmacook that the earl was again in Aherlow Wood, and had about three score gallow-glass with him, besides kerne in great number. For about two months the English harried him, so that his men never ate in the place where they cooked their food, or slept where they had eaten. One by one they fell away from their leader, till at length but four comrades remained to him.

Then on a dark night an English company, out hunting a prey of kine, spied through the trees the light of a fire. When they came to the mountain cabin where the fire was, they found only one old man, whose followers had all fled from him. The captain of the company drew his sword, and struck the old man, almost cutting off one of his arms. Another great blow did sore damage to his head. Whereupon the victim cried out for mercy, and that he was the Earl of Desmond. But still another blow was struck at the nobleman, and that severed his proud old head from his body. The one was sent to England, and raised on a pike on London Bridge; the other, now harmless carrion, was left to the wolves.

As a refuge from this stark reality, the Irish have built up a legend about the old earl's body. They comfort themselves with the belief that it lies in enchanted slumber under the waters of Lough Gur, near one of the Desmond castles. Every seventh year the earl awakes, they think, and rides forth over the surface of the lake on a horse shod with silver, attended by a knightly throng. When the horse's shoes are worn to the hoof, then the Earl of Desmond will return and restore all the lost glories of the Geraldines. And with his coming will come Irish freedom.

It was in 1583 that the Earl of Desmond was killed, and Munster left waste and desolate. "The sweetest soil in Ireland" it had been. Now that sweet soil was taken from its Irish owners, and parceled out to English undertakers. A quarter of a million acres soon passed from native to foreign landlords. Sir Walter Raleigh, more famous for sacrificing his cloak to keep the feet of his queen unmuddied than for his massacre of the Spaniards of the Golden Rock, was enriched with 42,000 acres in Cork and Waterford. Lesser Englishmen had tracts of from four thousand to twelve thousand acres, on which they contracted to plant families of English people, that the Irish might be overwhelmed.

Leinster was treated to some of Sir John Perrot's "precautionary measures." "I have in this castle the White Knight," he wrote to the Earl of Leicester, "the senechal, Patrick Condon, and Donnell McCormock, and have caused to have apprehended Mac Awley and Thomas Oge of the Island. I have sent for Patrick FitzMaurice. I have caused to be hanged Conell Mac Lysage O'More, Lisage Mac William O'More, three notables of the Kellys, and I have Connell McKedaghe O'More's head upon the top of the castle, so as there resteth not one principal of the O'Mores but Shane Mac Rosse, who was within these four days sore hurt and like to be killed, and so was Walter Roghe also, whose heads I am promised very shortly. I have also taken the young fry of all the Mores, saving one I am promised to have. So as I do not know one dangerous man of that sect left.''

In Connaught this is the picture, as recorded in the *Annals of Loch Cé* ''The person who was governor from the queen over the province at this time was Sir Richard Bingham, and of all the Clan William he did not hang he set at war with the queen, and the Clan Donnell in like manner, and he set the posterity of Hugh, son of Felim, and Muinter Flanagan and O'Rourke and Mac Dermot at war with himself and the queen. He made a bare polished garment of the province of Connaught . . . ''

And what of the people of the Pale? Nothing better for them. They were suffering as all Ireland was, from the impositions of the English garrisons. As the troops passed slowly through the country they ''wasted with their lingering journies the inhabitants' corn excessively with their horses, their goods and extortion . . . pleasing themselves at their pleasure, exacting meat and drink far more than competent, and commonly, money from them. . . . And if they be not satisfied with meat and money according to their outrageous demands, then do they beat their horses and their people, ransacking their houses, taking away cattle and goods of all sorts, not leaving so much as the tools and instruments that craftsmen do exercise their occupations withal, nor the garments to their backs, nor clothes to their beds . . . And if they do withstand or gainsay such their inordinate wills, then they do not only exercise all the cruelty that they can against them, in far worse sort than before, in nature of a revenge, so as whosoever resisteth their will shall be sure to have nothing left him, if he can escape with his life."

These were an Englishman's words.

What of Irish learning? It was being destroyed. What of the old religion? It was being persecuted. "We have neither rack nor other engines of torture to terrify him," the Council of Ireland complained to London of a cleric. They were advised to toast his feet against the fire, which they did till lumps of cooked flesh came away.

Is it a wonder that Ireland was sunk in misery and despair? Is it strange that her people would welcome any ray of hope? It came suddenly from the north.

In 1588, Lord Deputy Perrot had had a young nobleman kidnapped from Ulster, "brought hither by a stratagem," he reported gleefully to the queen. The boy spent four years in chains in Dublin Castle, with many other hostages taken in the same manner.

Now on a snowy winter night of 1592 he escaped, and all Ireland stirred at the news. For this boy, Hugh O'Donnell, was scion of the great family of O'Donnell of Tyrconnell; princes and patrons of learning the O'Donnells had been for a thousand years. Niall of the Nine Hostages was their ancestor, and St. Columba, called Columcille, was of their line. The famous *Battle Book* of the O'Donnells was supposed to have been written by the gray saint himself—the same psalter which had caused the battle of Cuildremne, and Columcille's exile. A priest free from sin carried the precious relic thrice sunwise around the O'Donnell army ready for combat, and it was supposed to bring the host back with victory. A prophecy as old as the *Battle Book* now made young Hugh precious to the Irish. When two Hughs, the legend ran, lawfully, lineally, and immediately succeeded each other as head of the O'Donnells according to the ancient customs, the second Hugh would be monarch of Ireland, and banish all strangers from her shores.

With the eyes of all Ireland upon him, Red Hugh O'Donnell set about fulfilling the conditions of the prophecy. His father was old and feeble, with thoughts more scholarly than warlike. He gave up the leadership of his clan to his son, and retired to a monastery. Young Hugh, known to the English as the Earl of Tyrconnell, was inaugurated as The O'Donnell, with all the ancient rites of his people.

His country was in ruins. The queen's agent, Captain Willis, had reduced the proud old family to the position of vassals. Hugh O'Donnell drove the captain out. The monastery of Donegal, which his ancestors had founded, he took from the English troops quartered there, and restored it to the clerics. He set about making himself a power in the north.

As of old, he had allies in the Maguires, Lords of Fermanagh. This great family, they of the lovely court of Enniskillen which the poet had sung of, was now headed by Hugh Maguire, greatest horseman in Ireland.

For centuries past the O'Donnells had fought the O'Neills of Tyrone, their greatest rivals in Ulster. Now Hugh O'Neill, Earl of Tyrone, by great personal affection for young Hugh O'Donnell, had wiped out the barriers that had kept the two houses apart.

All three of these princes had known Elizabeth's method of dealing with her enemies. They had had battle with her. They knew how disastrous the effects of her diplomacy could be. Each now, as their Ulster alliance became stronger, was put in active fear of his life. Their separate complaints of the actions of the queen against them are published in the State Papers for all to read. But the complaints changed nothing. The three men merged their forces, and a great confederacy was formed.

It was then that Elizabeth found that all Ireland had united. Princes forswore their family pride to think of their country. The people lifted their thoughts above the interests of their clans. For four hundred years England had dealt with separate Irish nobles. Now she had a nation to deal with. Now she was at war with a whole people. Ireland would fight now, not as Munster, not as Leinster, not as haughty Ulster, but as Ireland. Ireland. Ireland. It was a country born again. Born with agony, but born strong and brave and gallant.

The three Hughs were her leaders. O'Neill was a shrewd old general. He had been brought up in English ways, and had been used as a tool by the queen to keep Tyrone subdued. Whether he had been biding his time till a chance had come to strike at England no one knows. At any rate, he now held The O'Neill to be a better title than Earl of Tyrone, and all his skill and cunning were turned against the English. "He was of mean stature," says Fynes Moryson, the chronicler of this rebellion, in a book meant to be complimentary to the English, "but strong body, able to endure labors, watching and hard fare, being with all industrious, and active, valiant and affable, and apt to manage great affairs, and of a high dissembling subtile and profound wit."

He was now married to Joan O'Donnell, and her brother Red Hugh was betrothed to a daughter of O'Neill. But more than marriage ties bound the two men. O'Neill had many sons, but none who was his equal. O'Donnell's father was not worthy of his son. It was a strange friendship these two men had, the one old and crafty, the other young, gallant, and impetuous.

The strategic fortress of the Blackwater fell easily to O'Neill. Maguire took Monaghan. "The kernes," said Moryson, "shaked the English government in this kingdom till it tottered and wanted little of total ruin. By the victory of the Blackwater the rebels got arms and victuals, and the combined traitors on all sides puffed up with intolerable pride. All Ulster was in arms, all Connaught revolted, and the rebels of Leinster warmed the English Pale, while the English lay in the garrison, so farre from assailing the rebels as they rather lived in continual fear of being surprised by them."

Elizabeth temporized, and tried to effect a peace with each chief separately. But O'Neill was in charge of the Irish negotiations, and Elizabeth did not succeed. O'Neill did not mind the delay. He was waiting aid from Spain.

In the archives of Simancas lie the letters of Irish chieftains asking aid from the Spanish king. The signatures are O'Neill's and O'Donnell's, those of MacWilliam Burke, Brian O'Rourke, MacSwiney, and Neil O'Boyle, Bishop of Rapahoe. There is one signed "Don Mauricio Geraldino," a kinsman of the Earl of Desmond. "We know that these lords are Catholics," he wrote, "and amongst the strongest and most powerful in Ireland, and uniting thus of their own free will, they risk their lives and estates to serve God and your Majesty. . . . It would be a great pity that these lords should be lost for want of aid, as was the Earl of Desmond, who rose in arms in the same way."

While couriers passed to and fro between Spain and England (and lost many letters to English spies), Elizabeth and Tyrone played a waiting game. The people, meanwhile, were sure that Ireland had found its champion in the Earl of Tyrone. "There was no part of Ulster freed from the poison of this great rebellion, and no country, or chieftain of a county, whom the capital traitor Tyrone hath not corrupted and drawn into combination with him," Elizabeth was told.

She sent her best troops to Ireland, bright in uniforms of buff and scarlet, and captained by heroes from the Netherlands. O'Donnell defeated them in Connaught while O'Neill was engaged in Ulster.

At sunrise of August 14, 1598, an English army marched out of Armagh to go to the relief of troops at Portmore. The colors of dawn dyed their crested plumes, and tinted their armor with gold, but they met black defeat from O'Neill's gallow-glass and kerne. The battle of the Yellow Ford was the greatest conflict in the north, and a complete victory for O'Neill. Ulster was cleared of the English, and a great surge of exultation swept over Ireland. Freedom at last seemed in sight.

Elizabeth in London heard the news, and it angered her. Defeat was something she could not stand. She had been impatient for success before; now she became imperious. Robert Devereux, Earl of Essex, was sent to Ireland with the greatest force the island had yet seen, twenty thousand men and horses. His instructions were definite, and barbed with Elizabeth's anger. "We disdain to bear affront from a rabble of base kerne. In providing a remedy no expense shall be spared. . . . We will not suffer our subjects any longer to be oppressed by those vile rebels."

But Essex was courtier rather than soldier. "Sweet Robin" listened to the Council in Dublin, and instead of attacking O'Neill in the north, he wasted his strength on small encounters in other provinces. He had no keen desire to kill. He even had doubts of the holiness of the English cause. In 1599 he wrote Elizabeth, " 'Twere as well for our credit that we alone had the exposition of our quarrel with this people, and not they also."

Elizabeth answered with a reprimand. "Your two months' journey hath brought in never a capital rebel, against whom it had been worth to have adventured a thousand men . . . What displeases us most is that it must be the Queen of England's fortune, who hath held down the greatest enemy she had, to make a base Irish kerne to be accounted so famous a rebel . . . Little do you know how he hath blazed in foreign parts the defeat of regiments, the deaths of captains, the loss of men of quality in every corner. Surprises would have found better success than public and notorious marches. Regiments should not be committed to young gentlemen, and you have not informed us who they are that spend our treasure and carry places of note in our army . . . In order to plant garrisons in the north and assail that proud rebel, we command you to pass thither with great speed."

But Essex's forces were depleted from skirmishes, from sickness and desertion. Two thousand more men he asked from England, but even that was not enough. When he finally met Tyrone, it was a private parley on opposite banks of the Lagan. The two men, each on horseback, talked for half an hour, then whirled their mounts, and each returned to his own camp. Whatever had been said, it was soon evident that O'Neill had outwitted Essex. Not long afterward, without a battle, the young favorite of the queen abandoned his march to the north.

"Towards the end of July," says Moryson, "his Lordship brought his forces back to Leinster, the soldiers being wearie, sicke, and incredibly diminished in number, and himself returned to Dublin." Essex had resolved to go to London to see the queen. He soon paid for his blunders with his head.

O'Neill's army daily increased in number and courage. "At this time," wrote Moryson, "I may boldly say the rebellion was at its greatest height. The mere Irish puffed up with good success, and blouded with happy encounters, did boldly keep the field, and proudly disdain the English force."

O'Neill invaded Tipperary and Munster, and everywhere had victory. The English who had been planted in Ireland were also in rebellion, and more helpful to the Irish than to the crown. Kildare, Meath, and Dublin County south of the Liffey all belonged to the rebels, besides their territories to the north.

O'Neill issued a proclamation styling himself Defender of the Faith. He made a royal progress from the north to the south of Ireland, and met the southern gentlemen on the banks of the Lee. Everywhere he was acclaimed victor and hero.

Essex had not been able to subdue Ireland, but Elizabeth had other generals and other men. She was old now, and ill, but not less determined. She would have the rebels put down, Anglicized, and made submissive. She sent Charles Blount, Lord Mountjoy, to accomplish that purpose, and he came to his work with a will. He was young, brave, and ambitious, and aware of the tremendous advan-

tage that would be his in England if he could subdue
Ireland. Moryson, his secretary, admired him tremendously.
"The English soldiers he heartened and encouraged by
leading them warily. He bravely adventured his person."

He was a keen general. He compressed O'Neill on every
side, and kept him in Ulster while the English spoiled the
rest of the country. For Mountjoy, like Pelham, did not
trust to the sword alone. His policy was to starve the country. In the summer he cut their corn; in the winter he drove
off their cattle. He was commonly in the saddle five days
a week, routing the Irish. "This brake their hearts, for
the aire being sharpe, and they naked, and they being
driven from their lodgings into the woods bare of leaves,
they had no shelter for themselves."

In 1601, Mountjoy could write to the queen: "We have
seen no man in all Tyrone of late, but dead carcasses merely
hunger starved, of which we found divers as we passed.
Between Tullaghoge and Toome [a matter of seventeen
miles] there lay unburied one thousand dead, and since
our first drawing this year to Blackwater, there were about
three thousand starved in Tyrone. And no spectacle more
frequent in the ditches of the towns than to see multitudes
of these poor people dead with their mouths all colored
green by eating nettles, docks, and all things they could
rend up from the ground."

O'Neill was doing what he could, and fighting bravely
still. But Elizabeth had many resources. She honestly
considered the Irish dangerous reptiles, and no means too
unworthy to wipe them out. She was breaking up the
confederation of chiefs with offers of gold and land,
promised peace, high honors. The State Papers of the time
do not make pleasant reading.

As to O'Neill, Moryson marvels that his name is held in so much reverence that no man will betray him. This in spite of the fact that Elizabeth was "pleased again to renew her gratious offer that whosoever brought him alive should have two thousand pounds, and whosoever brought his head should have one thousand pounds for reward." These were tremendous sums in those days, but O'Neill was in his stronghold.

The three Hughs were holding Ulster alone. The old general, the bright-haired boy, and the splendid horseman could not be parted by any English machinations. Throughout the spring and summer they defended the north; O'Donnell, the coast; O'Neill, the southern border. In the fall came the long-promised help from Spain. Spanish ships sailed into Kinsale harbor, and landed men and arms. Hope was high for a time, till it was learned that three thousand men only had been sent, instead of the five thousand O'Neill had asked for if a landing was to be made in the south. It meant danger for O'Neill and O'Donnell to march through Ireland to meet the Spaniards, but the Spanish general insisted. He was surrounded by English troops on land, and English ships soon threatened him by sea.

O'Donnell was the first to set off on this journey, for it was through him that the Spaniards had been induced to send the Irish aid. O'Neill marched down by another way. When the two forces came to Kinsale they encamped a short distance to the north of the English, and settled themselves for a long siege. The enemy's position was a strong one, but their source of supplies was easily cut off by the Irish. Neither hay nor corn nor water could they bring in, and men and horses were soon starving.

Then the elements began their attack. The days were tempestuous with wind and rain, the nights bright with flashes of lightning, for all it was December. Soon to the misery of damp and cold and hunger was added illness. The English ranks were constantly depleted by death and desertion. Any strategist could see that the Irish had only to hold their camps, and the English would be defeated without a battle.

But as the Irish held their enemies in siege, so were the Spaniards held by the English. The Spanish general, Don Juan Aquila, was soon begging O'Neill to attack the English, that his own position might be bettered.

It was O'Neill's advice not to attack the other side immediately, but to keep them in their present straits until they perished by famine. "But O'Donnell was ashamed to hear the complaint of his allies without making some effort to aid them though defeat and destruction might come from it." Against the reasonable caution of the older man, the impetuous gallantry of O'Donnell had its way, and a night attack on the English was planned.

It was on December 23, 1601, that the deciding battle of the war was fought at Kinsale. Dawn was still hours away when the Irish columns began their march toward the English. Through the dark the flashes of the burning tow-matches each soldier carried coiled around his gunstock told the English of the movement of the Irish troops. Mountjoy, already well informed of the intended attack, had kept his men under arms through all the night.

The Irish advanced in three columns. There was some confusion in the ranks, as there is confusion in the stories of the battle. Either O'Donnell lost his way, or he was misled by his guides. When morning came the Irish army found itself in a bad position before the enemy's camp. Before they could rearrange their ranks for battle they were showered by fire from English cannon, muskets, and lock-guns. Then from the walls streamed the English horsemen, soon followed by well-ordered foot.

One charge of the cavalry was not enough. A second brigade came up in support and swept upon the Irish. The battlefield was a tangle of plunging horses, of confused and wavering men, of pleading captains. But in spite of the firmness of O'Neill, and the entreaties of O'Donnell, the Irish turned in defeat and left the English victors of the combat. Mountjoy returned to camp to give thanks for a victory which surprised no one more than himself. "If Tyrone had lain still and not suffered himself to be drawn to the plain ground by the Spainards' importunity all our horse must needs have been sent away or starved," said Moryson gleefully.

Whatever was responsible, the English had a great victory with small loss of men. The Irish left thousands on the field.

O'Neill retreated, bit by bit, to Ulster, his only hope in more help from the Spanish king. If Philip would send five or six thousand men, and a general more valiant than Don Aquila, Ireland might still be saved. O'Donnell under-took the mission, and O'Neill in the north waited for the news that would mean the life or death of the Irish cause.

O'Donnell wrote encouragingly from the king's court at Simancas. Philip, still antagonistic to Elizabeth, pro-mised more men, ships, and money. Then he wavered, and for a while the messages spoke only of delay. Finally came one that was alarming. O'Donnell was strangely ill, and there was a suspicion, later confirmed, that he had been poisoned. After a wait of weeks came the news of Red Hugh's death.

It was in the palace of the king in the town of Simancas that he died, and his body was taken in a four-wheeled hearse to the court of Valladolid, with great numbers of state officers and royal guards surrounding it. But all the accounts of the blazing torches that lighted the way, the bright flambeaux of beautiful wax tapers that were burned, and the many hymns and sweet canticles that were sung around his coffin could alter the fact that it was not only O'Donnell who was buried with such honor, but Ireland's hopes as well. In the Spanish monastery of St. Francis, in the most solemn manner, with great honor and respect, was celebrated the requiem of Hugh O'Donnell and Irish liberty.

O'Neill heard the news, and with sorrow and the bitterness of defeat mingling in his heart he put down his sword. The lord deputy offered terms, and he went south to accept them.

The day he went on his knees in submission came the news of Elizabeth's death.

Chapter XIV

THE FLIGHT OF THE EARLS

->>)<<-

HUGH O'NEILL, Earl of Tyrone, went back to Ulster "a new man" by royal pardon. The phrase was supposed to be significant of hope. For him it was just the contrary. He, who had been supreme, was now humbled. His lands, which had never know sheriff or king's writ, were now open to English officers. His rents were diminished, his powers curtailed. He was only another earl, instead of the Lion of the North.

All Ireland was now conquered by the English, but the victory had ruined the prize. A traveler, looking on the war-ravaged country with a compassionate eye, could see a likeness to a banquet table at the latter end of a feast. "Here lieth an old ruined castle, like the remainder of a venison pasty, there a broken fort like a mince-pie half subjected, and in another place an old abbey with some turrets standing like the carcass of a goose broken up."

The province of Ulster was so devastated by war that what people were left were hunger-weak. "Ulster, wherein at my first coming I found not one in subjection, hath now not one in rebellion," Mountjoy wrote the new king, James. Connaught was quiet, too. In all Leinster "scarce a thief was stirring, nor one rebel." But in Munster many towns, and Kilkenny and Wexford in Leinster, had, on news of Elizabeth's death, set up the public exercise of the mass. By fair means or by foul, Mountjoy promised, he hoped to leave them commanded by the king's garrison.

"If they make resistance, I was never worse provided. My companies are grown weak of English, for the miseries of this war are so intolerable, especially by this new coin, that all the best men forsake them."

"I cannot hope to bring things to any better pass than they already are," the victorious general explained, in asking leave to go to England to kiss the king's hand, "but with long time, that will polish what I have rough hewn. This kingdom is now made capable of what form it shall please the king to give it."

What the king wanted, it soon became apparent, was conformity in religion. To obtain that, James and his successors sacrificed "that addition of honor and commodity to the crown of England" that Mountjoy had said James might make of Ireland, and turned her, instead, into a land drained of her best blood, bereft of her poets, her trade suppressed, her people poor, miserable, and persecuted.

The towns which had joyfully celebrated mass in public on hearing of Elizabeth's death had done so in the belief that King James would be tolerant of the old religion, and allow the Catholics "freedom of conscience." They were soon disillusioned. Mountjoy marched against them, and when Waterford protested that by King John's charter they were not obliged to admit either English rebels or Irish enemy, the general answered that his army had suppressed both rebels and enemy, and that if resistance were offered, he would cut King John's charter with King James's

sword. What could they do but submit, proclaim Elizabeth's successor, and continue to hear religious services
secretly?

But Mountjoy had no sooner sailed away to England to
be made Earl of Devonshire than the country began stirring.
It would never lose hope of freedom so long as Hugh
O'Neill was alive. Already there were rumors that help
would come again from Spain; that Catholic Philip III
would ally himself with the earl against Protestant
England.

In September, 1603, the treasurer for war in Ireland
wrote Sir Robert Cecil, the future Lord Salisbury: "Of
late the country swarms with priests, Jesuits, seminaries,
friars and Romish bishops; if there be not speedy means to
free this kingdom of this rabble, much mischief will burst
forth in very short time. There are here so many of this
wicked crew as are able to disquiet four of the greatest
kingdoms in Christendom. It is high time they were banished, and none to receive or aid them. Let the judges and
officers be sworn to the Supremacy: let the lawyers go to
the church and show conformity, or not plead at the bar,
and then the rest will shortly follow."

He could not have been more mistaken. The Irish had
been unwilling to accept Henry VIII as the "only Supreme
Head on earth of the whole Church in Ireland," and all
the measures of his successors to make them Protestants
had been unsuccessful.

When Patrick had converted the Irish to Christianity
he had spent years traveling through the country; he had
preached; he had practiced diplomacy. If he had not used
the supernatural powers attributed to him, his eloquence
had often been weighted with promise of reward. He had

left behind him, not only chalices and bells and altars, and choirs trained in singing psalms, but the foundations of a great organization.

What did the "reformers" do? They issued edicts and manifestos. They said, "It is the law," and expected that plain statement of disputed fact to overbalance twelve centuries of tradition. They sent few preachers, and those with no zeal for their task. English officers in Ireland were always complaining of that. "It was the extreme negligence and remissness of our clergy here, which was the first cause of the general desertion and apostasy, and is now the impediment of reformation," the attorney general, Sir John Davies, no friend of the Irish, wrote in 1606. "Mere Idols [idles] and ciphers and such as cannot read," he had found them two years earlier, and the churches deserted and falling into decay. Another English Protestant critic of the Irish Protestant clergy had complained that they were "more fit to sacrifice to a calf than to meddle with the religion of God."

Elizabeth had ordered the people fined for not attending the Protestant church. James refused to give office to any who did not conform. But Barnaby Rich, in his *Remembrance of the State of Ireland*, could not tell of a city in all Ireland, "(no, not Dublin itself) that is able year after year, for two years together, to make choice of a mayor and two sheriffs that will take the oath of obedience to his Majesty, not to speak of inferior officers as notaries, sergeants, constables, jailers, and such other like. In Dublin, where they are most conformed, I know not any of these but is a Papist that on Sunday morning will first hear a mass, then after that will bring the mayor to Christ Church, and having put him in his pew they convey themselves to a tavern till the sermon be done, that they bring the mayor back again to his house."

It was in 1612 that this was written. It applied to all the early years of James's reign in Ireland. "The Jesuits, seminaries and priests swarm as locusts throughout that whole kingdom," Chief Justice Saxey of Munster wrote in 1604, "and are harbored and maintained by the noblemen and chief gentry of the country, but especially by the cities and walled towns within that realm, massing and frequenting all the superstitions of the people in their obstinate errors and contempt of God and his Majesty's laws ecclesiastical."

King James's proclamation of 1605, refusing liberty of conscience to the Catholics and ordering all priests and Jesuits out of the country, had no obvious effect, "for every town, hamlet, and house is for them sanctuary." "All the Irish," another English officer reported, "are solemnly vowed by sacrament to maintain their religion with their lives."

Sometimes the cost was a little less. At the Irish College in Salamanca in Spain is a paper written at Drogheda. It pictures " . . . such persecution as no man durst walk the streets that was a Catholic but presently they should be apprehended, and brought before the Lord Deputy [Sir Arthur Chichester] and Council to be examined of what religion they were. If their answer were that they were Catholics, then were they demanded if they would go to church. They answered that they would not, they were then presently sent to the jailer to be kept in prison. They were kept so close for half a year that nobody was let go towards them but those that carried them meat. Thus did they live in this miserable case till it pleased the judges to set them at liberty." These light punishments were for poorer people. Men of means and position were fined large sums for their "spiteful bravery" in defying the king's proclamation, and many others were made prisoners at Dublin Castle and in the Tower of London.

It was inevitable that in Irish minds "English" and "Protestant" had become synonymous with oppression and persecution.

They were all combined, now, in the person of a new Lord Deputy of Ireland, Sir Arthur Chichester. He had served under Mountjoy in fighting O'Neill, and the letters he wrote in that service are an index to his attitude toward the country. "We follow a painful, hazardous, and unprofitable way, by which the Queen will never reap what is expected until the nation be wholly destroyed, or so subjected as to take a new impression of laws and religion," he wrote in 1601, and a few months later was planning how the conquered nation should be ruled: by severe punishment, good laws, and the abolishing of old ceremonies and customs in religion. The people must be without arms, too, he supposed, and some port towns should be erected upon the northern harbors.

Unfortunately for the Irish, he was now in a position of power. Unfortunately for O'Neill, he was covetous and ambitious. Chichester was only one of a group of English officers who had endured the hardships of the Irish campaign with the expectation that if they won a victory they would be rewarded with the lands of O'Neill and O'Donnell. Now they were disgruntled and jealous that the earl had been restored to his estates, if not to his old powers.

No sooner had Chichester been made lord deputy than he turned his attention to O'Neill. All the indignities, annoyances, and humiliations that could be heaped on a man O'Neill knew. Spies intruded on him at all times, as well as on the the new Earl of Tyrconnell, Rury O'Donnell. The English officers were only too proud of the annoyances they created. "It is known not only how they live, and what they do, but it is foreseen what they purpose or intend to do, insomuch as Tyrone hath been heard to complain that he had so many eyes watching over him that he could not drink a full carouse of sack but the state was advertised thereof a few hours after," the attorney general, Sir John Davies, was pleased to relate. Chichester confided to Salisbury by letter that by means of the garrisons they had good espial in Tyrone.

The object seems to have been either to discover some plot of the earls whereby they might be accused of treason, and their estates forfeited, or to make their lives so miserable that they would give up their lands for pleasanter living abroad. The lord deputy even directed Sir Toby Caulfield to "sound" the Countess of Tyrone, "who may reveal her husband's secrets." She did not do so.

For four years the persecution lasted, during which time many a prisoner who had walked hopelessly up the steps to the gallows was promised that he might walk down again if he would implicate either O'Donnell or O'Neill. All the "intelligence" gained from the informers was duly forwarded to England. That it was of doubtful value may be gathered from a royal message of November 19, 1606. The king advised the Council in Ireland to be more cold [careful] in calling natives to testify against their fellows. Chichester and Davies had been blowing up the Spanish bogey to an enormous size. The king punctured it by his belief that the Catholic monarch was unable to engage in hostilities.

Tyrone had evidently meant to fulfill the terms of his submission. Though he was so poor that he could not cultivate a twentieth part of his lands, he had made his province the best governed in Ireland. If the eyes of the lord deputy had not been fastened on his holdings he would probably have spent his last days in Tyrone, and Ulster would have been spared its agony. But no Irishman could receive fearlessly the attentions that Davies and Chichester were pressing on O'Donnell and O'Neill. Too many Desmonds and Kildares and O'Kellys and O'Neills in the past had taken up residence in the Tower after similar preliminaries.

Tyrone began the year 1607 with a letter to the king. The king's advisers sought to bring him into disfavor, he wrote, and he asked his Majesty not to believe the reports without finding out the truth of the charges. Four months later he had to write another letter complaining that the Protestant bishop of Derry was seeking to claim a great portion of his lands. In this the clergyman was aided by O'Neill's own son-in-law, who had been allured to the English side. O'Neill was willing to go to London to argue his case before the king, as the lord deputy suggested, but before plans could be made for the journey there were new stirs in Ireland.

On May 18, 1607, an anonymous letter had been found at the door of the Council Chamber. It told, in the vaguest terms, of a plot of the Catholics in Ireland to seize the government. The writer of the letter was discovered to have been an adventurer with a reputation that was hardly savory, and details of his accusations were later acknowledged by Chichester to have been grounded, in all probability, "more in malice than good matter." "Some of the parties brought in support of it are not of sufficient honesty upon their words or oaths to condemn a horseboy," he added. Nevertheless, the plot, which some people have suspected of having originated in Salisbury's mind as a means of discrediting the Catholics, was used as a means for frightening the earls.

Whatever the truth of the matter may be, Irish lords in the Netherlands heard that O'Neill and O'Donnell were in danger of their lives. Cuconnaught Maguire, brother of the great horseman Hugh who had been killed in Elizabeth's war, had escaped the lord deputy's arrest and gone to Brussels, where O'Neill's son Henry was in command of an Irish regiment, and in high favor with the archdukes. With seven thousand crowns donated by them, Maguire purchased a vessel of eighty tons, loaded her with a cargo of salt, and good store of nets, so that she passed for a fishing ship, and sailed into Lough Swilly.

The captain of the vessel, one John Bath of Drogheda, went to warn the earls of their danger. O'Neill would be arrested if he went to London to see the king, he said. O'Donnell would have the same treatment at home. Even before this O'Neill had been in fear of his life. The two men made hurried preparations. They gathered their families about them, their poets and historians, their secretaries and captains and servants, and on a dark September midnight of 1608 they set sail for the open sea, and a lifelong exile.

The Maguires' historian, who was on that little ship, wrote afterward the history called *The Flight of the Earls.* "The entire number of souls on board this small vessel was ninety-nine," he records, "having little sea-store, and being otherwise miserably accommodated." After twenty-four days of contrary winds and ocean wanderings they landed at the harbor of Quillebœuf, at the mouth of the Seine, as weary and miserable as the two merlin falcons who had found refuge in the rigging of their craft.

The people of Ireland mourned the earls' going. Irish poets at home and abroad lamented the helplessness of the country left without its greatest princes, and the champions of their religion. "Woe to the mind that conceived that voyage, woe to the council that decided their setting out without knowing whether they would ever return to their native principalities or patrimonies to the end of the world," wrote the Four Masters. "Earthly joy has left Ireland," wailed another. "Her pomp and state are banished. Only the sea favors us, its size increased by our sad tears." And an exiled poet's vellum manuscript, stored even now in the British Museum, forecasts the state of Ireland after the Flight of the Earls: "Tonight it is that Ireland is desolate. Our earls are fled; a pall of hopeless dullness settles on the land. No more shall any laugh there, or children gambol; music is choked, the Irish language chained; no longer shall chiefs' sons so much as speak whether of the Winefeast or of hearing Mass; gaming is at an end, and all pastimes; the improvised panegyric shall not be poured forth, nor tales recited at bedtime; books will not be looked at, nor genealogies heard attentively."

The poet's prophecies were fulfilled with cruel exactness.

Within a few days of the earls' departure, five of the king's officers in Ireland, including Davies and Chichester, had written to their English king suggesting that the lands of the fugitive earls be seized, and given to others. "What a door is open to the king," Sir Geoffrey Fenton pointed out, "not only to pull down forever those two proud houses of O'Neill and O'Donnell, but also to bring in colonies of the English to plant both countries, to a great increase of his Majesty's revenues, and to settle the countries perpetually in the crown. Besides that, many well-deserving servitors may be recompensed in the district without charge to his Majesty."

Chichester professed surprise at the flight. They had found no evidence against O'Neill, he admitted, though O'Donnell was perhaps tainted with suspicion of treason. Later the lord deputy revealed that the writer of the famous anonymous letter had "put buzzes" into the ear of Tyrone that his life was in danger in Ireland. Whatever the real motives had been, of both the English officers and the Irish earls, the latter were now on the Continent, royally welcomed by France and the Netherlands, and eventually settled in Rome with pensions from the Pope and the Spanish king. Chichester obtained permission from James to have them watched by spies, and from that time on they were shadowed as persistently as they had been at home.

The earls were guilty of no treason, nor any other crime save the desire to save their heads. From the Continent, O'Neill and O'Donnell drafted long articles for the king, recounting the acts of government officers against them, and of the persecution to which they had been subjected. No answer to the complaint is to be found. Probably Salisbury, secretary of the Council, expressed the king's opinion of the whole matter when he wrote to Chichester concerning the flight, "I do think it of great necessity that those countries be made the king's by this accident."

None of the king's officers in Ireland made objection to that. It was the prize they had been playing for. When the great counties of the north had finally been escheated, and

parceled out, Chichester drew the whole barony of Inisho-
wen, twenty miles square, more lands in Antrim, and
Tyrone's own castle of Dungannon. His colleagues were
similarly rewarded. There was fine talk of providing for
the natives, but for the most part they were simply driven
from their lands, ordered to depart "with their goods and
chattels at or before the first of May next [1609] into what
other part of the realm they pleased." Of all the half million of Irish acres of escheated land, only fifty-eight thousand went to the native Irish, the awards in every case
being for some special subserviency. At that, they were
charged a double rent. The rest were simply uprooted.
"Many stubborn and stiff-necked people oppose the free
planting thereof, the word of removing and transplanting
being to the natives as welcome as the sentence of death,"
Chichester admitted.

How could they resist? The English lords in Dublin had
taken care that there were no men alive and at liberty who
would lead them in resistance. All the dangerous kinsmen
of O'Donnell and O'Neill who had been left behind were
gathered in on one excuse or another, or on none, and hung
or imprisoned. Hundreds of their young followers, "idle
swordsmen" in the eyes of the crown, were shipped away
to fight for the King of Sweden. "The levy of a thousand
men for Sweden," Chichester wrote to Salisbury, "came
very seasonably to give a better passage to the plantation
in general, and indeed, the invention was very good, for
it has discovered a possibility to compel those that live
idly and unprofitably to be transported into foreign countries, and will cause those who remain behind to learn to
labor in order to free themselves from such a just punishment." When the lord deputy, in 1614, was recounting

the details of his service in Ireland, he boasted that he had sent away to Sweden six thousand young Irishmen.

Their fair fields taken from them, their leaders gone, their young men fighting other wars, thousands and thousands of the Irish of Ulster retired to the bogs and woodlands, to live as wood kerne, miserable, starving, and cold. Mountain caves gave them refuge, from whose heights they could see their old fields now plowed by strangers, and the smoke of fires from hearths whose warmth they had long known. "We have lived to see heavy affliction," wrote one of the persecuted poets of the persecuted people, "The tribal convention plains emptied, the finny wealth perished away in the streams, dark thickets of the chase turned into streets, a boorish congregation in the House of the Saints, poets' and minstrels' bedclothes thrown to litter cattle." Sir Toby Caulfield, who had so unsuccessfully questioned the Countess of Tyrone about her husband's plans, reported with some understatement that there were no more discontented people in all Christendom than the Irish.

They never thought O'Neill would not return. It was their hope, as it was the English fear. Surely he would come back to free them. Surely an O'Neill would not accept defeat, and his people needing him. The earl must have thought that, too. He was always planning, always hoping. "The old man sleeps with a naked sword beside his bed," wrote one of his countrymen who was with him. But Rury O'Donnell had died within a year of their coming to Rome; O'Neill's oldest son, the young Baron Dungannon, had followed shortly after. Cuconnaught Maguire had died on his way to find service with the Spanish king. And O'Neill's old allies were no longer eager for more warfare.

There was a truce between England and the Spanish king. Philip had squandered too much blood in the Netherlands, to be able to afford anything but peace. So Ireland's cause was neglected, and her exiled champion grew old.

The Roman sunshine was dim for him in the eighth year of his exile. He could not see it at all in the spring of the following year. Fever racked him, and the miseries of age. Far from his Ulster hills and the sight of falcons wheeling in the Irish sky, he died July the twentieth, in the year sixteen hundred and sixteen.

At his funeral, as at O'Donnell's, were the greatest nobles of the land. They followed his body to the church of S. Pietro Montorio on the Janiculum to the chanting of monks, and the tolling of a hundred bells. As these sad sounds floated down toward the city of Rome, in far away Ireland three cheerful sounds had been hushed forever: the cry of the strainers a-straining ale, the cry of the vassals over the caldrons a-forking out meat for the banquet, the cries of warriors at the chessboards a-winning games.

The days of the great Gaelic princes were over in Ireland.

Chapter XV

POVERTY AND POTATOES

→»«←

Now you are helpless, indeed, Ireland. Now you are conquered and in chains. There is no longer a prince to come riding to your rescue. There is none to stay the victor as he stands over your beaten body. You are on your knees now, but that is not enough. Once you rode richly bridled. Now you will be driven into poverty, painfully, slowly, relentlessly. Once you were proud. The victor will try to shame you. Can he humble your spirit? Can he break your pride? He will try. He will nearly succeed.

Well would it be for you if you could sleep for a while, and find escape in dreams. Even nightmares are better than some realities. Better to think of what follows as a dreadful phantasmagoria than as happenings which were only too true. Better for you, Ireland; better for those who read of you. It will be a long dream, two centuries, almost, in time. But every acorn has to fall, said the Old Woman of Beare. Every dream must end.

Even nightmares begin quietly. For twenty-five years after Hugh O'Neill died in Rome, Ireland did not stir. Her people were poor. "Every county is full of determined cattle thieves, who are driven to thieve by poverty," wrote Lord Esmonde in 1629. The army, a "hungry, naked, mutinous crew," battened upon the entire country, Protestant and Catholic alike. Ulster was stripped of her old families, the O'Neills, the O'Donnells of the *Battle Book*, the Maguires who had been such splendid horsemen. Some were in their graves. Some fought in foreign lands. In their places were English and Scottish settlers.

Protestants, these, and many of them dissenters. Not great lords, as the old owners had been, except for a few government officers, "rewarded without charge to the king," but tradesmen, farmers, artisans. Strafford, the lord lieutenant who dominated Ireland for years till the eve of the 1641 Rising, started the linen trade for them in Ulster, after he had killed the woolen trade which rivaled England's own.

"All wisdom," he pointed out to Charles I, "advises us to keep this kingdom as much subordinate and dependent on England as possible, and holding them from manufacture of wool (which, unless otherwise directed I shall by all means discourage) and then enforcing them to fetch their cloth from England, how can they depart from us without nakedness and beggary?"

"A most cursed man to all Ireland, and to me in particular," the Earl of Cork was to say of Strafford, but he gave up the sword of state to him willingly enough. Strafford's main idea was to raise money for Charles, as much money as possible. The treasury was nearly empty. The army had pay for only a few months, and Strafford dared not reduce its strength. He could think of no better way to fatten the exchequer than to enforce the old fine of a shilling a Sunday against Catholics who refused to attend Protestant worship. By paying £20,000 the Irish escaped the levy for a year. Then, combining with the Protestants, they offered Charles £120,000 a year if Charles would grant them certain "graces." For this sum the Catholics would be allowed some leniency in matters of religion, the titles of Protestant newcomers would not be searched beyond sixty years by prying "discoverers," the exactions and oppressions of the soldiery on the people would be restrained. Charles took the money. He continued to take it year after year. But year after year he and Strafford contrived not to call a Parliament to approve the granting of the graces. Ireland paid, and had but little in return.

The dream begins to quicken. The prince lies dead, but little men try now to loosen Ireland's chains. The Catholics of Ulster, oppressed and poor, rise in a night, and drive out the settlers planted on the old estates. Blood flows, and flesh is wounded. Not your blood, at first, sleeping Ireland. The blood of those who took your land. An O'Neill, the beloved Owen Roe, foreign born and foreign bred, comes back to the land of his fathers, a Spanish sword in his hand. He leads an Irish army. But the Irish victory is soon over. Reprisals are bitter and bloody. Is there an ogre moving through your dreams, Ireland? That is Cromwell, called The Protector in England, but whose sword in Ireland is for women and children, citizens and soldiers alike. Do you hear sounds of massacre from churches? That is Drogheda, and again the Rock of Cashel. Are praying women cut down around a cross? That is Wexford. Do you see men shot out of trees like blackbirds? Those are your defenders, brought down by English snipers.

Do you see soldiers muttering before the paymasters' empty coffers? There is no money for Cromwell's soldiers. "Adventurers" with greedy eyes advance some. The soldiers take the rest of their pay in promises. Promises of what? Promises of Irish land when the war is over. So the ogre strides about, his great hands snatch the Irish from their lands as Gulliver caught up Lilliputians. Do you hear the blare of trumpets? They call your people to the reading of declarations depriving them of their land for the benefit of soldiers and adventurers. The Cromwellian Settlement deprives all gentle Irish folk of their estates unless they can meet the almost impossible requirements of an Innocent. Farmers and artisans stay to work for the newcomers. The rest are banished to the rocky wastes of Connaught. Do you see frail ladies starving on makeshift farms, sleeping Ireland? Do you see children preyed upon by wolves? Do you see old men dying of hardship on their way over the Shannon? The children of Jordan Roche "have nothing to live on but what they earne by their needles, and by washing and wringinge." Cromwell's Life Guards have their father's estate. Poorer, poorer, always poorer, you and your people. Soon troopers will tell, of a rarity, of smoke they saw by day, or candle by night.

The dream moves on. England, after the Restoration, has a king again, and then a Catholic king. What do you dream now, Ireland? Your country is a battleground where two men fight for the English throne. You back the Catholic king. Do you see him flee in cowardice? Do you see the Boyne run red? Do you hear Sarsfield's angry challenge, "Change kings, and we'll fight you over again"? Do you see him, later, dying on a French battlefield, and mourning that his blood is not shed in your defense?

Do your hear drums beating, Ireland? They recruit your men to fight in foreign wars, for French or Polish kings. Do you hear the Wild Geese call farewell as they leave your shores? They are your defeated soldiers, sailing away to other lands. They are your young men, who see no future, no living, before them in Ireland, and so they seek their fortunes elsewhere. Do you see slave ships setting out for the West Indies with Irish men and women, and Irish children, too, on board?

Do your chains hang heavy, Ireland? They are weighted now with the Penal Laws. Your people who are Catholics cannot practice their religion, or hold office, educate or be educated, they cannot keep arms for their protection, they cannot own land, or rent any but the poorest, they cannot own a horse whose value is above five pounds. Children are bribed to turn against their parents. Do you see bloodhounds on the track of a man in black? That is a priest, fleeing for his life. And there—that figure moving through the woods at night. That is a schoolmaster, guilty of teaching Catholic children. The hounds will find him, too.

You moan in your sleep, Ireland. Do not lose heart. The Protestant Wolfe Tone will throw away the "foolish gown and wig" of the lawyer, and take up pen and sword for you. See his fine forensic gestures. Hear his orator's voice as he pleads for you. "To subvert the tyranny of our execrable government, to break the connection with England, the never-failing source of our political evils, and to assert the independence of my country, these were my objects. To unite the whole people of Ireland, to abolish the memory of our past dissensions, and to substitute the common name of Irish in place of the denomination of

Protestant, Catholic, and Dissenter, these were my means.''

He is poor, humble, unknown. With a hundred guineas in his pocket he sails away to plead with the French for you. The French are a republic now. They have just helped America to become a republic. They listen, and promise aid. Wolfe Tone sails with French ships into Bantry Bay. But the wind, the wind, it blows them all away. More ships sail in, and meet defeat. Do you see Wolfe Tone in chains? Do you hear him sentenced to be hanged? That is a penknife in his hand. He thinks death is more honorable that way.

Do you see English troops again ravishing the land, stirring the people to revolt? The English are planning to take your Parliament away, and they must drive you to rebellion first. Do you see burning pitch caps on men's heads? Do you hear the screams of the lashed? Do you see an English general lay down his sword and refuse to torment you further? That is Abercrombie, whose humanity revolts at what he sees done to you. "Every crime, every cruelty that could be committed by Cossacks or Calmucks has been transacted here.''

Do you see gold passed, and coronets given? Castlereagh and Cornwallis are taking your Parliament from you, by bribery, and there is nothing you can do.

The figure of a young girl now, half-hanged, and then cut down, her firm breasts streaming red. Anne Devlin, that, who will not betray young Robert Emmet to the English. A traitor does. Do you see that pool of blood on a Dublin street? Do you see dogs lap it up? The blood of Robert Emmet was shed for you there, Ireland, and he was glad to shed it.

You are cold, Ireland, and your bed is poor. But sleep a while longer. We must talk in a while of your poverty. You were once so rich and proud. It would hurt your pride to hear us.

Long ago Elizabeth had written to her ministers in Ireland, "Consideration to be had of the counties of Leix and Offaly, how they may be reinhabited with good subjects, and the rebels O'Connors and O'Mores expelled." Her ministers considered, and the rebels gave way to English settlers. Munster had been planted after the death of the old Earl of Desmond. When the Earls O'Donnell and O'Neill fled over the sea in 1608 most of Ulster had been seized, and planted with English and Scots. Connaught titles had been broken for the benefit of the government in the reign of Charles I on the plea that they had not been properly registered fifty years before. When Cromwellian soldiers and adventurers could not be paid, all Ireland had been surveyed, and parceled out to meet the government's debts. All the people to whom the land had formerly belonged were banished to Connaught, exiled to the wastes of that rocky province. One-sixth of the land of Ireland was all that was left to them.

So the country assumed a new aspect. Not only were there strangers with new customs, but the land itself was transformed. "Isle of the Woods" the Milesians had called Ireland when they first landed from Spain. Now, with titles so dubious, the planters hurried to draw all the wealth possible from the land before they could be dislodged. The woods vanished almost overnight. "In twenty years there will hardly be left an oak in Ireland," one observer wrote in 1697. A thousand years before, the sound of the axe on his beloved oaks of Derry had been fearful to Columcille. When Ulster was settled with strangers, fifty thousand oaks and twice as many ash were cut down for the making of Londonderry, which was the name the new English gave to the town they built there. Whole hillsides were ravished of their woods, which were sold for as little as sixpence a tree. The forests went to make English ships, to build towns for the English, to fire iron-works. Hillsides which had been mantled in green were beautiful no longer, but ravaged and scarred.

That was not a matter of concern to the newcomers. They regarded with disdain everything Irish, except, as one observer remarked, Irish land and Irish gold. If their estates were large enough, they lived in England on the rents derived from Irish land. If not, Dublin was their second choice. Some, through necessity, had to dwell on the land which had been granted them. Owing everything to the government, as they did, they would do anything to help that government retain its power. The Ascendancy Party, they were called. Their platform was the belief that anything English was better than anything Irish. They lived lives patterned on English models. In Dublin, they aped London, though the gentlemen's coats were called "French frocks." A sword, a queue, and a three-cocked hat went with evening attire, and any gallant so careless as to wear boots into a lady's box at the theater was in danger of being challenged to a duel. Their chief occupation was "plowing the half-acre," their euphemism for the cultivation of their own interests with the government at Dublin Castle.

They had a chronicler in Sir Jonah Barrington, a government official of impeachable integrity, who admitted a love of power and social standing. His ancestors had been some of those "good subjects" who had taken the places of the O'Connors when Leix was being "settled" by Elizabeth. They were "gentlemen every inch of them." Let Sir Jonah explain the phrase.

The common people, said Sir Jonah, in his *Personal Sketches*, divided the gentry into three classes. "Half-mounted gentlemen" were the descendants of the small English planters who had come to Ireland to improve their fortunes. These lived on farms of a few hundred acres and were admitted to the hunting group of society chiefly because of their "good, clever horses." These animals, said Sir Jonah, could leap anything, but never felt currycomb or trimming scissors. Their riders wore buckskin breeches, boots well greased, but never blacked, carried large thong whips leaded at the butt ends.

"Gentlemen every inch of them" were members of reasonably old families, once wealthy, but whose finances were now not in the best of order.

"Gentlemen to the backbone" were the very oldest families and settlers, respected and obeyed by the peasantry. Their word was law, as it had been in the days of the great Kildares and Desmonds.

The Barrington fortunes led Sir Jonah to Dublin, and finally to exile in France, but in his youth he lived in Leix, called then Queen's County, by the transplanted and grateful English. We are indebted to him for a gay picture of county life as it was lived by the Ascendancy Party.

"Gentlemen to the backbone" were great hunters, but sometimes the weather prevented their following that sport. Once Sir Jonah's brother, "justly apprehending that the frost and snow of Christmas might probably prevent their usual occupation of the chase, determined to provide against any listlessness of the shut-up period by an uninterrupted match of what was called 'hard-going' till the weather should break up.

"A hogshead of superior claret was then sent to the cottage of Quin the huntsman, and a fat cow, killed and plundered of her skin, was hung up by the heels. All the windows were closed to keep out the light. One room, filled with straw and numerous blankets was destined for a bed chamber in common; and another was prepared as kitchen for the use of the servants. Claret, cold, mulled or buttered, was to be the beverage for the whole company, and in addition to the cow above mentioned, chickens, bacon, and bread were the only admitted viands. Wallace and Hosey, my father's and my brother's pipers, and Doyle, a blind but famous fiddler, were employed to enliven the banquet, which, it was determined, should continue till the cow became a skeleton, and the claret should be on its stoop.

"My two elder brothers; two gentlemen of the name of Taylor; a Mr. Barrington Lodge, a rough songster; Frank Skelton, a jester and butt; Jemmy Moffat, the most knowing sportsman of the neighborhood, and two other sporting gentlemen of the county, these composed the permanent bacchanalians. A few visitors were occasionally admitted.

"As for myself, I was too unseasoned to go through more than the first ordeal, which was on a frosty St. Stephen's Day, when the hard-goers partook of the opening banquet, and several neighbors were invited to honor the commencement of what they called the 'shut-up pilgrimage.'

"The old huntsman was the only male attendant, and his ancient spouse, once a kitchen-maid of the family, now somewhat resembling the amiable Leonarda in Gil Blas, was the cook; whilst the drudgery fell to the lot of the whipper-in. A long knife was prepared to cut collops from the cow; a large turf fire seemed to court the gridiron; the pot bubbled up as if proud of its contents, whilst plump white chickens floated in crowds upon the surface of the water; the shimmering potatoes, just bursting from their drab surtouts, exposed the delicate whiteness of their mealy bosoms; the claret was tapped, and the long earthern, wide-mouthed pitchers stood gaping under the impatient cock to receive their portions. . . .

"At length the banquet entered; the luscious smoked bacon, bedded on its cabbage mattress, and partly obscured by its own savory steam, might have tempted the most fastidious of epicures, whilst the round trussed chickens, ranged by the half-dozen on hot pewter platters, turned up their white plump merry-thoughts exciting equally the eye and appetite; fat collops of the hanging cow, sliced indiscriminately from her tenderest points, grilled over the clear embers upon shining gridirons, half-drowned in their own luscious juices, and garnished with little pyramids of congenial shallots, smoked at the bottom of the well-furnished board. A prologue of cherry-bounce [brandy] preceded the entertainment, which was enlivened by hob-nobs and joyous toasts."

It was too much for the young man. "My reason," he confesses, "gradually began to lighten me of its burden, and in its last efforts suggested the straw chamber as my asylum. Just as I was closing my eyes to a twelve hours' slumber I distinguished the general roar of 'stole away' which rose up almost to the very roof of old Quin's cottage.

"At noon next day, a scene of very different nature was exhibited. I found on waking two associates by my side, in as perfect insensibility as that from which I had just aroused. Our piper seemed indubitably dead, but the fiddler, who had the privilege of age and blindness, had taken a hearty nap, and seemed as much alive as ever. . . . "

After breakfast had been served for the survivors, "it was determined that the room should be ventilated and cleared out for a cockfight to pass time till the approach of dinner.

"In this battle royal every man backed his own bird, twelve of which courageous animals were set down together to fight it out, survivor to take all. . . . In about an hour one cock crowed out his triumph over the mangled body of his last opponent—being himself, strange to say, but little wounded. The other eleven lay dead.

"Fresh visitors were introduced each successive day, and the seventh morning had arisen before the feast broke up. As that day advanced the cow was proclaimed to have furnished her full quantum of good dishes, the claret was upon its stoop, and the last gallon, mulled with a pound of spices, was drunk in tumblers to the next merry meeting."

It was probably not far off. . . . Barrington gives another "ludicrous instance of dissipation" which indicates that such revels were not confined to holidays alone.

This was life among the Ascendancy Party. With the Irish, things were sadly different. They owned so little of the land now; only a sixth, say most of the estimates. Strangers held the rest of it, aliens who had no interest in the country but what riches it would yield them. The system of rack rent which they devised pressed down on the Irish tenants like a vise. There were no leases. Land, except in Ulster, was held at the will of the owner. Every six months he could raise the rent, and deprive the tenant of any improvements he had made, and even seize unharvested crops.

Observers, Irish, English, and French, looked on Dublin— which was the magnet of all Ascendancy people who could not afford to live in England—and found it gay and prosperous. They stepped beyond the Pale, and saw a picture so desolate, so hopeless, that they could scarcely believe their eyes. The descendants of the transplanted Irish, trying to live upon the rocky wastes of Connaught, led lives hardly more miserable than those who had, as Swift said "worked to the last gasp rather than leave their native country. These starve to pay racking rents and (as they call it) keep both ends together as long as their small stock shall hold out, till at last they have been turned out of their tenements, with, almost always, a wife and several children, to the inclemency of the weather, and all compelled to live in unroofed churches (for there are plenty of them in the country) stables, dog-kennels, hedges and under trees. . . . If they happen to hear of the death of a horse they run to it as to a feast, and often quarrel among themselves for the just partition of the booty. . . .

"This wretched state of the poor is not confined to the north, or any one part of the country, but is now spread over the whole face of the kingdom, to the entire depopulation of several estates.

"Nor has this calamity kept itself within this class of people, and disturbed none but the lowest of our brethren. No, it has already ascended some stages higher, and has reached those in whose power it was to help and relieve the common poor, and who maintained their families decently, according to the bigness of their farms."

"The old and the sick," Swift went on to say, "were dying with cold and famine. The young laborers cannot get work, and pine away for want of nourishment to such a degree that if at any time they were accidentally hired to commence labor, they have not the strength to perform it."

This was not the picture of a country suffering only one or two famine years. It was the mark of the whole time, one stage of a progressive decay of prosperity which had started centuries before, and would continue for more than one to come. Twenty years after Swift's *Letter to the Irish People*, a "country gentleman of Munster" wrote his Grace, the lord primate: "I have seen the laborer endeavoring to work with his spade, but fainting for want of food, and forced to quit it, I have seen the aged father eating grass like a beast, and in the anguish of his soul wishing for dissolution. I have seen the helpless orphan exposed on the dunghill, and none to take it in for fear of infection, and I have seen the hungry infant sucking at the breast of an already expired parent."

After another twenty years an English traveler in Ireland noted poverty no less pitiful. He did not, as some have done, blame it on the Irish as the just reward for refusing to submit willingly to English rule. "Upon my word, sir," he wrote to a friend, "the inhabitants, in general, of this kingdom, are very far from being what they too often and unjustly have been represented by those of our country who never saw them, a nation of wild Irish. Since I have been in Ireland, I have traveled from north to south, and from east to west through the provinces of Ulster and Leinster and Munster, and generally found them civil and obliging, even amongst the very lowest class of the natives. Miserable and oppressed as by far too many of them are, an Englishman will find as much civility in general, as amongst the same class of his own country . . . I never met with such scenes of misery and oppression as this country in too many parts of it, really exhibits. What with the severe exactions of rent, even before the corn is housed, a practice that too much prevails here among the petty and despicable landlords, third, fourth, and fifth from the real proprietor (of which inferior and worst kind of landlords this kingdom abounds infinitely too much for the reputation of the proprietors, or the prosperity of agriculture), of the parish priest, in the next place, for tythes, who, not content with the tythe of grain, even the very tenth of half a dozen or half a score perches of potatoes, upon which a whole family probably subsists for the year, is exacted by the rapacious, insatiable [Protestant] priests. I am sorry, to tell you the truth, that too many of them are English parsons. . . Add to these, the exactions of the, if possible, still more absolute Catholic priest who though he preaches charity by the hour on Sunday, comes around with the terrors of damnation and demands his full quota of unremitted offerings. For, unhappily, for them, the inhabitants in the south and west parts of the kingdom are generally Catholics, and by the time that they are all satisfied, the poor reduced wretches have hardly the skin of a potato to subsist on. The landlords, first and subordinate, get *all* that is made of the land, and the tenants, for their labor get poverty and potatoes.

"Ireland would, indeed, be a rich country if made the most of; if its trade were not reduced by unnatural restrictions and an Egyptian kind of politics from without, and its agriculture were not depressed by hard masters from within itself.

"To prohibit the importations of such commodities as our country shall be sufficiently provided with, must, even to an Irishman, appear just and reasonable, but that they should be excluded from, or restricted in their trade with almost all the rest of the world, is a species of policy, the wisdom of which, with deference to our administration of the Hibernian department, is to me, I own, not easily intelligible."

The observing gentlemen had forgotten, as a French traveler a few years later did not, that the Irish were being punished for not conforming to the Protestant religion and English ways. Fleeing from the French Revolution in 1792, a M. De Latocnaye recorded in his journal that "guided by capable men who are actuated by motives of public welfare there is no people I have known so easily led for good. If the government would only give up at once and absolutely the attempt to Anglicize the Irish at any cost, and would lead them through their prejudices and customs, it would be possible to do with them anything that could be wished."

It is unfortunate that such a policy did not appeal to the English. Having seized most of the land, and with the government, as always, in the hands of their own party, their determination was still to make Ireland give up its Irishness. "The speech being Irish, the heart must needs be Irish too" Spenser had said in Elizabeth's time. He was not wrong, but he did not go quite far enough. It was something more than speech that kept the Irish Irish. Into the making of their people had gone an element which would keep them always from a complete merging of themselves with others, which would maintain them as an individual people even under oppression. It was more than the realization of their great capabilities, and their rich heritage. It was more than love of beautiful sights, and sweet sounds, and brave deeds. It was more than the intellectual passion which from the beginning had marked Irish civilization. "Seeds of fire," the Irish poets had called that particular quality, but the name could as well be applied to that element which held the essence of things Irish. Let us use the word in that broader sense, and see how it survived the English attack.

Their poverty was hard for the Irish to bear, but there was something worse. It was being put in the position of inferiors by people the Irish did not regard as superior, but only as a stronger race. One of the peasant poets of the eighteenth century put it into a quatrain which can be translated only literally. " 'Tis not the poverty I most detest, or being down forever, but the insult that follows it, which no leeches can cure." The poet who wrote that was proficient in Greek and Latin and English, besides his native Gaelic, but he had to earn his living as a spáilpin, a spade laborer, or by teaching school, or by soldiering. Owen Roe O'Sullivan was his name, Owen of the Sweet Mouth. He was as wild a rake of a man as ever fled before a shotgun, and he burned his brilliant life out before he was forty. But the poems he wrote are the brightest things which came out of a cruel century, and today the words of them are in the mouths of the peasants of his native Munster, peasants who, because of the meagerness of their educational advantages, can scarcely read or write.

For three centuries the poets of Ireland had known persecution. Edward VI began it, fearful of the power they had over the Irish people. Elizabeth had followed her half-brother's example. But in those days the princes had still been powerful; they had "raised a forest of lances" about their learned men. The princes were gone now, and the poets were thrown on their own resources. The old schools of poetry which they had fostered had perished, too. No longer could young men gather at Michaelmas in the house of some chief poet, and have instruction in his craft until the first cuckoo sang in the spring. Until the seventeenth century the bardic schools had lasted, and the life that the scholars lived there was a pleasant one, in spite of the hardness of their literary labors, and the long days each spent alone in his dark room, composing poetry to a theme set by the master. "No better life in Ireland," said one of them, nameless and undated, though he probably lived in the seventeenth century. "Over him no prince or king, for him no church's due, no fines for misdemeanor. Not for him the little hardships of early rising or watching at night, or the weariness of turning soil. His harvests all are poems. Backgammon is his delight, and the harp so sweet, and sometimes wooing and love-making with a fair woman."

But though the bardic schools crumbled beneath the weight of poverty, the poetic fire was still aflame. When poets were no longer subsidized by princes, and were forced to earn their living by other means than their learning and genius, they still thought of themselves as poets, and not as the farmers or brewers they might have become. Occasionally they met together in some tavern or Gaelic home which had managed to survive the general destruction, and held the Courts of Poetry which took the place of the bardic schools. There, for a few hours, they could talk with fellow poets, hear their verses, and recite their own.

Such changes were bound to have an effect on their work. No longer was there training to be had in the intricate meters of old Gaelic prosody. Style was necessarily altered, the meters became simpler, and poems on new subjects began to appear reflecting the new occupations of the authors. When Owen Roe O'Sullivan needed a new spade, he did not ask for it bluntly, crudely, as any ordinary peasant would have done. In his poem of request to the smith his requirements were set forth dexterously and daintily, and his poetic genius sounds in every line. The last, perhaps, is best. "And crowning all, let it have the sweetness of a bell."

Those were the days when learning was hardly bought, when children, deprived of schooling, copied with chalk the letters on their fathers' tombstones, when the blaze of a furze fire lighted the pages of treasured manuscripts for some scholar in his poor cabin, when vagrant masters taught Greek under the hedges, when poetry was the only consoling pleasure the poor Irish could enjoy. They did enjoy it. It was so much a part of their lives that it remained with them long after their learning had lessened, even though it remained as an oral tradition only. It was not more than twenty years ago that Daniel Corkery, whose book, *The Hidden Ireland*, itself a lovely piece of prose, which tells of these peasant poets, found the words of one of the poems of those dark days in the mouth of a peasant woman of Munster. She did not simply quote it, as something learned by rote, but deftly changed a word here, and a name there, so that the poem, written perhaps a hundred and thirty years before, was made to apply to the Great War then being waged in Europe.

"In their reaching out towards poetry there was a two-fold impulse," says Mr. Corkery, of these peasant poets of Munster of the eighteenth century. "However untowards their fortunes, they were still the residuary legatees of over a thousand years of literary culture, and this drinking in of poetry was an effort to satisfy in the way that had become second nature with them, the needs of the human spirit . . . From the nightmare that existence had become for them, they rose into the clear, perfected, rounded, unified life that is art. Thus poetry had for them the double gift of the drug; it put pain aside; it raised vision."

A vision that the poets often raised was that of Ireland as a woman, beautiful and bereaved, a woman to whom they gave lovely names, Dark Rosaleen, and Kathleen ni Houlihan, and Dear Dark Head. They saw her "weeping, torn, woeful, bruised, humble, full of wounds," a woman garbed in grief and poverty. Her plight was a challenge to her people's gallantry, to their honor, to their pride. Themselves in poverty, her poverty was more grievous to them, her oppressions more burdensome than their own. They knew humiliation, and bore it. That humiliation should be heaped on their Dear Dark Head engenderd a resentment common to them all, a resentment which bound them together when the miseries of hunger and poverty were sundering them, when an ordinary feeling of nationalism would have been killed. So the poetically invoked vision of their country as a woman united the Irish people, and the seeds of fire were kept aglow.

Chapter XVI

THE RAGGED COAT

->>><<<-

THE STORY of Ireland in the nineteenth century is the story of a people robbed, who
are fighting to regain their rights; of a
nationality being crushed; and struggling
to retain its life. The first day of the year
1801 saw the Irish Parliament killed, and
the beginning of the legislative Union between England and
Ireland. The last day of the century would see the Irish
people still opposing that Union.

It was a dark, unhappy hundred years. Hunger and poverty walked the land, and on their heels came pestilence.
Bitter reading the story of Ireland makes now, bitter and
dreary. But the dreariness is lightened by the men who
fought to redress the wrongs of the Irish people: O'Connell
with his swinging cape, young Percy Shelley, standing for
a moment on the stage of a Dublin theater, the "fine, falcon
face" of the poet Mangan, and all his comrades of the
Young Ireland party, the Fenians of the sixties, the tall,
proud figure of Parnell, whose love for a woman was to
undo in the end all his work for Ireland.

As the century began, Ireland was still a rich land, many
of whose people were sunk in poverty. Irish soil grew

abundant crops, but these were sent over the sea to England to pay the grievous rents. The Established Church still exacted its tithes, the Catholic Church the support of its priests. The rents of the absentees, and the pensions of people who had no right or claim to support by the Irish people, still drained from the country the money that would have meant prosperity and employment. Taxes were increasing. Though the penal laws were much relaxed, the Catholics of the country were still denied the ordinary rights of citizenship and education.

The country presented a picture of such unnecessary and desperate need that more than one Englishman was moved to plead for her. The young poet Shelley crossed the Irish Sea, and spoke to a Dublin audience. He had come to Ireland, he said, standing on the stage of the Fishamble Street Theatre, for the sole purpose of interesting himself in her misfortunes. He was deeply impressed by the sense of the evils which Ireland endured, which he considered to be due to the legislative Union. The oppressions of the Catholics also moved him to remonstrance, and he could see no reason why the religious opinion of a man should exclude him from the rights of society.

His printed pamphlets reiterated his spoken words, but it was in his private letters that the real intensity of his emotion was shown. "I am sick of this city," he wrote from Dublin to a friend in England, "and long to be with you in peace. The rich grind the poor into abjectness, and then complain that they are abject. They grind them to famine, and hang them if they steal a loaf." A month later, in April of 1812, he wrote to Godwin: "We are no longer in Dublin. Never did I behold in any other spot a contrast so striking as that which misery and grandeur form in that unfortunate country."

Shelley was unknown then, and his words had little weight. But Ireland had in her midst a champion who was speaking for her in a voice of increasing authority: Daniel O'Connell, affectionately called the Counselor and later the Emancipator, worshiped in Ireland, vilified in England, respected throughout the world. He was to win for the Catholics their long-withheld rights; he was to lead an almost successful struggle for the repeal of the Union. The reasons why he won the first and lost the second battle are to be found in the story of his life and character.

Limerick had been the original home of the O'Connells. The Cromwellian Settlement had found them a prosperous family, headed by an aged father. The old patriarch had died on his way to banishment in the west, but his surviving children and servants had found refuge beyond the mountains of West Munster, in Kerry, where they rented land from the Earl of Cork. In the Emancipator's day the ancestral mansion they had built there was held in the name of a Protestant friend of the family, and their estate was larger and more prosperous than those of most Catholic families.

"Ivied oaks" some translated the name of Derrynane, but others said it meant St. Finian's Oakwood. At any rate, the rambling old house knew the shelter of great trees and thick vines. It was well that it did. For this was one of the old Gaelic "Big Houses" that Daniel Corkery writes about in *The Hidden Ireland*. Stray survivors in the battle against things Irish, these occasional Big Houses were able to carry on life in the old manner chiefly because the officials in Dublin did not know of their existence. Such large holdings were not legal for Catholics. Whether leased or owned, the houses sought safety in obscurity, and in remote valleys and on rocky coasts their gray stone walls and slate roofs welcomed the shelter of vines and trees.

Not to be compared with the grandeur of the Kildares' and Desmonds' castles, or the court of the Maguires at Enniskillen, Derrynane was still a large and comfortable old house, which sheltered an enormous family and many servants. Its master and mistress overlooked the preparation of every article of common use. Corn was threshed with flails, and winnowed by the wind which blew over the winnowing crag. Servants ground it in querns probably much like the one old Cormac Mac Art's mistress had used when she was in bondage to his jealous queen. Others kneaded it into bread to be baked in the great ovens. Laundresses, dairymaids, gardeners, cooks, spinners, carders, turf-boys, pump-boys, all these had to be kept busy, fed, and clothed. Every laborer had a salted hide each year to make himself two pairs of brogues. There were, besides, says Mr. Corkery, "cowboys, drovers and thatchers. There were smiths, carpenters, weavers, plowmen, tinkers—all these had their own workshops and meeting places. Before the dawn had risen, the farmyard was loud with activity; and when darkness had fallen, lanterns went swinging across it, over and thither, from byre to shed, and from shed to barn."

Derrynane was on the coast, almost within wash of the great waves of the Atlantic. Like many of its neighbors, it had a landing cove, and a smuggler's cave, and the O'Connells were not ashamed of the fact that they carried on an illegal trade with the Continent. Most of the members of the Grand Jury were their customers for smuggled goods.

Silks and velvets and carpets and wines came in, and salted hides and beef and young men for the Irish brigades of Europe went out in O'Connell boats. At one time there were no fewer than seventeen O'Connells in foreign military service.

Young Daniel went abroad, too, but not to fight. He sought the education that was still denied to Catholics in Ireland. General Count O'Connell, his uncle, found a school for Dan and his brother Maurice in France, but the Revolution drove them away before long. What Daniel did see of the Revolution gave him a horror of it, and fixed in him the conviction that no constitutional concession was worth the shedding of a single drop of human blood. It also fired him with a love of royalty, and a belief in their benevolence which his experience with them was not to justify.

Life at Derrynane, where English authority was not held in awe, had given Daniel plenty of self-assurance. Ambition must have been born with him. "Sometimes," he records in his journal as a young man, "I am led away by vanity and ambition to imagine I shall cut a great figure on the theater of the world." He also confessed, "I have a relish for happiness." He was large and handsome, he wore his good clothes easily, and his hat at a jaunty angle. He was a leader born, and two great causes awaited him.

He was a young man when the Act of the Union was passed. Years later he related to his friend O'Neill Daunt: "I was maddened when I heard the bells of St. Patrick's ringing out a joyful peal for Ireland's degradation, as if it were a glorious national festival. My blood boiled, and I vowed on that morning that the foul national dishonor should not last, if ever I could put an end to it." But it was

the Catholic's cause he took up first, the endeavor to get
for them the ordinary rights of citizens.

Hundreds of years of persecution, and the long agony of
the Penal Laws had not weakened the Catholics' faith in
their church, but they had accustomed them to being regarded as inferiors. Only a decade earlier, the Catholic
leader of that day, John Keogh, had said that one could tell
a Catholic by his timid gait. O'Connell had no such sense
of inferiority. His manner bordered more on bravado. In debate and in duel he took the Catholic side, and pleaded the
cause as it had not been pleaded before.

No one questions the greatness of O'Connell's ability,
but it is probably true, as related, that half his legal
victories were won by his splendid voice. "His tones were
melody," says Charles Gavan Duffy, one of his severe
critics. "The music of his voice associated itself with every
mood of his mind, as if it were created for that special
purpose alone." His religion kept him from practicing at
the Inner Bar, but the cases he tried in the lower court were
soon famous. When the editor of a nationalist newspaper
dared to criticize the career of an outgoing official, and was
sued for libel, O'Connell took his defense. He knew the jury
would be packed, and an acquittal impossible. He used the
occasion to show the corruptness of the government and the
shamefulness of their treatment of Catholics. He browbeat
the attorney general and the presiding judges, and his defense of the prisoner was, said young Robert Peel, a far
greater libel on the government than the one for which the
defendant was tried.

But the Catholics were delighted. Here was the most
gifted lawyer of the country, an eloquent orator, a witty
debater, fighting for their emancipation. He soon had all

Catholic Ireland in his grasp. He would lead them, he promised, he would win for them their freedom, using only peaceful, legal methods. He would form associations to demand repeal of the laws against Catholics.

The Protestants were naturally against this, as it would lose them the monopoly of power that they had held for so long. O'Connell's association was legal. Parliament made it illegal for any association of the sort to last longer than two weeks. But O'Connell could not be outwitted. He is said to have boasted that he could drive a coach and six through any law that was passed against him. So when one Catholic Association died, O'Connell formed another, and when its short life was run, another still. The people who attended the meetings constituted the great mass of the Irish population. They were determined, under their able leader, to secure their rights. The time came when the English government, warned by its Irish officers that unless Emancipation were voted Ireland would revolt, had to give in, and pass the measure; George IV signed it in a rage, and O'Connell became a national idol.

Now Irish Catholics could vote and hold office, Catholic barristers could advance from cotton gowns to silk and ermine. But Emancipation could not remedy Ireland's economic ills, or lighten the poverty of the Irish peasants.

Their condition was desperate. Most of them lived in one-roomed cabins, with no ceilings, nothing between them and the sky but thatch, and what cobwebs were on it. Few of them had bedsteads; a little straw and one blanket for many was the rule. Their fare was potatoes and salt. When the old crop went bad in early July they had to live on weeds and greens till the new one was dug in August. Meat they had only twice a year, at Christmas and Easter. A laborer was considered well off if he got a drop of milk with his potatoes. "Aye, and blue milk, too, that if you threw it against a wall, wouldn't color it." It was not an invigorating fare at its best. "We're only just kept breathing. Our eyes are only just kept winking."

Why potatoes all the time? Why not bread, or beans, or any other fare? "Potatoes by night, potatoes by day, and should I rise at midnight, potatoes still I'd get," a poet had remonstrated a few decades before. The answer is that potatoes yielded the largest crop that could be grown on the small plots which were all that the Irish peasants could keep for their own use. All the other produce, the grain, the rye, the barley, cattle and bacon, these were shipped away to England to pay the enormous rents. But an acre of potatoes would feed a family of ten the year round, except for the hungry weeks before the new harvest. Did they like potatoes, as their landlords have claimed in justification for the monotonous Irish fare? Let one of them answer for them all. "Arrah, sir, and why should we prefer what we feed our pigs on, to better food? Don't you like it better, yourself, and shouldn't we? Never believe that we'd eat but lumpers, if we could get good bread."

The man who asked that question, and, not like jesting Pilate, waited for an answer, was a government commissioner sent to Ireland to conduct an agricultural investigation. His report did not make pleasant reading for his superiors. "Ireland," said Mr. Binns, after describing the poverty of the people, the lack of profit in raising even a "slip of a pig" when feed must be paid for (for garbage was a luxury the poor Irish did not know), the desolation of their dwellings, and the lack of employment, "Ireland presents to those who contemplate her peculiar condition a striking and fearfully disgraceful anomaly. Possessing a singularly fertile soil, capable of abundantly repaying the labor bestowed upon it, she also possesses a population depressed by more than ordinary destitution, and dishonored by a long catalogue of more than ordinary crimes. . . . Ever since her connection with Great Britain Ireland has been a grievously oppressed country, that for the ignoble purpose of extinguishing her religion, and seizing upon the property of her votaries, she has been deprived of those political privileges that were her right, and which sooner or later she *will* possess, that so far from the Irish being naturally a turbulent people, they are made so by circumstances under the control of England, and that, dissatisfied as they are and have been, the wrongs they have endured, the insults they have suffered, would have justified a course of conduct incomparably more violent than any which Ireland, even in her most excited moments, in her wildest paroxysms of resentment, has displayed. The terms of the Union, let us remember, promised an equality of civil rights, and until these terms are rigidly complied with, Ireland never will, and Ireland never ought to be, a contented country."

"Injustice, doubt it not, abounds, or Ireland would not be miserable," said Carlyle in 1840. "The earth is good, and bountifully sends food and increase, if man's unwisdom did not intervene and forbid."

Five years later one James Grant traveled through ailing Ireland. Beautiful to the eye, he found her, "affluent beyond every other land in all those natural resources which, when developed, constitute a country's commercial greatness; but the unjust policy of men has prevented the development of the natural capabilities of Ireland. The purposes of providence have been defeated by the mischievous measures of those who for centuries have had the rule over her. Hence Ireland is poor and miserable, when she ought to be rich and happy. She is in a state of degradation, when she ought to be a great, glorious and free nation."

James Grant was only one of many who noted in Ireland laborers willing to work for sixpence a day "without diet," and not finding constant employment even then, who saw harvesters walking weary Irish miles to take ship to England, and there to walk equal distances for a few weeks' work, the wages of which they carried back to Ireland sewed up in the sleeves of their ragged coats, who spoke to women anxious to help with the support of their families, but who could earn only eightpence a week by spinning, who learned of little herd-girls who tended cattle half a year for a wage of eight shillings. He was one of many who saw Irish roads dark with old and infirm beggars "dragging sorrow after their heels." He was one of many who saw the needy going into pawnshops to raise money on anything from a needle to the family blanket. "We used to go in the dusk," said one woman questioned by Mr. Binns, "but now I would not care if all the people on the market cross saw me; they know it is a weighty pressure makes me do it."

Poverty is a weighty pressure, indeed. There were few who really doubted the cause of it in Ireland. Ireland's population, steadily increasing, made land necessary because English laws had killed her commerce. The land rents went largely to England, to be spent by absentee landlords, who had no interest in improving the condition of the country. The Duke of Wellington, who never showed any affection for the land of his birth, had written to a friend in 1830: "The annually recurring starvation in Ireland . . .

gives me more uneasiness than any other evil existing in the United Kingdom. . . . The proprietors of the country, those who ought to think for the people, to foresee this misfortune, and to provide beforehand a remedy for it, are amusing themselves in the clubs in London, in Cheltenham, or Bath, or on the Continent, and the government are made responsible for the evil, and they must find a remedy for it where they can, anywhere except in the pockets of the Irish gentlemen."

If the government thus "made responsible" for the welfare of the Irish people had undertaken that responsibility honestly, all might have been well for Ireland. But it did not. The government held the old belief that Ireland was English property, to be handled for English gain. Some few individuals in England, to their honor, decried the spoiling of the smaller island, and championed the rights of the Irish as a people, but they were in the minority. In the *Life of Lord Campbell*, that statesman, once lord chancellor of England, recollects "how essentially Ireland is hated by the English nation, and what a lenient view is taken of any measure which tends to degrade the mass of the Irish population."

That being the case, it is not strange that the Irish people should not be content to be governed by a parliament to whom they could send so few representatives that they were always outvoted by interests hostile to their own. They wanted a parliament of their own, a parliament free to introduce all measures necessary for the good government of their land. Back in the reign of Henry VII the Irish Parliament, weak instrument of a weak government, had passed the famous Poyning's Law which prohibited the Irish Parliament from considering any legislation except that

which had the preliminary sanction of the English Privy
Council. This act limited the power of the Irish Parliament
for nearly three hundred years. It would have continued to
limit it had not the weakness of England during the
American Revolution permitted the Irish to demand successfully the easing of that restraint. In 1779 Free Trade for
Ireland had been won, while the cannon of the Irish Volunteers was pointed at Dublin Castle. Three years later
England, fearful that it would lose Ireland as it had just
lost America, agreed to a modification of Poyning's Law,
whereby the Irish Parliament might originate and pass bills
without the previous consent of the English Privy Council.
Thereupon poor Ireland's poverty was lessened for a few
brief years, only to be increased by the Act of the
Union.

To repeal the Act of the Union, and give Ireland once
more an unbound government of its own, now became
O'Connell's great desire. Forty years after the bells of
St. Patrick's had rung out in celebration of the Act of the
Union, O'Connell took up the task he had vowed then. In
1834 he had undertaken a similar task, which for various
reasons had had little success. In the years between he had
not made Repeal an issue on the hope, if not on the under-
standing, that England would pass ameliorating measures
for Ireland. O'Connell, for all his cleverness, was sometimes
misled by the promises of English statesmen. But now, in
1840, he had given up that hope. Repeal of the Union was
a necessity.

He undertook to form a Repeal Association, open headquarters, and hold weekly meetings. For a year things went
slowly. O'Connell was aging now, and his great popularity
was somewhat diminished. With his old speeches, his old

familiar arguments, he could not weld the people into a powerful group.

The fire necessary for that welding came from a new source, and one for which O'Connell was not responsible. Indeed, he feared it as something that might grow beyond control. He was to benefit by it, and to use it for himself and for Repeal, but he could not claim credit for it. A group of young men joined the Repeal Association and went earnestly to work. They were middle-class young men, barristers, some of them, with leanings toward literature and patriotism. Half of them were Catholics and half Protestants.

It was easy to see that O'Connell was not stirring the country. But why? Because, these young men believed, the Repeal arguments were all materialistic. They believed that Irish pride and imagination should be appealed to. "The complaint of Ireland had been contemptuously described as a beggar's petition," said Charles Gavan Duffy, the editor and chronicler of the Young Ireland movement. "They were of the opinion that it ought rather to be presented as a new petition of rights; the claim of an ancient historic nation, which had been robbed of its constitution, stated with scrupulous fairness, but stated as from equal to equal, and persisted in to all extremities."

But the lower classes of the people were in a woeful state of ignorance about their country's past. Irish history was not taught in the schools, though English history was. In the cabins of the poor the old Gaelic songs were sung, and the words of the poets were handed down as an oral tradition, but neither of these was known in taverns and workshops. The English attack on all things Irish kept statues of Irish heroes from Irish streets, and their names from the mouths of the people. Duffy reported that beyond a vague sense of disaster and injustice the mass of the people knew little of their past.

To bring back that knowledge, and revive the pride of the great mass of the Irish people, was the aim of the group of new members of the Repeal Association. Their method was the printed word. With Charles Gavan Duffy as owner and editor, they started a weekly newspaper called *The Nation*. The prospectus which advertised the first issue stated that the great object of the editors was nationality, "a Nationality which will not only raise our people from their poverty, by securing to them the blessings of a domestic legislature, but inflame and purify them with a lofty and heroic love of their country—a Nationality of the spirit as well as the letter—a Nationality which may come to be stamped upon our manners, our literature and our deeds—a Nationality which may embrace Protestant, Catholic and Dissenter,—Milesian and Cromwellian,—the Irishman of a hundred generations, and the stranger who is within our gates."

The articles and editorials which appeared in the new paper fulfilled all the promises of the editors. *The Nation* became immediately popular, and increasingly important. "Ireland," said a writer in the Leeds *Times*, "has at length, after weary and dumb ages of suffering and of wrong, found a voice which speaks to some purpose. Five centuries of pain and injustice plead sternly and eloquently to God and to man for redress." But what gave the necessary fire to the Repeal movement was the publication in *The Nation* of patriotic poems. Clarence Mangan, one of the contributing editors, he of the "fine, falcon face," made translations in verse of poems of older days, poems of Kathleen ni Houlihan and Dark Rosaleen, the poem the O'Donnells' poet had written in Rome lamenting the death of the two great earls, O'Hussey's "Ode to Maguire," keening the death of the Lord of Fermanagh. Week after week his verses appeared, sometimes translations, sometimes originals. They were soon augmented by the works of countless volunteers known and unknown.

It was not in Gaelic that poets wrote now, but in English. But that the writers were the spiritual descendants of the old Gaelic bards was evident in more ways than one. Duffy tells of the fine peasant verses of John Keegan, done in a handwriting "on which the scythe and spade had left their broad mark." One pictures him a less rakish Owen Roe O'Sullivan; less rakish, but no less proud. His "Irish Reaper's Harvest Hymn" is a cry of rebellion against the assumption of superiority of the English, and the poverty of the Irish peasants.

> *From the home of my fathers in anguish I go*
> *To toil for the dark-livered, cold-hearted foe*
> *Who mocks me, and hates me, and calls me a slave,*
> *An alien, a savage,—all names but a knave. . . .*
>
> *The land that I fly from is fertile and fair,*
> *And more than I ask or I wish for is there,*
> *But I must not taste the good things that I see—*
> *There's nothing but rags and green rushes for me.*

The first issue of *The Nation* appeared on October 15, 1842. "Repeal rent"—the small voluntary contributions which financed the movement—amounted that week to less than £60. By spring of the following year "Repeal wardens" all over the country were sending in the rent at the rate of about £300 a week. "Repeal Reading Rooms" were started throughout the country, and soon there was hardly a parish without one. A copy of *The Nation* went to each. But the Reading Room copy was not the only one, even in small towns. One of the editors of *The Nation*, visiting a small village in Mayo, wrote back to Dublin that no less than twenty-three copies of the paper came to that place alone, a town which boasted hardly a score of houses, and those poor ones.

England had told the Irish that a small country could not survive. *The Nation* refuted that statement. "Look at Portugal," it said. "Look at Holland. Look at Sweden and Prussia." Every issue of the paper was tonic for the Irish pride. Every page was education for a people who had been deprived of it. The national spirit flamed anew. After O'Connell debated Repeal before the Dublin Corporation the cause obtained many new recruits from sections in the middle class which had hitherto been hostile.

The landed gentry became alarmed at the extent of the movement. They inquired of the government what was to be done to suppress this menace to their superiority and prosperity. Their fear was that the Irish people, awakened to a sense of their political rights, would not continue for long to pay their "feudal exactions." Sir Robert Peel, the lord lieutenant, reassured them. Her Majesty's government he said, would use all power, all authority, to maintain the Union. If the existing laws were not enough, he would ask new powers of Parliament. Civil war, he said, would be preferable to dismemberment of the empire.

This threat of coercion O'Connell answered immediately at one of the regular Dublin meetings at the Corn Exchange. "I belong," he said, "to a nation of eight millions, and there is besides a million of Irishmen in England. If Sir Robert Peel has the audacity to cause a contest to take place between the two countries we will put him in the wrong, for we will begin no rebellion, but I tell him from this place that he dare not begin that strife against Ireland."

It was soon after this that one of the great county meetings took place at Mullingar. The soil of Westmeath shook to the marching of 100,000 feet. Parish after parish sent in its delegates, each group headed by temperance bands. Two meetings in Tipperary, and one at Cashel, drew enormous crowds to listen to the man who, as one of the Young Irelanders later put it, was more of a god than a guide. Repeal rent amounted now to more than two thousand pounds a week.

While the English Parliament debated an arms bill for Ireland, to make risings of the people there impossible, and met unexpected resistance to it, the monster meetings continued. On June 11, 1843, the great Mallow meeting was held, when according to the newspapers, half a million people came together in order and amiability. The squadron of hussars and the two companies of infantry the government had sent to keep peace were not needed. At the banquet which followed the meeting O'Connell repeated his determination to violate no law and to assail no enemy. But he warned his audience that they would be much mistaken "if you think others will not assail you. . . . Are Irishmen to be called slaves?" he asked. "Are we to be trampled under foot? . . . They may trample me, but it will be my dead body they will trample on, not the living man."

To the Tara meeting another half million came, if not to hear the leader—for that was a physical impossibility for them all—at least to demonstrate their sympathy with his cause. Even Ulster turned out a hundred thousand.

For the great meeting at Clontarf, where Brian Boru had broken the power of the Danes, the greatest number of all was expected. It was to be the final, conclusive meeting. The will of the people had been undeniably shown. If Parliament denied Repeal to the Irish people now, it was a violation of all constitutional rights.

As Sunday, October 5, 1843, approached, the atmosphere of all England and Ireland was electric. Peel was in a delicate position. The landed gentry were fearful, and looked to the lord lieutenant for support. Would he dare to put down this giant meeting by force? And if he did, would O'Connell keep his implied threat, and fight? There was no doubt at all that if he did he would have the Irish people joyfully behind him.

In this great crisis, with this great power at his command, with his challenge given and his honor pledged, O'Connell disappointed his country. On Saturday, October 4, the English Privy Council issued a proclamation, a thing having no force in law, forbidding the meeting, "as calculated to excite alarm and lead to a breach of the peace."

If ever there was proof of O'Connell's power, it was shown then. Already hundreds of thousands of people were setting out for the great meeting. They would have gone as gladly to battle if O'Connell had given the word. He did not give it. Instead, he sent forth word to cancel the meeting. "The time for resistance has not come," he said. Was he thinking of the bloodshed of the French Revolution? Was he letting his respect for legal methods of reform deny his plighted word? Was he merely unwilling to grasp the opportunity which presented itself, and become warrior instead of orator? In all the printed records of his thoughts and convictions there is none that satisfactorily answers these questions.

"Ireland was won at Clontarf," said one of his followers, "and she is going to be lost at Clontarf."

The evidence which time slowly turns up seems to indicate that the English were not relying on their proclamation alone. It had not been issued until three o'clock of a Saturday afternoon in October, when only two hours of daylight by which it could be read remained. If the news of the proclamation did not reach the people, or if O'Connell's word of cancellation did not spread quickly enough, then the Repealers meeting on the site of an ancient battlefield would meet the armed troops of an oppressive authority.

Under the circumstances a certain entry in Raikes's *Diary* is significant. It describes the entry of the Duke of Wellington into a London drawing room, bearing a copy of the proclamation issued at Dublin Castle, and the Duke's reading of it, "with emphasis on the words 'tending to overthrow the Constitution of the British Empire by law established.' I could see that he was much pleased with this exercise of authority, and that he thought the government had been dilatory in not adopting these strong measures at an earlier period. He said, 'We must now show them that we are in earnest; there must be no paltering or truckling with O'Connell; and as we are prepared for every emergency I have no fears of the result. Ten years of misrule in Ireland have rendered our task more difficult, but we must now bring the rascals on their knees; they give us now a fair pretext to put them down, as their late placard invites the mob to assemble in military order, and their horsemen to form in troops. This order was probably not written by O'Connell himself, but by some eager zealot of his party, who has thus brought the affair to a crisis. Our proclamation was well drawn up, and avails itself of the unguarded opening which O'Connell has given to set him at defiance.' He then turned to me and said, 'Do you know what the Pope's nuncio, Gravina, said at Lisbon at the time of the insurrection? 'Pour la canaille, faut la mitraille.' As he went in to dinner, he repeated the couplet two or three times."

"Muskets for the mob." That was Wellington's answer to a people lawfully assembling to petition for their rights.

That was the great climax of the movement. What if Repeal agitation did go on? What if the government, denied the excuse to use their muskets, did sue O'Connell and the Young Irelanders for libel, and try them with packed juries? What if the Young Irelanders, splitting with O'Connell on the matter of force, finally unsheathed the sword he would not draw in the abortive rebellion of '48? A fighter cannot stay for long in the pink of physical condition. A nation's emotions attain their peak, and then subside. On October 4, 1843, Ireland's destiny was in the balance, and the man she loved and trusted swung the scales the wrong way. It would be many a long year before Ireland's hopes would again appear so close to realization.

Sore saddened in spirit must one become who reads the pages of history of this time. Treason laws tried Irish patriots, and banished them in chains. O'Connell died in 1847 of the brain affliction which was the reason for his retirement during the last few years of his life. Famine came to dampen the fires of nationalism already diminished.

Is it right to speak of famine in terms other than those of harsh reality? Is it right to soften the picture of an already starving people losing what little sustenance they have left, and that not by act of God, but by greed of man? If it is, here are the words of Speranza of *The Nation*, who, as Lady Wilde, was to reap her own sorrow nearly fifty years later:

"Weary men, what reap ye?" "Golden grain for the stranger."
"What sow ye?" "Human corpses that wait for the avenger."
"Fainting forms, hunger-stricken, what see you in the offing?"
"Stately ships to bear our food away, amid the strangers scoffing."
"There's a proud army of soldiers—what do they round your door?"
"They guard our master's granaries from the thin hands of the poor."
"Pale mothers, wherefore weeping?" "Would to God that we were dead—
Our children swoon before us, and we cannot give them bread."

It was "the exigencies of verse" that made Speranza use that final word "bread." Bread was a luxury that was seldom known to Irish peasants. What the lady meant was potatoes, a word she found difficult to fit into her composition. In September of 1845 farmers along the coast of Wexford noticed brown spots on the leaves of their potato plants. When they harvested their crop, half were found to be decayed, and the part that seemed sound when dug were decayed three weeks later. The parish priest of Kells, a most fertile potato-growing locale, noted on October 24 his fear that "one family in twenty will not have a single potato left on Christmas day next. With starvation at our doors, grimly staring us, vessels laden with our whole hopes of existence, our provisions, are hourly wafted from our every port. From one milling establishment I have seen no less than fifty dray loads of meal moving on to Drogheda, thence to go to feed the foreigner, leaving starvation and death the soon and certain fate of the toil and sweat that raised this food." The landed proprietors, warned that the Irish potato crop was blighted, were hurrying the shipment of the rent-paying crops.

The Dublin Corporation, alarmed at the threat of famine, appointed a committee to report on the blight. The propositions they advanced to avoid a national catastrophe were presented to the lord lieutenant, who replied coldly to the committee that there was "no immediate pressure on the market," and that the queen's advisers must be consulted. Ireland began to know the pinch of hunger.

John Mitchel, one of the Young Ireland group, who was later banished halfway round the world in chains for upholding the rights of the starving people to retain their crops, wrote in his exile *An Apology for the British Government in Ireland*. It advances the theory that the British government deliberately allowed millions of Irish people to starve to death, because in that way the "surplus population" which had been alarming the English government for several years would be diminished. There were nine million people in Ireland. Only four million were required to raise the crops which helped feed England.

"When the Irish nation, then being nine millions, produced by their own industry, on their own land, good food enough to feed eighteen million, one cannot well say that providence sent them a famine, and when those nine million dwindled in two or three years to six and a half million, partly by mere hunger and partly by flight beyond the sea to escape it, and when we find all these same years the English people doing well and feeding well, upon that very food for want of which the Irish died, I suppose the term British famine will be admitted to be quite correct . . . "

Even people with less drastic accusations against the British government admit that Ireland, during all the famine years, was producing double the amount of food necessary to feed her people, and that if she had had a national government her ports would have been closed to the export of grain. But Ireland was ruled from England, and this simple measure was not taken. Instead, Peel passed the corn laws, which merely lessened the return the Irish got for their produce, and hindered rather than helped the Irish situation. Even Wellington admitted that. Speaking of Peel's change of policy about the corn laws, he told a friend that he was totally unprepared for it, "nor do I comprehend how the repeal of the corn laws can remedy the potato famine in Ireland, where the want is not of food, but the money to buy it."

But if the British government would not pass the measures necessary to avoid the famine, societies and individuals in other lands were quick to send relief to ameliorate its miseries. Subscriptions were raised to help the starving people, and ships loaded with American maize sailed for Irish ports. When they reached there, they found a British policy which handicapped their work. All relief was to be administered through the government. All other relief bodies were induced to act in subordination to it. Ten thousand blank books and fourteen tons of paper were sent to Ireland to carry out the new poor law decision, by which a farmer applying for aid had to give up his land before he was given relief.

Few landloards, even the occasional Irish ones, showed any leniency to their tenants. The rent must be paid. If it was not, whatever livestock the poor farmer had was "driven," to make good the deficit. William Bennett, in Ireland as relief representative of the Society of Friends, tells of one man who was short in his rent but twenty-five shillings: he had a horse and four sheep "driven" and sold for twenty shillings to satisfy his landlord. The tenant got nothing.

With the generous impulses of strangers thwarted by British red tape, it is easy to understand why millions died with food in sight. By February in 1847 O'Neill Daunt was writing in his journal: "The horrors of the famine are such as would almost seem fabulous if we read of them in books. The tax collectors find houses shut up, the inmates having died. Great numbers are buried without coffins. Miserable creatures, crawling up the rocks on the coast in search of edible weeds, fall into the sea from inanition. The coffinless bodies that have been interred in kitchen gardens are rooted up by pigs and dogs and devoured. Pestilence is generated by the stench of unburied carcasses. The cereal crops have been very abundant; of oats, wheat, barley, and also of pigs, sheep and cattle there are within the four seas of Ireland more than enough to feed all the inhabitants. But these commodities are not for the people whose industry produced them."

During the famine Daunt was impressed by the patience of the starving peasants, and their forbearance from robbery, and spoke to a neighboring farmer about it. "We do not know how soon we may die," the man answered, "and it is better to suffer hunger than to put our souls in danger by thieving."

But some few of the poor hungry people did endanger their souls in order to fill their stomachs. The records of

Bantry Sessions of 1847 tell of the indictment of Timothy and Mary Leary, "for that they on the fourteenth day of January, at Oakmont, did feloniously steal twenty turnips and fifty parsnips, the property of James Gillman." They were found guilty, and sentenced to transportation for seven years.

Two more observations of Mr. Daunt on the famine, though made a few years later, are worth ferreting out. In 1850 he tells of a talkative old gentleman he met in a coffeehouse, who "had seen six carloads of dead sent daily out of the Cork workhouse in 1846."

In an entry in his journal for the year 1853, Mr. Daunt tells of a conversation with one McCarthy, whose father had been physician to the Sultan of Turkey. "He told me that the Sultan had intended to give £10,000 to the famine-stricken Irish, but was deterred by the English Ambassador, Lord Cowley, as her Majesty, who had only subscribed £1,000 would have been annoyed had a foreign sovereign given a larger sum."

An American woman who had spent some years in Ireland, before the famine, went back to carry relief in a small way to the people she had grown fond of. She tells, in a quietly realistic way, of the fat, sleek dogs of Arranmore, and why they were so well fed in a starving country, of soldiers standing guard over grain to be shipped to England, of the awful look of the starving people.

"The first stage of starvation is somewhat clamorous, and will not easily be put off, the next is patient, passive stupidity; and the last is idiocy. In the second stage they will stand at a window for hours, without asking charity, giving a vacant stare, and not until peremptorily driven away will they move. In the last state, the head hangs forward, and they walk with long strides, and pass you unheedingly."

Mrs. Nicholson's description is not quite accurate. In the last stage, a starving person crawls into some quiet place to die. Mrs. Nicholson surely knew that. One morning she learned that nine poor wretches had died in the yard beneath her window during the night before.

There was no red tape about Mrs. Nicholson's charity. She took what money she had, and spent it carefully for people who were dying of starvation all around her. She sent back to America for more funds. She taught the Irish peasants how to use the corn meal which American generosity sent, and about which they knew nothing, so that they sickened by eating lumpy, half-cooked porridge. She consoled the bereaved. She saw one mother whose son had been drowned three weeks before, "as fine a lad as ever put oar across the curragh, and who had the larnin' entirely."

The years of the famine were four, from 1846 to 1849, and each year the misery and poverty became greater, more millions died, more fled across the Atlantic. When Carlyle went to look at Ireland in 1849 he found it an ugly spectacle. "The whole country figures in my mind like a ragged coat; one huge beggar's gabardine, not patched or patchable any longer, far from a joyful or a beautifying spectacle." Derry, rising red and beautiful on a hill, "the prettiest looking town I have found in Ireland," won most of his scant approval. Two starving children, coming out of their cabin dressed in rags, to beg for a bit of food, stirred no sympathy in him, only anger and contempt. He thought the rags theatrical—beggars' paraphernalia worn to arouse pity. It aroused none in him. "Gave them nothing," he coldly records.

It was an emaciated Ireland which began the second half of the nineteenth century. Her poor people were hungry, hundreds of thousands of them had died in the famine years, and as many more had emigrated. In the six years from 1845 to 1851 the population of Ireland shrank from eight and a half millions to six and a half millions. O'Connell had died with his glory dimmed. Almost to a man the leaders of the Young Ireland movement were dead or banished from Ireland. Duffy of *The Nation* was left, and for a while he carried on the fight. The odds were all against him. "For seven years I have kept the green flag flying alone, or but with a handful of friends," he said in 1855. That was his valedictory as he sailed for Australia. A friend had just written him that all hope for the poor of Ireland was dead.

At the time it doubtless seemed so. But when one man gives up the struggle in Ireland, there is always another to carry it on. The next fifty years were to see two groups who raised the nation's hopes—groups sometimes working separately, and sometimes merging their efforts—that Ireland might not always know poverty and hunger. One was the parliamentary group, who trusted to the power of speech to win reforming laws. The other was the sword group, even though that shining word often represented in reality an old rifle, or a pike whose blade had been hammered out at the village smithy.

It was in the early sixties that word was passed from mouth to mouth of a secret organization whose aim was the founding of an Irish republic. Rumor said that two men who had been "out" in the rising of '48, and who had escaped to Paris, had fathered the movement there. John O'Mahoney had carried the plan to America; James Stephens had brought it to Ireland. The Irish Republican Brotherhood it was named, but members who joined its oath-bound ranks were soon called Fenians, or IRBs. America was to send money, and officers from the disbanded ranks of the armies of the Civil War. Ireland would arm, and strike for her rights.

Eventually the plans were changed, and a force in America crossed the border into Canada to try to set up an Irish government there. But the United States authorities closed the frontier, and the military phase of America's Fenian outbreak was soon over. Still, money kept coming into Ireland from America. Rich and poor sympathizers bought Fenian bonds, not as an investment. Many a laborer's wallet held one or more, to become in time creased and dirty, and valued only for the ideal it represented. Many a servant girl, holding in a hand rough and red from scrubbing the small wages that her work had earned, passed by the temptation of a new bonnet or a warm shawl, and hoped that the poverty which had sent her to a strange land would soon be over for her brothers and sisters at home.

In Ireland the IRB recruits were numbered by the thousand. In 1865 the army in Ireland was honeycombed by Fenians. Thirteen thousand had taken the oath, and would desert the queen's officers at a word from their own leaders. More were in the militia, and many in the police. Things seemed promising, till Stephen's orders to the country to prepare to strike fell into the hands of the police. The government had not been unaware of what was going on. It suspended the habeas corpus act, filled the jails with would-be rebels, and felt confident that the danger was over.

But the IRB could not be killed. In exile, in prison, "on their keeping" in the hills, the men who had had the courage to defy their church and a powerful hostile government kept before them the hope of an Ireland free from England, an Ireland free to achieve her own destiny. The roots of the movement were many and deeply imbedded in the life of the country. "No greater self-deception could we practice on ourselves than to imagine that Fenianism is the folly of a few apprentices and shop-boys," wrote Cardinal Manning to Lord Grey. "Fenianism could not have survived for a year if it were not sustained by the traditional and just discontent of the whole people."

The cardinal wrote in 1867, just after another Fenian outbreak had failed. The subject of his letter was the land question. The land question, he informed Lord Grey, "means hunger, thirst, nakedness, notice to quit, labor spent in vain, and toil of years seized upon, the breaking up of homes, the miseries, sickness, deaths, of parents, children, wives; the despair and wildness which spring up in the hearts of the poor when legal force, like a sharp harrow, goes over the most sensitive and vital rights of mankind. . . . It is this which spreads through the people in three-fourths of Ireland with an all-pervading and thrilling intensity. It is this which has driven thousands to America, there to bide the time of return."

Ever since the lowering of the price of corn, tillage in Ireland had been less profitable than pasturage. With the disfranchising of the forty-shilling freeholders tenants were less useful to the landlords. So Irish fields made way for pastures, and the farmers who had worked small holdings were put out on the road. In the words of Lord Carlisle, Ireland was to be "a fruitful mother of flocks and herds." Cattle and recruits were the approved Irish products, and the falling population of Ireland was not a source of concern

to English officials. No hindrance was offered to the landlords who added to their already-great power by obtaining
from the English Parliament laws which made evictions
easy. A farmer could be dispossessed from his holdings for
six months' arrears of rent. A bailiff served notice, the
landlord's crowbar brigade leveled the delinquent's dwelling to the ground, and a family was left shelterless.

Physical force movements are always followed in Ireland
by peaceful agitation. In 1870 the IRB was far from dead
but it planned no insurrection for the near future. Its leaders
were willing to substitute speech for the sword for a while.
Among the men who met at the Bilton Hotel in Dublin on
May 19, 1870, to form the Home Rule party were several
Fenians. For a time Isaac Butt was the leader of the party.
The platform was the belief that the true remedy for the
evils of Ireland was the establishment of an Irish Parliament
with full control over domestic affairs. Their method was to
elect Irish members to the House of Commons pledged to
work for such a parliament. At the election of 1874 sixty
of the hundred and five successful candidates were Home
Rulers.

Parliament did not listen sympathetically to the plea for
Home Rule for Ireland. It was the opinion of the House of
Commons that Home Rule was only a step toward total
separation. "If we have to deal with discontent now we
have to deal only with individuals. But what would be the
position if we had to deal with an Irish Parliament having
the resources of government at its command?" The question
was asked by Lord Hartington, leader of the opposition in
Parliament.

As a matter of fact, Parliament was not greatly worried.
Irish members were in too small a minority to count in the

House. They knew it, and most of them did not waste efforts in proposing legislation which was bound to be voted down. They were elected, and they sat, generally in silence. Cornelius O'Brien, of County Clare, never made a speech in all his thirty years in Parliament. "The best representative Ireland ever sent to Westminster," said Lord Palmerston approvingly.

The quiet of the Irish benches was broken by a little man named Biggar, on whom inactivity had palled. If Irishmen could not get laws passed for Ireland, he would keep Englishmen from getting laws passed for England. So he heckled and questioned, and made himself a nuisance to the outraged House. Butt urged in vain the "duty of maintaining before the civilized world the dignity of the Irish nation and the Irish cause." In 1874 a new member adopted the obstruction policy, and made it a mighty force.

Charles Stewart Parnell was the new member's name. He came from Avondale, in Wicklow, of old Ascendancy stock. His grandfather had been chancellor of the exchequor at the time of the Union. Though offered the usual bribes of money and title, he had refused to vote for the Act, and had lost his office in consequence. Charles Stewart Parnell's maternal grandfather was Admiral Stewart of the United States Navy. His enemies used to say that Parnell hadn't a drop of Irish blood in his veins, but that was not the truth. The Stewarts had gone to America from Ulster.

The portrait of Parnell by Sidney Hall which hangs in the National Gallery in Dublin is worth a careful study. No one can look at that picture of the pale, bearded man and not see the icy intensity of his being, and the almost hypnotic power of his eyes. No one can note that fine brow, and doubt his intellectual gifts. No one can glimpse the slender, chiseled perfection of his nose, and not know that it belonged to a man as proud as Lucifer. Pride was the dominant characteristic of Charles Stewart Parnell; and it contributed largely to every important decision of his life.

He went into politics suddenly, soon after being rejected by an American girl of wealth and position. She is said to have reproached him for lack of distinction, for being only an idle Irish gentleman. Within a short time he entered politics, and distinction was not long in coming to him.

The voice of the new member of Parliament was not silent in the House. He not only adopted Biggar's policy of obstruction, but made it a constructive force. "I have shown the country," he replied to Butt in 1877, when the old leader attacked his methods, "that they have a power which they little know of, to use if they desire for the enforcement of their just claim." The just claim, of course, was for Home Rule.

The movement was strengthened when a young Fenian named Michael Davitt was released from Dartmoor with a plan for winning self-government, which he had formulated during his seven years of penal servitude. It was to link the land or social question to that of Home Rule by making the ownership of the soil the basis of the fight for self-government.

Land was as dear to Davitt as were power and pride to Parnell. He had been four when his family was evicted from their holding during the famine of the forties. At twelve he had lost an arm in a machine in a Lancashire mill. At twenty-four he had been arrested in London while on IRB business, and sentenced to fifteen years' penal servitude. His release on ticket of leave after seven years in prison was just in time to let him see Ireland suffer under another famine. There was a bad harvest in 1877, and again in 1878, and again in 1879. The impoverished farmers knew again quick hunger, and eviction from their homes.

"There are many houses in this parish at present," wrote one priest in 1880, "in which the last pound of meal has been consumed, the last bed-covering worth a shilling has been deposited in the pawn-office, and the last fire of turf collected from the saturated heap upon the bog has died away upon the hearth, the dying embers being a vivid emblem of that death from starvation which is already creeping upon the threshhold."

This description prefaces the story of a land war in Drumlish. Three hundred people of that town were supported by alms alone, collected by the parish priest. The bad harvests had made it impossible for the tenants to pay their rents. So when evictions were imminent the church bell and the drums of the Land League summoned the people of the district to repulse the bailiffs. The peasants of the countryside poured out, armed with pikes and sticks, and crying that they would not die of starvation, but would die fighting like men.

In County Longford, Lord Larton ordered the whole population of Ballinamuck to be swept away, and the entire village to be razed.

These are not isolated cases, but examples of the social state of much of rural Ireland. If they had been the exception rather than the rule, the name of Captain Moonlight would not have been so well known. He was the mythical champion who warred for the farmers against landlords, magistrates, and bailiffs. He was scorned by the Parliamentarians, who were trying to remove the basic cause of these troubles, but loved and applauded by the poor people. "Rally round from sea to sea," they sang. "Raise your voice and chorus me. We'll sing the song of liberty, and Captain Moonlight's Army."

But the material question of land was not the only issue in Ireland. Parnell would never have attained his great power if the people had not felt that he was leading them toward greater things than peasant proprietorship. They had Parnell's word that the fight was a national one. In a speech in America he said: "I feel confident that we shall kill the Irish landlord system and when we have given Ireland to the people of Ireland, we shall have laid the foundation upon which to build up the Irish nation." His slogan was "No man can set bounds to the march of a nation."

Through the eighties his power grew. He built it up with speeches of icy passion directed against a hostile Parliament. He augmented it by appearances among the people of Ireland, aloof, autocratic, but still an idol. Gladstone jailed him for a while in Kilmainham, and he lived there in almost royal comfort, while gifts from the people poured in upon him. When he decreed in 1886 that a certain Captain William O'Shea would be elected member from Galway, and Timothy Healy led the revolt of Parnell followers who did not want the spruce and dapper little man, Parnell appeared suddenly among the hostile crowd at Galway. How he forced his will upon the electors and upon Healy has been told in a book which was published in 1888. The date is important, as will be seen later. "I was in Galway when he came over there suddenly to quell the revolt organized by Healy," says the narrator. "The rebels were at white heat before he came. But he strode in among them like a huntsman among hounds, marched Healy off into a little

room, and brought him out again in ten minutes, cowed
and submissive, but filled, as anybody can see, ever since,
with a dull, smoldering hate, which will break out one of
these days, if a good and safe opportunity offers."

Mr. Parnell could return his gray mare to Parliment, if
he wished, the same witness believed, although he admitted
that there were people who thought it would be midsummer
madness to hand over Ireland to the Home Rule of the
Uncrowned King of Ireland.

Midsummer madness or not, Parnell's power was now so
great that Home Rule seemed inevitable. He was in absolute
control of the Irish Parliamentary party, and that party,
under his leadership, could play the game of politics in such a
way that a majority of votes for Home Rule was practically
conceded.

But the game of politics has strange rules, and these allow
a man's actions as a private individual to be made the basis
of attack as a public leader. Sir Alfred Robbin's book
Parnell—The Last Five Years, makes some interesting dis-
closures which seem to justify suspicions which were
current at the time. The author, as a newspaper correspond-
ent of ability and discretion, had enjoyed, he says, the
confidence of Parnell, Chamberlain, and Morley . . . "as
well as of certain very active wire-pullers in every political
camp, who largely at that period pulled strings which did
more than move puppets—they strangled politicians." In
August of 1889 Robbins was asked by one of the inside of
the Liberal Unionist machine whether Parnell would be
politically ruined by a divorce. "Captain O'Shea, it was
added, being believed to be willing to take proceedings."

"I pointed out the risk of the Unionist leaders seeming
to countenance such a proceeding, all the greater a risk by

their dependence on so bruised a reed as O'Shea, who had already twice 'double-crossed' Parnell. Besides, I added, the scandal was not new. It had not merely been talked of in private, but alluded to in print for at least seven years; had been on every political lip during the Galway election episode of the spring of 1886; had been clearly hinted at in the *Times* the following year; and had been revived by the appearance of O'Shea before the Special Commission as a witness, not only politically but personally hostile to Parnell."

On December 30, 1889, the news was made public that Captain William O'Shea had filed a petition for divorce against his wife, Katherine O'Shea, and that Charles Stewart Parnell had been named as corespondent. On November 17, 1890, a jury found a verdict against Parnell, and the divorce was granted.

That same day Parnell called a meeting of his party for November 25, to consider the business of the coming session of Parliament, in which session he could ordinarily have hoped, with the aid of Mr. Gladstone and his party, to have the Home Rule Bill become law. But Mr. Gladstone, who had entertained Parnell at his home, and who had, by Mrs. O'Shea's own assertion, known of the relationship between Parnell and herself for ten years, now decided that Parnell was not the man to lead his party in Parliament. He wrote John Morley a letter which was to form the basis of a hint to Parnell that he was to resign that position. The wording of the letter was diplomatic in the extreme. "Notwithstanding the splendid services rendered by Mr. Parnell to his country, his continuance at the present moment in the leadership would be productive of consequences disastrous in the highest degree to the cause of Ireland. I think I may be warranted in asking you so far to expand the conclusion I have given above, and to add that the continuance I speak of would not only place many hearty and effective friends of the Irish cause in a position of great embarrassment, but would render my retention of the Liberal party, based as it has been mainly upon the prosecution of the Irish cause, almost a nullity."

At the party meeting Parnell was again chosen leader, and Mr. Morley himself gave the news of his reelection to the astonished Gladstone. "He stood at the table, dumb for some instants, looking at me as though he could not believe what I had said. Then he burst out at me that we must at once publish his letter to me: at once, that very afternoon." *The Pall Mall*, he told Morley, would bring out a special edition. The letter was published that night.

Now Parnell found what it meant to be in politics. He had known its powers before, and his pride had relished them. Now his pride and his iron will would not allow him to give way; to go into the quiet of retirement. "My private life shall never belong to any country, but to one woman," he had once told Mrs. O'Shea. And another time he had said to her: "You do not learn the ethics of kingship, Queenie. Never explain, never apologize. I could never keep my rabble together if I were not above the human weakness of apology."

He did not apologize for his love now. It had lasted long. Years before, Mrs. O'Shea had asked her husband for a divorce. He would not allow it, and insisted on the appearance of a marriage long after it had ceased to be one in fact.

Gladstone's letter had its effect. In the famous Committee Room Fifteen, at a party meeting on November 25, Parnell's leadership was challenged. John Morley, to whom the letter had been sent, has left a description of the scene, though he was not present personally. "The party interest of the scene was supreme, for if the Irishmen should rally to their chief, then the English alliance was at an end, Mr. Gladstone would virtually end his illustrious career, the rent in the Liberal ranks might be repaired, the leading men in important sections would all group themselves afresh. 'Let us all keep quiet,' said one important Unionist. 'We may now have to revise our positions.'

"Either way, the serpent of faction would raise its head in Ireland, and the strong life of organized and concentrated nationalism would perish in its coils."

Parnell stood at the head of the committee table, his face pale in the lamplight. In a speech famous for its impassioned oratory he urged his followers not to allow the cause of Home Rule to be wrecked when success was so near. He cried out against being thrown to the wolves. "I am going to ask you, before my deposition, to be sure you are getting value received for it. I know what Mr. Gladstone will do for you, I know what Mr. Morley will do for you, and I know there is not a single one of the lot to be trusted unless you trust yourself."

The motion was put to vote, and lost by 44 to 29. Parnell's leadership was over. The seceding faction of the party was led out by Timothy Healy.

On December 28, 1890, after a Parnell candidate had been defeated at Kilkenny, Gladstone wrote to John Morley: "Since your letter arrived this morning, the Kilkenny poll has brightened the sky . . . We are now free from the enormous danger of seeing Parnell master in Ireland." To Lord Aston a fortnight later he wrote: "I consider the Parnell chapter of politics finally closed for us, the British Liberals, at least during my lifetime."

Ireland did not get Home Rule.

Chapter XVII

SEEDS OF FIRE

→»×«←

THE ENCHANTMENT that Parnell had put upon Ireland was suddenly broken. The excitement into which he had stirred the people subsided, the noise of parliamentary debate died away, and in the quiet that followed Ireland turned back her eyes from Westminster to look once more upon herself.

It was only natural that she should be critical, and she was. She saw with dismay that a nationality which found utterance in politics only was a poor thing, indeed. In Parnell she had felt she was following a star, and she found the star to be a torch that had flickered out. For how could speeches in Parliament ever cure Ireland's ills? England had shown herself to be Ireland's enemy still, though she was carrying on the conquest along unwarlike lines. "Three things show the mark of a successful conquest," one of Elizabeth's ministers had written, "customs, laws, and language." The discerning ones in Ireland suddenly realized that her old customs were vanishing, that she was governed by English laws, and that her language was all but dead. "A new England named Ireland," one of the O'Neills' poets had feared his country would become, and so it seemed it might.

In the beginning the invaders had wanted of the Irish treasure and tribute and lands, and they had taken as much as they could of them all. For centuries they had made laws to cripple Irish trade, that it might not be a menace to their own. Ireland of the nineteenth century, with her wealth diminished, was still necessary to England as a producer of cattle and recruits, and as a military possession. Ireland was too close to England to have it controlled by any but English authority. For the Irish people and their culture England cared nothing. The less nationalized and the more subservient the Irish were, the easier English rule would be.

So all English effort, when it was not actually engaged in putting down Irish rebellions, was directed toward making the Irish tractable and tame, and removing all traces of their nationality. The National Schools were instrumental in accomplishing this, and never were two fine words more maligned. For they did not fit the Irish people for the fullest kind of life, as real schools should, but for the unthinking existence of subservient people. And instead of making them proud of their country, and its past, all knowledge of Ireland was kept from them. It must be admitted that "national" is a sardonic word to apply to an Irish school which does not teach Irish history.

"For myself," said a woman whose education had been along these lines, "I believed that Ireland had no history but a history of disgraceful tribal squabbles of half-naked people, who had to be held down by a civilized conqueror, and who, wherever I caught a glimpse of them in the histories of England were turbulent and barbarous. There was nothing to feed my imagination in their uneventful lives, neither romance, nor heroic deeds. They were always the rebels."

It was more than tales of Irish heroes which the National Schools withheld from the Irish people. Other things they took from them gradually and imperceptibly, so that it was not until a great void had been created that their going was noticed. It was a scholar who noticed the void, and listed the things which had filled it. "In the first place," Douglas Hyde accused the Schools, "they have taken away [from the Gael] his language, and with his language has gone his music, for they were bound together, and with his music has gone his light heart. They have taken from him his poems, and his songs, and his old sayings, and his stories, and they have taken away his knowledge of the history of his country, and of his forefathers, for they, too, were bound up with the language, and when it was taken from him they went also. They have taken from him his wit and his quickness and his deep thinking, for he can never bring out the deep things that are in him in the broken English that has been put in his mouth; and the man that is without stories, without music, without poems, without traditions, without knowledge of the history of his country, and of his forefathers—it is not usual for that man to have any thought at all, except the trivial thoughts that come to him from the wants of the hour."

But while this devitalizing influence had been at work on the great mass of the Irish people, Irish scholars had also been at work, and from their labors was to come one of the remedies for Ireland's ills. The Irish language still lived on among the peasants in Gaelic outposts of Ireland. It still lived on with great students of Gaelic, both at home and abroad.

So the century that saw the greatest havoc wrought upon the Irish language saw also the *Annals of the Four Masters* translated; it saw the publication of Gaelic texts and translations of old tales of Finn and his companions, and other old Irish heroes; it saw Eugene O'Curry's works on *The Manuscript Materials of Irish History* and *The Manners and Customs of the Ancient Irish* published in four great volumes.

"Dry pages," a poet was to call these works, while admitting their importance. But from these pages Standish O'Grady was to get the material for a retelling of old Irish tales, which helped to revive interest in Irish history and literature, and which was a factor in the great Gaelic revival of the 1890's.

"When I read O'Grady," wrote George Russell under his nom de plume of AE, "I was as such a man who suddenly feels ancient memories rushing at him, and knows he was born in a royal house, that he had mixed with the mighty heaven and earth, and had the very noblest for his companions. In O'Grady's writings the submerged river of the national culture rose up again, a shining torrent, and I realized, as I bathed in that stream, that the greatest spiritual evil one nation could inflict on another was to cut off from it the story of the national soul."

O'Grady's first books appeared in 1878 and 1880, while Parnell's enchantment was on Ireland. It was not until twelve years or more later—when Parnell's epoch had ended and disillusioned Ireland was sickened of politics, and was thinking once more of its national culture—that the force of their influence was felt. By that time, boys who had read them in their teens were men. One was William Butler Yeats, and the enthusiasm which the books had inspired in him was augmented when John O'Leary of Fenian fame returned to Ireland from long years of prison and exile. To the young poet Yeats, O'Leary personified romantic Ireland, and Finn could still move this youthful imagination. It seemed to him that a new kind of romance, a new element in thought, was being molded out of Irish life and tradition. He became the leader of a movement whose aim was to create a literature for Ireland written in the English language, and inspired by Irish themes and traditions.

No one depreciates Yeats's influence on the Gaelic revival, but his first interest, at least, in Gaelic things had come from books. There was another side to the revival which had its roots in the native language and the living Irish people. Douglas Hyde and other scholars had learned the language from native Irish speakers, and then found, as Spenser had done, that "the speech being Irish, the heart must needs be Irish too." And more than that, that "when you've learned to speak Irish, you want an Irish hat on your head, and an Irish coat on your back." To revive Irish customs, art, and industry, and most of all, the Irish language, Dr. Hyde and six other scholars founded the Gaelic League in 1893.

It grew with inspiring swiftness. Within ten years there were eight hundred branches throughout Ireland, and the sale of its language textbooks sometimes reached fifty thousand copies a year. "Gan teanga, gan tir," had been an old Irish proverb, meaning "Without a tongue, without a country." The warning was widely heeded. Young boys who were to be heroes in the second decade of the twentieth century were in the nineties studying Gaelic with their Latin and Greek, and going on holiday to the Gaelic-speaking districts of the west. Clerks and teachers and housewives studied in their spare time. Gaelic is a difficult language, but they went to its mastery eagerly, and after the evening grammar classes were over there was much midnight talk about Ireland's future. Many a street-lamp in a quiet country town or Dublin street shed its light on a group of homeward-bound Gaelic Leaguers, lingering for a few minutes more to talk of plans and hopes. One of them nearly forty years later recalled those days of youthful enthusiasm: "We believed that if only Ireland's soul could be saved her body would somehow take care of itself."

The Gaelic Leaguers, laboring with the intricacies of grammar, had more concern than the mere speaking of another language, even though that language was rich and beautiful and enshrined in an ancient and unique literature. They studied the Irish language because it was bone of their bone and flesh of their flesh, because its growth had been the growth of the Irish nation, because it was part and parcel of the Irish nationality, which they had determined was not to be blotted out.

Fifty years before, Thomas Davis, of the Young Irelanders, had said, "It is time for the Irish people to learn the Irish language," and he had forecast for the Gaelic League its watchword: "The language which grows up with a people is conformed to their organs, descriptive of their climate, constitution, and manners, mingled inseparably with their history and their soil, fitted beyond any other language to express their prevalent thoughts in the most natural and efficient way.

"To impose another language on such a people is to send their history adrift among the accidents of translation, it is to tear their identity from all places, it is to substitute arbitrary signs for picturesque and suggestive names, it is to cut off the entail of feeling, and separate the people from their forefathers by a deep gulf, it is to corrupt their very organs, and abridge their power of expression.

"The language of a nation's youth is the only easy and full speech for its manhood and its age, and when the language of its cradle goes, itself desires a tomb."

The Gaelic League was not the only evidence of the vigor which filled Ireland at the turn of the century. The country was as full of energy as a boiling pot, Yeats said, and a vigorous country does not look upon its faults with complacence. Discontent stirred and found voice. Let us bring back some of the voices which express this discontent, voices which are significant for the trends they represent. Listen to Michael Davitt as he leaves Parliament forever: "For five years I have tried to appeal to the House of Commons on behalf of Ireland. I leave convinced that no just cause, no cause of right, will ever find support from this House of Commons unless it is backed up by force."

Listen to James Connolly, young Socialist Republican, as he speaks at the anti-Jubilee Celebration demonstration in Dublin: "During this glorious reign [of Victoria Regina] Ireland has seen a million and a quarter of her children die of famine, starved to death while produce of her soil and of their labor was eaten up by a vulture aristocracy, enforcing their rents by the bayonets of a hired assassin army in the pay of 'the best of the English queens,' the eviction of 3,668,000, a multitude greater than that of the entire population of Switzerland, and the reluctant emigration of 4,186,000 of our kindred, a greater host than the entire population of Greece. At the present moment 78% of our wage earners receive less than a pound a week, our streets are thronged with starving crowds of the unemployed, cattle graze on our tenantless farms and around the ruins of our battered homesteads, our ports are crowded with departing emigrants, and our workhouses are full of paupers."

Listen to Arthur Griffith, speaking editorially in his paper, *The United Irishman:* "There exists, has existed for centuries, and will continue to exist in Ireland, a conviction hostile to subjection, or dependence of the fortunes of this country to the necessity of any other; we intend to voice that conviction."

Davitt's voice was the voice of those who had lost faith in parliamentary measures, Connolly's voice was the voice of Labor, and Griffith was expounding the theories of the policy which came to be known as Sinn Fein. It was a policy of self-reliance for Ireland, a policy of passive resistance to English rule, of denial of the English claims to the right to rule Ireland.

Griffith was no militarist. When he had been in South Africa the Kaffirs had called him Cuguan, The Dove. He curbed Connolly's warlike ambition at the time of the war on the Transvaal Republics, and answered his declaration that "the people must become case-hardened to conflict," with the answer, "People do not become case-hardened to being dead. A succession of conflicts in which the people always get the worst of it will not strengthen their confidence in themselves. A tradition of abortive insurrections has already shaken their faith in physical force. The wolfdog must be ready, but he must be chained and concealed until the moment comes for slipping the leash."

The Irish Parliamentary party had not recovered the power it had lost at the time of the Parnell split. Even when the two factions which had stood for and against the old leader were reunited in 1900 under John Redmond, the party had neither the force it had had under Parnell nor the entire confidence of the Irish people. There was a feeling that the Irish members of Parliament were merely a section of the British Liberal party. Those who held this belief looked naturally elsewhere than to Westminster for a solution of Ireland's problems, and to many of them Sinn Fein seemed the answer. Its policy looked toward a self-contained and independent economic existence for Ireland, a policy which could be condensed into the Gaelic words "Sinn Fein," which some translated "We Ourselves," and others "Ourselves Alone." Sinn Fein as a political party was inaugurated in 1905.

Sinn Feiners claim that it was their growing power which revived the Home Rule question. At any rate, in 1910 John Redmond felt that there was again hope for a Home Rule bill to pass in Parliament. Asquith and Lloyd George needed the votes of Irish members to pass a bill curbing the House of Lords. That bill, supported by the members of the Irish Parliamentary party, became law in August of 1911, and a Home Rule bill for Ireland was offered to the House soon after.

It was a poor measure in itself, that Home Rule bill of 1911, but it evoked a mighty furor in England and in Ireland, and out of that furor was to come a change greater than anyone thought possible at the time.

Ulster had always met any suggestion of Home Rule with the phrase "Ulster will fight, and Ulster will be right." It had been coined by an English statesman, Lord Randolph Churchill, in Belfast Hall, when speaking against Home Rule in Parnell's day.

We have had little to say of Ulster since the Flight of the Earls bereft it of its princes, the O'Donnells, the O'Neills, and the Maguires. Their lands had been declared forfeit to the king, and parceled out "that many well-deserving servitors may be recompensed in the district without charge to his Majesty." And in addition to the large estates thus bestowed upon the king's high officers lesser folk had been planted in Ulster, too. It was from England that they received their land, and it was to England that they gave their grateful loyalty. They were Protestants, and it was traditional for them to look down upon Catholics. They did not merge with the proud and hardy native Irish who had survived the plantation. This suited England well. With a Protestant majority in Ulster remaining unassimilated, Ireland would always be divided, and so weaker and less formidable than an Ireland politically entire. "The worst of this," a Protestant archbishop of Armagh had said at the beginning of the eighteenth century, in speaking of some agitation about coinage, "the worst of this is that it tends to unite Protestant with Papist, and whenever that happens, good-bye to the English interest in Ireland forever."

One might hesitate to take a Catholic's explanation of the Protestant point of view. Fortunately, a Protestant's is available. "It is true to say," wrote Stephen Gwynn, "that Ulster Protestants have regarded Irish Catholics as a separate and inferior caste of Irishman. The belief has been ingrained in them that as Protestants they are morally and spiritually superior to those of the other religion. The whole political attitude is determined by this conviction. They refuse to come under a Dublin Parliament because in it they would be governed by a majority whom they regard as inferior. It is in their deliberate view natural that Roman Catholics should submit to be controlled by Protestants, unnatural that Protestants should submit to be controlled by Roman Catholics."

If this seems like exaggeration, one has only to turn for confirmation to an Anti-Home Rule bulletin, published by the Canon of St. Columba's Cathedral, of Londonderry. In it, the canon calls the men to whom the government of Ireland would be entrusted under Home Rule devils, tyrants, and blackguards, and a Catholic secret society which he assumed would rule Ireland "a sinister and murderous society." One hundred thousand copies of the bulletin had been sold by 1914.

At a conference of Unionist clubs and Orange lodges held at Belfast on September 25, 1911, the delegates passed a resolution embodying their fears that Home Rule would "inevitably lead to disaster to the Empire and absolute ruin to Ireland, the degradation of our citizenship in the United Empire, and the destruction of our material prosperity and of our civil and religious liberties."

Three days before these fears were expressed, the Duke of Abercorn, unable to be present at a great anti-Home Rule demonstration at Craigavon, had written a letter to be read at that meeting. Assuming, quite incorrectly, that Ireland was dependent upon England to the extent of five million pounds a year for the expenses of government, he pictured the terrible poverty which would result in Ulster if Ireland were left without imperial aid.

"The taxes will have to come from Ireland alone. Look for one minute at what will be the result. In the first place, the Home Rule government would tax Ulster to the uttermost degree." Employers could not keep up their establishments . . . Lower wages or a reduced number of employees would result. Wives and daughters would be forced into poor houses. "Misery and hunger and poverty would be their lot."

The Duke of Abercorn, useful as he was, was not the chief Unionist leader in the fight against Home Rule. The conduct of the campaign had been placed in the hands of an able Irish politician of Italian descent, Sir Edward Carson. He had been principal crown counsel under Arthur Balfour, that Balfour sent to Ireland to administer "twenty years of resolute government," and called Bloody by the Irish for the way he administered it by means of the strongest Coercion Act ever introduced into Parliament. Carson had entered the House of Commons in 1892, and his biographer says that Balfour was his "dear friend and patron."

It is said to be axiomatic with historians that they do not quote the statements of men in office. But sometimes the public utterances of public men are illuminating, whether they be based on honest conviction or expressed simply as a matter of political expediency. In a speech made in 1914, Sir Edward Carson said: "Proud as I am of being an Irishman, I was taught to look upon England as the great prototype of justice-loving, religion-loving, and in every respect a trusted nation, which in colonization brought all its great qualities to bear on securing the happiness of the people."

Following the Churchill tradition that "Ulster will fight," Carson set about forming an Ulster army. He hinted at war against the Empire, and the possibility of seeking German aid. He stated that a provisional government would be declared in Belfast the day Home Rule became a law. Colonel Hickman, a Unionist Member of Parliament, in a speech made at Wolverhampton, November 27, 1913, stressed the seriousness of purpose of the Ulster Volunteers. Said he: "You may be quite certain that these men are not going to fight with dummy muskets. They are going to use modern rifles and ammunition, and they are being taught to shoot. I know, because I buy the rifles myself."

In March of 1914 some of the officers of British regiments quartered at the Curragh of Kildare threatened to resign if ordered to Ulster, and possible duty against the Ulster Volunteers. Mr. Bonar Law, in the House of Commons, declared that "The House knows that we on this [the Tory] side have, from the very first, held the view that to coerce Ulster is an operation which no government, under existing conditions, has a right to ask the army to undertake. And in our view, of course, it is not necessary to say it, any officer who refuses is only fulfilling his duty."

Brigadier-General Gough, in the *Daily Telegraph* for March twenty-fifth, reported: "I got a signed guarantee that under no circumstances shall we be used to force Home Rule on the Ulster people. If it came to civil war, I would fight for Ulster rather than against her."

While these activities had been going on in the north of Ireland, in the south the people who were opposed to English rule rather than in favor of it had not been idle.

The Gaelic League had never had political aspirations. William Butler Yeats and his colleagues were concerned with literature and drama, and not in firing the Irish people with desire for freedom from England. Even the keen and kindly AE, expounding his views on the aims of a national literature, had not wanted to make rebels of Irishmen in a military sense.

But in studying Gaelic the students of the language felt

themselves inheritors of brave old traditions. No one could see or read Yeats's "Kathleen ni Houlihan," with its tall woman of the queenly walk symbolizing Ireland, and not feel a divine wind fanning the embers of patriotism, and all AE's beautiful prose, pacific though its composer was, led inevitably to the conclusion that to fulfill her own destiny Ireland must be free.

For how could the future AE envisioned be attained, and Ireland England's vassal still? Would England give the Irish people the liberty of shaping their own social order to reflect their own ideals, and to embody the national soul which had been slowly incarnating in the Irish race from its dawn in the cloudy ages before Christ? "To reveal Ireland in clear and beautiful light," AE had written in *Nationalism and Cosmopolitanism in Literature*, "to create the Ireland in the heart, [which is the Ireland that kindles enthusiasms, and for which Irishmen work and make sacrifices] is the province of a national literature. Other arts would add to this ideal, thereafter, and social life and politics must in the end be in harmony." Could this be done in Ireland under the English rule?

There were those who did not think so. They were not many compared with the great mass of the Irish people, but in matters of the spirit mere numbers do not count. Ireland has always bred her precious few who know that freedom is a holy thing, and who have been glad to give their lives in the struggle to attain it. They have carried in their hearts the seeds of fire, and from small buds of flame have blossomed mighty things. Against them the laws of empire are of no avail, and the armies of great nations cannot overcome them, for when they gird themselves for battle they triumph even in defeat.

Seventeen years of servitude in an English prison for his national activities had not dampened the Fenian faith of Thomas Clarke. Quiet, patient, still hopeful that a chance would be given to Ireland to strike for her freedom in his lifetime, he had come back to Dublin from prison and exile, and was the chief figure in Irish plans and hopes for independence in the first decade of the new century. With Sean MacDiarmada and other members of the Irish Republican Brotherhood, he had founded a newspaper. *Irish Freedom* it was called, and it voiced the philosophy that Ireland was entitled to complete freedom, that the government best suited to Ireland was a republic, and that the best method of securing that form of government was by armed revolution. Every editorial it printed was aimed toward the achieving of that end. "There is need in Ireland," it said in its first issue, November, 1910, "a great need that our nationality shall become a more intense and a more consuming thing, a faith to be lived for, to be followed in adversity as in prosperity, without hope of gain or reward for ourselves. We shall endeavor in *Irish Freedom* to revive and rekindle that faith. With that faith animating our people, national independence is not only possible, but even easy of achievement."

Not at all opposed to the separationist ideals of Clarke and MacDiarmada was James Connolly, the same Connolly who had cried out against celebrating in Ireland the Jubilee of Queen Victoria. But his projected program for Ireland went a step further than separation. "If you could remove the English army tomorrow, and hoist the green flag over Dublin Castle, unless you set about the organization of the Socialist Republic, your efforts will be in vain," he had written in 1897, and he never changed his mind. He knew poverty himself, and all his life he worked to improve the conditions of the laboring people of Ireland. The country as distinct from its people was nothing to him, and he had words of scathing sarcasm for people who "bubbled with love and affection for their country," but could pass unmoved through streets whose poverty was bitter and degrading.

He was editor of the *Workers' Republic*, and in its columns was found repeated day after day his conviction that English rule and the freedom and prosperity of the Irish people could not exist in Ireland at the same time.

To Padraig Pearse, Ireland must be not free merely, but Gaelic: and not Gaelic merely, but free. To him, as to O'Donovan Rossa, whom he admired and praised, the Gael and the Gaelic ways were splendid and holy, worthy of all homage and service. Pearse had known Gaelic from his early childhood. It had been taught him by a great-aunt, and from her he learned also of old rebellions, and was taught songs which immortalized the Fenians of the sixties, and were "musical with the names of O'Donovan Rossa and Hawk of the Hill." The old heroes of the Gael were his early heroes, and at St. Enda's, the school he founded to teach the youth of Ireland as it had been taught in the days of the Red Branch knights, the mural of Cuchulain which adorned the walls of the dining hall was a constant, silent admonition to remember old Gaelic ideals. "I care not if my life has only the span of a day and a night, if only my deeds be spoken of by the men of Ireland," ran the legend under the mural.

A grave and gentle man was Padraig Pearse, gentle with the restrained and controlled power of greatness, and grave from the realization that he had a part to play in Ireland which would lead inevitably to his death. He was so sure that Ireland must be freed. If she would not herself seek freedom, he must drive her to it.

He saw two ways of righting wrong: reform and revolution. Reform he knew to be possible only when those who inflict the wrong can be got to see things from the point of view of those who are wronged.

He prepared for revolution. In the unfinished story of his life, which he has left behind, he confesses that sometimes in the midst of military plans and organizations he found himself suddenly recalling bright images of his youth—that he watched himself as a child come out of a certain green gate into a certain sunlit field. One understands why he did so. The small hedged fields of Ireland hold peace itself on a sunny day, and Pearse was a poet who forced himself to be a man of action.

Two things constantly pulled at cross-purposes in him: one, the "desire beyond words to be at home always with beloved faces and familiar shapes and sounds," about him; the other, "the impulse to seek hard things to do, to go on far quests and fight for lost causes."

He fought for Ireland because he loved her, and because for him patriotism was at once a faith and a service. Not for him to say, "I believe," and not be able to add, "I serve."

When Carson was arming Ulster, and threatening to use the Ulster Volunteers against the rest of Ireland if Home Rule were passed, Pearse was saying that even if Home Rule came, there would remain still the substantial task of achieving the Irish nation. "I do not think it is going to be achieved without stress and trial," he said in November of 1913, "without suffering and bloodshed; at any rate it is not to be achieved without work. Our business here and now is to get ourselves into harness for such work as has to be done."

He was glad, he said, that the North had armed. It was a goodly thing to see arms in Irish hands. "We must accustom ourselves to the thought of arms, to the sight of arms, to the use of arms. Bloodshed is a cleansing and a sanctifying thing, and the nation which regards it as the final horror has lost its manhood. There are many things more horrible than bloodshed, and slavery is one of them."

When it was announced that a meeting would be held on November 25, 1913, at the Rotunda Rink in Dublin to start a volunteer organization for Nationalist Ireland, seven thousand people surged through the doors of the hall, and as many more crowded the streets outside. The Irish Volunteers enrolled people of all parties, Sinn Feiners, Parliamentarians, Gaelic Leaguers. They all subscribed to the policy expounded in the manifesto issued by the new organization: "At a time when legislative proposals universally confessed to be of vital concern to the future of Ireland are being put forward, and are awaiting decision, a plan has been deliberately adopted by one of the great English political parties, advocated by the leaders of that party and by its numerous organs in the press, and brought systematically to bear on public opinion, to make the display of military force and the menace of armed violence the determining factor in the future relations between this country and Great Britain. If we fail to take such measures as will effectually defeat this policy we become politically the most degraded population in Europe, and no longer worthy of the name of Nation . . . Such is the occasion, not altogether unfortunate, which has brought about the inception of the Irish Volunteer movement."

The manifesto was signed by Professor Eoin MacNeill, who had been chosen chief of staff of the new organization. Chosen by whom? By the members of that spontaneous meeting which had inaugurated the movement, thought the general public. They were only partly right. MacNeill had, earlier that fall, suggested the forming of national volunteers to safeguard the rights of Irishmen against the menace of Carson's activities. He was a quiet, scholarly man, one of the greatest authorities in the world on early Irish history and laws. No organization under his chairmanship would arouse the suspicions of the British government.

But MacNeill's selection had also been determined on before the Rotunda meeting was held, and determined on by a body of men who would have been instantly suspect by the government. They were the members of the Supreme Council of the Irish Republican Brotherhood, that organization called the Fenians in the sixties, and which most people thought out of existence long ago. But the IRB had never died. P. S. O'Hegarty, who was a member of the Supreme Council for six years, from 1908 till he was deported from Ireland in August of 1914, tells how the organization did its work: "It had members everywhere, its tentacles went into everything; it maintained a footing in every organization and movement in Ireland which could be supported without doing violence to separatist principles. And when money was needed at a pinch for any of the organizations which it regarded as key organizations— the Gaelic League, Sinn Fein, the Gaelic Athletic Association, the Fianna, and the Irish Volunteers—it found the money. Strange and transient Committies and Societies were constantly cropping up, doing this or that specific national work. The IRB formed them. The IRB ran them. The IRB provided the money. The IRB dissolved them when their work was done. The major portion of its funds, without which the home organization would have been helpless because of its paucity of numbers and poverty of its members, came from the Clan na Gael of America, which played the same part in Irish-American organizations that the IRB played at home, and to which no appeal for money for an object even remotely separatist was ever made in vain. . . .

"That was how the Irish Volunteers came to be started. Before ever there had been so much as a public whisper of a Volunteer force the Council had discussed it. It decided that any such force started by physical-force men or by advanced nationalists would be suppressed, but it felt also that the Ulster force made it difficult to suppress a Southern force which would be sponsored by unsuspectable people. And that is how Eoin MacNeill and Larry Kettle and other unsuspectable people started the Irish Volunteers. They thought they were acting on impulse, and they were acting on suggestion. Everything they did, then and thereafter, was supervised. Tom Clarke, standing behind his counter [of his little shop on Parnell Street] on the night the Irish Volunteers was launched, could smile and go home happy. The cheers, the overflow meeting, the nonsuppression, were meat and drink to him. He had been one of the strongest of us in wishing that no desire on our part to get in on the movement should be allowed to jeopardize it."

Padraig Pearse spoke at that meeting. He was on the governing body of the Volunteers, who within a week had fifteen companies drilling in Dublin. He was one of those who decided definitely that the Volunteers should, if the opportunity ever arose, strike for Irish freedom. He would not have them unprepared. So, while he wore an academic gown in the daytime, concerned himself with educational problems, and was called "The Head," by the teachers and pupils of the two schools he had founded, in the evenings he wore uniform, and administered military matters.

In both roles he had two able assistants. One was William Pearse, two years his junior, sculptor, and teacher of art at St. Enda's, whose love for his brother was so great that he was content to live and die in Padraig's shadow. The other, no less devoted, was Thomas MacDonagh, another teacher of the school. Beside the tall, grave figure of Padraig Pearse there often moved the small, gay soldier-poet. He was always so wordy, always so ready to argue about anything and everything, that one forgets that it was Thomas MacDonagh who left behind him one of the most beautiful sentences of Anglo-Irish literature. It is found in his book, *Literature in Ireland*. "To us, as to the ancient Irish poets, the half-said thing is dearest," he wrote, and in spite of his own loquacity on frivolous topics, it is quite true. He was versed in the literatures of many languages, and his book on the English poet Campion is recognized as an authority.

One mentions these things here because when Thomas MacDonagh and Padraig Pearse and the other leaders of the rebellion of Easter week of 1916 were holding Dublin by force of arms, news accounts concerning it sent out from England to the rest of the world said that the rising was an inconsequential one, hatched in the cellars of Dublin, and an editorial in *The New York Times* spoke of "the weak character and blind folly of the leaders."

How the Countess Markiewicz would have laughed if

she had seen those notices. Anglo-Irish aristocrat by birth,
Polish countess by marriage, Irish patriot by inclination,
she had formed the young boys of Ireland into an organization called the Fianna, after the tall warriors of Cormac
Mac Art's time, to train them mentally to achieve the independence of Ireland. "Madame," they called her, and when
she moved into battle with all the militant spirit of another
Queen Maeve, there wasn't a boy who wouldn't have risked
death to be with her, and many of them did.

The English had let the Ulster Volunteers arm, and had
done nothing about it. Before the Irish Volunteers were
two weeks old the importation of arms into Ireland was
forbidden. On April 24, 1914, more arms were landed a
Larne in Ulster for the Ulster Volunteers, and no one was
brought to account.

On Sunday, July 26, a little yacht came sailing into the
harbor of Howth, a few miles north of Dublin, with a
woman in a red skirt standing near the helm. As the little
craft moved gracefully up to the end of the long pier a
brigade of Volunteers went marching out to meet it. "There
was beauty in their movements, and amazing beauty in
their extreme punctuality," said a man who had been
concerned in loading a cargo on that yacht, and who was
anxious about its unloading. It went off well. While the
harbor master, under arrest by a Volunteer officer, fumed
futilely, the first arms to come to Nationalist Ireland since
the Fenian risings of the sixties were handed up to the
waiting Volunteers. There were tears in men's eyes as they
worked, and no man passed a rifle down the line until his
own was safely under his foot.

The rifles reached their ultimate destination safely, but
the King's Own Scottish Borderers, who had been marched

out of Dublin in an effort to disarm the Volunteers, marched unsuccessfully back again to meet the jeers of a Dublin crowd. At Bachelor's Walk the regiment halted, and fired without warning on that civilian gathering, killing four and wounding thirty-eight others.

Within a week England was at war. Tell us, England, what will you do about Ireland now? You need peace in Ireland now. You need Irishmen to fight in your army.

"Oh, we'll pass the Home Rule bill quickly," says England. "We'll put it on the Statute Book. We'll say it's there for all to see. But (lean near me while I whisper this discreetly) we'll pass a suspensory bill, too, that nullifies the law. We'll promise the Unionists to alter the bill to make it acceptable to them before it's put into operation. We'll say that the coercion of Ulster would be an unthinkable thing."

What will you do now, John Redmond, leader of the Irish party in Parliament, what will you do now? Many of the Irish people still trust you, though there are some who think you care more for the Empire than you do for Ireland. The majority of the Irish people are asking for their freedom. Will you be true to your trust? Will you get it for them?

"Oh, John Bull's a jolly old sort," says John Redmond. "I'll just go recruiting for his army."

Redmond found that he could not deliver all the recruits he had counted on. He had not approved of the forming of the Irish Volunteers, but when they had become a force to be reckoned with he had induced them to let him have a controlling voice on the governing body. Under his patronage the Volunteers had grown amazingly, and numbered a hundred and fifty thousand men or more by August of '14. With a lavish gesture Redmond presented these to England; England could remove all her regiments from Ireland, he said, and the Volunteers would guard the Irish shores.

England had other ideas, and she turned the offer down. It better suited her plans to have Irish Volunteers in France, and English troops in Ireland. But less than twenty thousand of the Volunteers responded to Redmond's recruiting pleas, and his power began to suffer for making them. The support of the New York *Irish World*, which had been financial as well as political, was withdrawn, Redmond lost the backing of the Ancient Order of Hibernians, and was denounced bitterly by nationalist papers in America and Ireland. The original founders of the Volunteers disclaimed the right of Redmond to make promises for the Volunteers, and led off a minority hotly opposed to his imperialistic views. In their opinion, it was the duty of Irishmen, and especially of Irish Volunteers, to remain in Ireland. MacNeill was henceforth chief of staff of the Irish, and Redmond of the National, Volunteers.

Undoubtedly, John Redmond was a sincere and honest man. But he had been out of touch with his country for years, and he did not know the Ireland that had been growing up while he had been in London. He was leading a party of old men, and young men with ideals differing from his own were taking charge in Ireland. They were not impressed with the speeches of English statesmen such as Asquith, that "this is a war for the Emancipation of the smaller states," and Winston Churchill, that "England wants to settle the map of Europe on national lines, and according to the true wishes of the people who dwell in the disputed areas." These Irishmen knew only too well that such fine words were meant for foreign consumption, and did not apply to Ireland.

While England spoke optimistically through Lord Grey, calling Ireland the "one bright spot," and Asquith praised Redmond for his recruiting activities, *Irish Freedom* was asking why Irishmen should fight for England? "Is it in gratitude for the priest-hunters and the rack of the Penal days, the gibbet, the pitch-cap, the half-hangings and all the horrors of '98? Is it in gratitude for the Famine, when a million of our people were slowly starved to death, and Christian England thanking God that the Celts were going, going with a vengeance? Is it in gratitude for the blazing homesteads and the people half-naked and starved to death by the roadside?"

Such pointed questions hindered recruiting, though Ireland in the end lost more men in the Great War than Belgium did. *Irish Freedom*, as well as all Republican, Sinn Fein, and labor papers, was suppressed three months after the war began, and the *Gaelic American* and the *Irish World* were refused circulation in Ireland. But stray pamphlets still appeared which voiced the antirecruiting sentiment. One went straight to the heart of the whole matter. "No rainbow chasing for us out in Belgium, or Gallipoli, while the chains bind and fetter our own dark Rosaleen."

The war was hardly well started when the Supreme Council of the Irish Republican Brotherhood held a meeting and came to a grave decision. It was that their organization would strike a blow for Irish freedom before the war was over. At the close of the Boer War Salisbury had taunted Ireland with the fact that England had been able to hold Ireland "with a handful of cripples," while she was fighting in South Africa, and that Ireland had not risen to take her

liberty. Now the successors of men who had been willing
to fight a mighty empire armed with homemade pikes
decided that Ireland's honor would be stained if this opportunity passed and Ireland remained quiet.

There was, for them, no question of loyalty for England.
England had never held Ireland on such terms. She had
held her with cruel and oppressive laws, she had held her
with troops, but she had not held her on terms which made
love and respect possible, and it is only from love and respect that loyalty is evoked.

The element of English civilization which likes to speak
of fair play and a sporting chance was to decry the rebellion
which the IRB now decided on as a stab in the back, and as
taking a most unfair advantage of England's preoccupation
in France. The criticism brought forth a letter in the *Daily
News* from George Bernard Shaw. "Until Dublin Castle is
superseded by a National Parliament, and Ireland volun-
tarily incorporated with the British Empire, as Canada,
Australasia and South Africa have been incorporated, an
Irishman resorting to arms to achieve the independence of
his country is doing only what Englishmen will do if it be
their misfortune to be invaded and conquered by the Germans in the course of the present war. Furthermore, such
an Irishman is as much in order morally in accepting
assistance from the Germans, in his struggle with England,
as England is in accepting the assistance of Russia in her
struggle with Germany . . . I remain an Irishman, and
I am bound to contradict any implication that I can regard
as a traitor any Irishman, taken in a fight for Irish independence against the British Government, which was a
fair fight in everything except the enormous odds my
countrymen had to face."

It is true that the Rising, if its military phase only is viewed in retrospect, seems a gallant, futile thing. It is true, too, that the leaders of that Rising were of the discerning few who knew that without it Ireland's soul would perish, and the country sink into slavery. And it is also true that from the first they worked and planned and hoped to make it a success.

The detailed story of those plans is written elsewhere. Here one can only say that through the Military Council of the Irish Republican Brotherhood that body devised a scheme of remote control of the Irish Volunteers. Their Military Councils were almost interlocking, and the IRB men saw to it that their colleagues held all possible posts and commands in the Volunteers. Needless to say, there were many IRB men in the ranks. But the IRB men did not, and could not, have complete control. MacNeill as chief of staff of the Volunteers was their concession to Dublin Castle, a symbol of academic deliberation and coolheadedness to divert suspicion from the corps.

Without his knowledge, and the knowledge of his colleagues who wished to limit Volunteer activities to defense tactics, the Republicans planned a rising.

They had the help of James Connolly and his Irish Citizen Army. It was a body small in size, but invincible in valor, and it symbolized the social discontent of the Dublin working classes. When the Dublin Metropolitan Police had batoned spectators, parading workers, and band instruments alike during the Great Transport Workers strike of 1913, Union leaders had learned to send out men armed with hurleys to guard the pipes and drums, and from this beginning had grown the ICA, trained and drilled by an ex-officer of the British Army, Captain Jack White.

Connolly for years had been urging the necessity for breaking away from English rule. He held it the first requisite for the free development of the national powers needed for the bettering of the laboring classes. If he did not look on Germany as a possible ally, at least he did not look on her as an enemy. For him, Ireland had but one enemy—the country which held her in subjection.

He was as determined as the IRB not to let the war pass without making an attempt to set Ireland free. He preached the necessity for that in the columns of many papers, including his own *Workers' Republic*. As the war progressed, and the people as a whole did not move toward insurrection, he saw the necessity as only more urgent. "Deep in the heart of Ireland has sunk the degradation wrought upon its people—our lost brothers and sisters—so deep and humiliating that no agency less potent than the red tide of war on Irish soil will ever be able to enable the Irish race to recover its lost self-respect or establish its national dignity in the face of a world horrified and scandalized by what must seem to them our national apostasy. Without the slightest trace of irreverence, but in all humility, that of us as of mankind before Calvary, it may be truly said, 'without the shedding of blood there is no redemption.'"

And Pearse held the same belief. What was peace, unless it was the peace of freedom? "Ireland will not find Christ's peace until she has taken Christ's sword," he warned. "What peace she has known these latter days has been the devil's peace, peace with sin, peace with dishonor. It is a foul thing, dear only to men of foul breeds."

As Pearse wrote these words, in December of 1915, the IRB was deciding that it must strike soon if it was to strike at all. There was always the danger that the Volunteers would be disarmed, and that the government would imprison the men who were to be the leaders of the Rising. In the Defense of the Realm Act, England had an instrument of inquisition and persecution which she used constantly against Ireland. Men of known nationalist sympathies were deported from Ireland from the fall of 1914 on. Men, women, and boys were arrested, and many were held without trial. There were in custody men against whom the government had no charge except that they had spoken Irish.

It was only natural that Connolly's warnings to the people that they must rise were also warnings to the government that it must suppress Connolly and all who held his views.

These are little dangers, Ireland, but you face a greater one. Pearse and Connolly have spoken truly. England holds you to your dishonor. Your body is used for England's pleasure, and for England's need. For your soul's sake you must strike against her. You must make some move to show that you are not complaisant. Will you rise from apathy? Will you heed the voices of your prophets? There is more than victory of arms to be decided as men march out on a bright spring morning. These men risk something more than death, but they risk it bravely, knowing that even in apparent defeat they may arouse you to action as a nation. They risk it gladly, hoping that the sacrifice of their blood, devoutly made, will not be without reward. They risk it confidently, believing that you will prove yourself worthy.

They risk it gravely, too, for all has not gone well with their plans. The Rising had at first been set for Easter Sunday of 1916. Word had gone to America, and arms and ammunition, but no money, were asked from Germany.

But a slight change of date had been decided on later. On Easter Monday many British officers stationed in Dublin would leave town to attend the Fairyhouse Races. It seemed a better day to strike. But now the arms which had been looked for at dawn of Easter Saturday must not arrive before Easter Sunday night. Word of that change of plan reached Germany too late. The *Aud*, with its cargo of twenty thousand rifles, had already left Germany, and she had no radio on board. She expected lights on the Irish coast near Tralee to signal her, and a pilot boat to meet her at the entrance of Tralee Bay. After a hazardous ten-day cruise through enemy water she reached her rendezvous on the afternoon of April 20. No lights signaled her that night. No pilot boat appeared. But next day English patrol boats came to question her, and presently the *Aud* was surrounded by English men-of-war. The *Bluebird* put a shot across her bow, and ordered the *Aud* to follow her to port. Rather than submit to capture the captain of the munitions ship set time-bombs in the hold, and ordered his crew to take to the boats.

More disaster followed. The Volunteer authorities, not knowing that it had been impossible to inform the captain of the *Aud* of the postponed date for landing arms, counted on receiving them Sunday night. The men ordered from Dublin to meet the *Aud*, and superintend the unloading and distribution of its arms, were traveling to the Kerry coast by car. At Ballykissane their driver made a wrong turning in the dark and drove off a pier-end. The news of the drowning of the passengers of the car reached Dublin at about the same time as the news of the blowing up of the munitions ship, and of the capture of Sir Roger Casement. He had followed the arms from Germany in a submarine, for the purpose of warning the leaders of the Rising that Germany was sending no men, and no officers to lead the Volunteers. He was not aware that the Volunteers were not depending on such aid.

It was only the week before Easter that Eoin MacNeill learned that the mobilization orders which had been issued to the Volunteers over Pearse's signature for Easter Sunday really masked plans for an armed insurrection. He went at once to Pearse's house, and warned him that he would do everything in his power to prevent the Rising, short of giving information to the government. Constitutionally, he was within his rights in doing so, as he was, in fact, the Volunteers' chief of staff. But the matter had now gone beyond a point when it could be stopped by a mere technicality, and Pearse undoubtedly felt that the wishes of the Volunteers were for a Rising rather than against it.

MacNeill followed his warning with actions. That they were wavering, influenced by conflicting counsel, and sometimes contradictory only made matters worse. Readers saw in the *Sunday Independent* an announcement signed by MacNeill rescinding all orders given to the Volunteers for Easter day. Volunteer headquarters throughout the country received by couriers orders confirming the countermanding order, and warning the Volunteers not to rise.

But six men ready to stake their lives on the righteousness of a Rising, and the necessity for it even in the face of overwhelming odds, met in Liberty Hall in Dublin on Easter Sunday morning. It was not possible for Thomas Clarke, who presided at that meeting, to face the prospect of turning back. For seventeen years of English prison life he had kept before him the hope of striking a blow for Irish freedom. For as many more in America and Ireland he had worked to bring the chance about. He knew it would never come again. Not in his lifetime; perhaps not in many years thereafter.

Sean MacDiarmada would not turn back. "In his steady eyes and delicate features a spirit shone that looked beyond all ruin, giving him an intense beauty, a beauty born of discipline and vision, clear and of compelling charm, like a flame shining in a slight crystal-like lanthorn of a body," a friend had written of him. He looked beyond all ruin now, and saw Ireland redeemed by the effort which seemed so hopeless to outsiders.

Proud Eamonn Ceannt would not turn back, nor Thomas MacDonagh, whose gaiety was a mask. Certainly Padraig Pearse would not turn back. Had he not looked forward to this day, and prepared himself for sacrifice? "There are in every generation those who shrink from the ultimate sacrifice, but there are in every generation those who make it with joy and laughter," he had written. And James Connolly, impatient for action, would lead them all, or gladly go alone.

When Joseph Plunkett, poet friend of Thomas MacDonagh, heard of the decision of the members of the Military Council he left the nursing home where he was convalescing from an operation and joined them, as determined as they were to go ahead with their plans. It was the unanimous decision of these seven men that they would lead the Volunteers and the ICA into battle against England, following all civilized rules of war. Orders went out that night to mobilize Monday morning.

In Dublin less than a thousand men answered the call. Many of the special orders MacDonagh had sent to the Dublin battalions had not reached their destinations in time, and the Volunteers for whom they were intended obeyed MacNeill's countermanding order. Between seven and eight hundred Volunteers appeared, a hundred and eighteen of Connolly's ICA, and an unexpected dozen men from the Hibernian Rifles.

Through the carefree atmosphere of bank-holidaying Dublin these men went to take up posts which had been determined in advance: railway stations, strategic buildings, bridges, and barracks. Up Abbey Street from Liberty Hall marched Connolly and Pearse with units of their two forces, now united as the Irish Republican Army. They seized the General Post Office on O'Connell Street, and prepared it for military occupation.

At noon a tall man in uniform, holding a paper in his hand, appeared at the main doorway. Only mildly curious were the holiday crowds as he stopped at the head of the steps, and two other men came to stand beside him. For a moment Pearse and Clarke and Connolly stood there silently, looking down at the people in the street. Perhaps it was the realization of the tremendous odds they were facing which made Pearse's voice, usually so compelling and charged with magnetism, for once flat and thin as he began to read from the paper he held in his hand.

It declared the right of the people of Ireland to the ownership of Ireland, and the unfettered control of Irish destinies to be sovereign and indefeasible. Standing on that fundamental right and again asserting it in arms in the face of the world, the Irish Republic was proclaimed as a sovereign independent state. "And we pledge our lives and the lives of our comrades-in-arms to the cause of its freedom, of its welfare, and of its exaltation among the nations . . . The Republic guarantees religious and civil liberty, equal rights and equal opportunities to all its citizens, and declares its resolve to pursue the happiness and prosperity of the whole nation and of all its parts, cherishing all the children of the nation equally, and oblivious of the differences, carefully fostered by an alien government, which have divided a minority from the majority in the past . . . In this supreme hour the Irish nation must, by its valor and discipline, and by the readiness of its children to sacrifice themselves for the common good, prove itself worthy of the august destiny to which it is called.''

When the reading had ceased, and the three men had gone back into the Post Office, others came out with pots and brushes, and pasted up posters proclaiming the Republic. They were signed in this manner:

Thomas J. Clarke

Sean MacDiarmada	Thomas MacDonagh
P. H. Pearse	Eamonn Ceannt
James Connolly	Joseph Plunkett

There was little fighting that day, though skirmishes at Stephen's Green, the North Wall, and at the Castle showed the people that an insurrection had really begun. Barricades began to appear in the streets, telegraph wires were cut by the insurgents, and communications were established between the Republican posts. But the telephone exchange had not been taken, and from it messages went out ordering military reinforcements to Dublin.

On Tuesday, Trinity College, in the center of the city, established by Elizabeth "principally for breeding upp the natives of that kingdom in civility, learning and religion,'' after she had suppressed to the best of her ability all Irish civility, learning, and religion, became in fact what it had long been figuratively, an English fort. It was manned as a British garrison by students of the Officers' Training Corps, and then taken over by the military themselves. From its impregnable walls the British established posts to Dublin Castle and on to Kingsbridge Station, thus cutting the Republican forces in two.

On Wednesday field guns went out from Trinity to demolish Liberty Hall, and a gunboat on the Liffey opened fire on the city. Buildings crumbled under its attack, and incendiary shells set the ruins on fire. The upper story of the Post Office was wrecked. In the evening a battalion of Sherwood Foresters reached Kingstown Harbour from England. As one column marched toward Dublin by the Ballsbridge road they met fierce resistance by Eamon De Valera's Third Battalion of Irish Volunteers.

All this time the Post Office had been the center of attack by machine guns, snipers, and artillery. James Connolly was wounded there on Thursday, but continued to superintend the defense of the building. Friday morning the upper story was in flames.

From the first day, men in the ranks at the Post Office had known that the situation was hopeless. One of the older boys from St. Enda's who was a member of the Volunteers lived through all the perils of that week, and the time of executions which followed, to tell of the feelings of the men there. "We were frightened the first day," he said, "but after that we got used to being fired on. But we knew it was no use, except when Pearse was talking to us. For half an hour after he'd been around we'd believe we could do anything."

Friday it was seen that the Post Office would have to be evacuated. It was almost all in flames. Pearse and Connolly decided to try to get their men to Parnell Street, and establish communications with the Republican forces in the Four Courts. They did not know how thoroughly all surrounding streets were covered by machine-gun fire, nor that communication with the Four Courts was impossible. A retreat under fire was made as far as 16 Moore Street, and headquarters established there. Seventeen casualties were suffered on the way.

The flames of burning Dublin that night lighted a city as war-wrecked in portions as any in France. General Sir John Maxwell had arrived from England that morning and taken supreme command of the British forces. "If necessary I shall not hesitate to destroy all buildings within any area occupied by the rebels," he declared, and O'Connell Street in the vicinity of the Post Office he laid in ruins.

It was evident that the Republican Army was defeated. On Tuesday, Pearse, as commandant in chief of the forces of the Irish Republic, and president of the provisional government, had issued a proclamation calling on "all citizens of Dublin who believe in the right of their country to be free" to give their allegiance and their loyal help to the Republic. The call had not been answered. Saturday morning the leaders from the Post Office held a meeting around Connolly's stretcher, and decided to surrender.

At half past three on Saturday Pearse surrendered his sword to Brigadier General Lowe in Parnell Street. He sent instructions to commandants of other commands: "In order to prevent the further slaughter of Dublin citizens, and in the hope of saving the lives of our followers now surrounded and hopelessly outnumbered, the members of the Provisional Government present at Headquarters have agreed to an unconditional surrender, and the Commandants of the various districts in the city and country will order their commands to lay down arms."

Some did not want to do so. MacDonagh would not, until he had seen Pearse, a prisoner in Richmond Barracks. De Valera's position was so secure that his men could hardly be persuaded to ground their arms. Commandant Brennan's men of County Wexford, one of the few county units to rise, had held the town of Enniscorthy in military occupation, and then had retreated in good order to historic Vinegar Hill. Not until two officers had been escorted to Dublin and seen Pearse himself would Commandant Brennan order his men to surrender. Galway under Liam Mellowes had been successful, too, and so had the Volunteers of Ashbourne. But the countermand order had had its effect elsewhere, and these small successes did not alter the fact that the Rising as a whole had been a failure.

General Sir John Maxwell did not believe in suppressing revolts of this kind by kid-glove methods. He said so in a letter to the *Daily Mail*. He proved it by the way he took command of the Irish situation. Martial law for Dublin. Arrest, imprisonment, sometimes deportation, for every person in Ireland suspected of Republican sympathies. For the leaders of the Rising, the seven men who had signed the proclamation proclaiming the Irish Republic, court-martial and death. Death, too, for nine other Republican leaders.

Pearse and MacDonagh and Clarke were the first to be shot. On the evening of May 3 a brief official announcement was made of their trial, sentence to death, and prompt execution. Joseph Plunkett was next. Day after day came news of other shootings. William Pearse . . . Sean MacDiarmada . . . Eamonn Ceannt . . . James Con-

nolly. Gravely ill and weak from his wounds, Connolly
was carried on a stretcher to his execution, and propped
up on a chair to face the firing squad. That was the way to
treat rebels in Ireland, thought Maxwell. He was a military
man, and this seemed to him a simple military matter. He
believed that by the execution of the leaders of the Rising,
and their burial in a common quicklime grave, he could
instill fear into the hearts of the Irish people, fear that
would keep them quiet, then and in the future.

But the May mornings that saw men led out into the
gray-walled yard of Kilmainham Gaol to face English
muskets saw a change come over the Irish people. Martyrs'
blood is fiery red. It does not dampen a nation's spirit, it
inflames it. That was what Clarke and Connolly had
known. That was what Pearse had counted on. As day
followed day, almost every one with its tale of a brave man
shot down by English bullets, the temper of the people
changed. The anger and disgust with which they had seen
Dublin shelled and burned subsided. Sympathy for men
who met death bravely gave birth to interest in the cause
for which they had died.

Gradually the Irish people began to understand the Rising. What had seemed a foolish flourish of arms which had
resulted in the wrecking of a city they saw to be a blow for
Ireland's pride and honor, an effort to free her from chains
she had almost come to kiss. Who would not be proud
and grateful for the sacrifice that saved them from such
indignity? After Sean MacDiarmada's memorial mass, the
congregation, coming down the steps of the Pro-Cathedral
at the back of battered O'Connell Street, heard for the
first time a song which sounded a keynote to which they
were only too eager to respond:

Who fears to speak of Easter Week,
Who dares its fate deplore?
The red-gold flame of Erin's name
Confronts the world once more!
So, Irishmen, remember then,
And raise your heads with pride,
For great men, and straight men
Have fought for you and died . . .

The storied page of this our age
Will save our land from shame;
The ancient foe had boasted low
That Irishmen were tame;
They'd bought their souls with paltry doles,
And told the world of slaves;
That lie, men, will die, men,
In Pearse and Plunkett's grave.

The seeds of fire were now well aglow. The flames which blossomed from them warmed and heartened the whole island. The bonds that had bound the nation's spirit were burned away, and Ireland's soul was free again.

A skylark, when it is released from captivity, will rise straight up and sing. The feeling of spiritual release and exaltation which now came welling up in Irish hearts found its most natural expression in song. Whom did the songs praise, but Ireland's new heroes? For AE, they turned life's water into wine. They "ribboned with gold the rags of this our life," for the Countess Markiewicz's sister. William Butler Yeats chanted of a glorious transformation, "A terrible beauty is born." The American Joyce Kilmer, chiding Yeats for an old poem which had lamented that romantic Ireland was dead and gone, and with O'Leary in the grave, spoke with exultant appreciation of the Easter sacrifice:

> *Romantic Ireland never dies:*
> *O'Leary lies in fertile ground,*
> *And songs and spears throughout the years*
> *Rise up where patriot graves are found . . .*

The English executed sixteen men for their part in the Easter Rising, including Sir Roger Casement, hanged in England for "treason without his Majesty's realm." "Sixteen Dead Men" was the subject of Dora Sigerson Shorter's song:

> Hark! in the still night. Who goes there? . . .

> Sixteen dead men! What on their sword?
> *'A nation's honor proud do they bear,'*
> What on their bent heads? *'God's holy word;*
> *All of their nation's heart blended in prayer.'*

> Sixteen dead men! What makes their shroud?
> *'All of their nation's love wraps them around.'*
> Where do their bodies lie, brave and so proud?
> *'Under the gallows-tree, in prison ground.'*

> Sixteen dead men! Where do they go?
> *'To join their regiment, where Sarsfield leads:*
> *Wolfe Tone and Emmet, too, well do they know.*
> *There they shall bivouac, telling great deeds.'*

> Sixteen dead men! Shall they return?
> *'Yea, they shall come again, breath of our breath.*

They on their nation's hearth made old fires burn.
Guard her unconquered soul, strong in their death.'

Long before all these poems were published England
began to see that something was wrong, that Maxwell had
made a bad mistake. Sir Cecil Spring-Rice, England's
ambassador to the United States, wrote home that it was
"most unfortunate that it has been found necessary to
execute the rebels." It lessened the possibility that England
could get American help in the war. "The attitude toward
England has been turned for the worse by recent events in
Ireland." He urged an immediate settlement of the Home
Rule question as "the announcement will have a most
beneficial effect here."

But even the astute Spring-Rice could not measure the
extent of Maxwell's mistake. The punishment of the Irish
rebels was more than a simple military matter. It was a
spiritual one, far beyond the comprehension of English
army officers or Foreign Office officials. How could those
earthly ones know that by their heroic deaths the dreams
of freedom of the Irish rebels would become the dreams of
the Irish people? Had they ever heard that "those who die,
in so far as they have imagined beauty or justice, are made
a part of beauty or justice, and move through the minds of
living men"? And if they had heard, would they have
understood the philosophy, or thought it pertinent?

Baffled and uncomprehending, the English knew only
that their methods of punishment in Ireland had all failed.
What good did it do to shoot rebels who died saying, "Our
blood will rebaptize and revitalize our land," and whose
prophecy came true? What good did it do to imprison men,
when they preached their patriotic beliefs to their fellow

prisoners, and made converts to the very cause the English were trying to suppress? What good did it do to try to discredit the Volunteers, when every day their hold in Irish hearts became stronger?

An Irishman returning to his country after the Rising found a remarkable change. "Political boundaries had disappeared, having been submerged by a rising tide of sympathy and indignation. The Irish Volunteers, instead of being a cause of division, had become a symbol of a new unity."

This new unity organized itself around the old Sinn Fein party, and gave it life and a new objective—the founding of an Irish Republic, or rather, the reaffirming of the Republic proclaimed by Pearse on the Post Office steps on Monday of Easter Week.

"The enthusiasms of the young was wonderful," Michael O'Flanagan wrote, "but the enthusiasm of the old was more wonderful still. To the young it was love's young dream. To the old it was the return of the prodigal son. To the great mass of the young it was the first time that they had got a glimpse of the royal face of Kathleen ni Houlihan. To the old their mother Erin, who had for the past forty years dressed in the rags of a beggar, had donned her queenly robes again. No longer would she bargain in a foreign parliament for crumbs of liberty; she would boldly stand before the world and demand a Nation's right."

As one election after another came along, Sinn Fein men were put up as candidates, and the Sinn Feiners won. De Valera was a stranger when he stood for a seat in a County Clare election, but he stood for the new national ideal, and he was elected by a significant majority. One verse of a street ballad, political propaganda though it was, is a fair index of the feeling of the time:

'Tis my grief that any Redmondite should show his face again,
With their jobbery and recruiting and their slanders on Sinn Fein.
Faith, we want no lying speech-makers, but men to fight and dare,
And the hero De Valera is the man for County Clare.

In December of 1918 came a General Election for England and Ireland. All Sinn Fein candidates were pledged to refrain from taking their seats in the British Parliament; they would, instead, form their own government in Ireland, and govern the country from Dublin. England realized the seriousness of the situation. She suppressed the entire Republican and Sinn Fein press, conducted raids on political headquarters, arrested Sinn Fein leaders and deported them without trial. Still, Republican Ireland triumphed at the polls, and elected seventy-three of a hundred and five candidates.

True to their word, the elected men stayed in Ireland, and met as Dail Eireann at the Dublin Mansion House, January 21, 1919. The proceedings were conducted in Irish. Only twenty-six deputies answered the roll as their names were called. "Under the lock of the enemy," was the explanation given by the secretary for the absence of thirty-five others.

Almost the first business of the Dail was to ratify, in the name of the Irish People, the establishment of the Irish Republic.

AFTERWORD

→>>≪←

THE *Manhattan* sailed for Hamburg, January 29, 1936, with Queenstown listed among its ports of call. Again the wind inside the harbor was cold and unwelcoming. Dark of night kept all sight of land from me, and the rain that came cutting through the winter air seemed the final discomfort which would alienate a weary, sleep-starved stranger.

But again, as it had ten years before, something called to me. Some mystic tie tugged at my heart. As I stepped from the tender, I felt no sense of strangeness, but something of the joy and exaltation the returning traveler knows on reaching home. The thin, gray or green silhouette that is all many Atlantic voyagers see of Ireland no longer hid a country strange and unknown, but one that had been the object of my study and research for some years.

Ten years before I had had no idea of the significance of the change of name from Queenstown to Cobh. The language revival of which it was a part had seemed to me a rather childish gesture of the Irish people. Now I knew it to be a vital factor in a government program whose aim was the de-Anglicizing of Ireland.

Ireland, it was true, was not a republic, but a country with two governments: Northern Ireland and Saorstat Eireann, in English the Irish Free State.

The Republic proclaimed by Pearse, and ratified by the elected representatives of seventy-five per cent of the Irish people in 1919 had not been able to maintain itself against English arms. As the members of Dail Eireann elected Eamon De Valera as their Executive, and began peaceably supplanting the alien government of the British with a *de facto* government of their own, they met English opposition which developed into an Anglo-Irish war. The treaty which concluded that war, a treaty forced on the Irish delegates to the Peace Conference by Lloyd George's threat of "immediate and terrible warfare" if it were not accepted within three hours without consulting the Irish government in Dublin, had partitioned the country. Six counties of the north, with large Protestant planter-stock population, were split off from the rest of Ireland to be governed by a separate Parliament under English supervision. In the south the remaining twenty-six counties made up the Irish Free-State.

"Free State" is not an exact rendering of the Gaelic word Saorstat, and the translation implies an independence which the terms of the treaty did not allow. The Irish Republic had recognized no authority other than its own. The Free State, under treaty terms, was to have something less than dominion status within the British Empire. Its officials were pledged to take an Oath of Allegiance to the English crown, a governor general was to represent the king, and certain air and harbor defenses in Ireland were retained under British control.

It was hardly to be expected that the Irish people would accept such terms as the final and complete settlement of all their hopes and efforts, especially considering the circumstances under which the peace delegates had signed the treaty. Called on to ratify or reject it, the members of Dail Eireann were not voting so much for or against the treaty as for or against a continuation of the Black and Tan terror they had known for two years. Civil war followed the ratification of the treaty by a small majority of Dail Eireann, and Ireland knew the bitterness of brother fighting brother, and comrade turning against old comrade. It is a chapter of Irish history which every Irishman regrets, and which no outsider, at present at least, should attempt to explain.

The winter sun rises very late in Ireland. As the boat train carried me toward Dublin through the sleeping countryside I had plenty of time to ponder on the differences I might find between the "Ireland of the heart," which I had been creating through my years of reading and research, and the actual, living Ireland of the present. Would I be disappointed? Would I find the country less beautiful, less inspiring, less devoted to its ideal of liberty than I had thought it?

The English government had been removed from Ireland for hardly fifteen years. For more than seven centuries the country had known foreign rule. It was too much to expect to find the country as thriving, and as articulate in its art, as one that had been allowed a natural national development. It was too much to expect a government policy exactly suited in all details to the needs of the country, or what government there was functioning perfectly in all departments. I knew that I must look below surface annoyances and discontents to find the real feelings of the Irish people. I knew that images are always blurred when viewed from short distances; that one must have perspective to see any picture clearly.

The ancient Ireland of the saints and of the great Celtic princes had been of almost equal vividness in my mind with the Ireland of more recent years. The feeling of another age still clings to many spots in Ireland, but I had to learn to assign the old Ireland to its proper place in the centuries. I had to learn to think of the Shannon less as the river which marked the boundary of the exile country into which Cromwell had forced the gentlefolk of Ireland in the seventeenth century than as the center of a great electrification project. I had to learn that the pride which the people of Clondalkin have in the old round tower which still stands in the center of the town, uncrumbled after a thousand years, is of one kind, and that the pride they have in their modern factories is of another. There is no truth, I was to find in that town, in the criticism that the Irish people live in the past, and have no thought for the future.

Sometimes, on the surface, the emphasis does seem to be on the past. One finds great eighteenth-century drawing rooms where the name of Parnell is still living and loved. But even there one meets the people who are working to make the new Ireland the rich and lovely country she can become by expressing herself artistically and by developing her own resources. The Ireland of tomorrow will be related to the Ireland of the past, and the artists and scholars and statesmen of Ireland who are doing the most for her are aware of that relationship.

Unhappily, there are those in Ireland to whom their racial inheritance means nothing, or who have bartered their loyalty to it for earthly things. "Voices of the dust," AE called them. I found them, speaking insistently and with English accents, within the walls of Trinity, in the Dail, at social gatherings of every sort. But their insistence, it soon became obvious, was that of weakness and wishfulness. Every day it became more and more apparent that in Ireland at the present, *quite aside from the divisions of party politics*, and ignoring for the moment the inevitable social and economic adjustments which face Ireland as well as many other countries, there are only two divisions of thought: that which wishes to maintain the imperial connection, and that which hopes ultimately for an independent Irish Republic; and of these the first is small and weakening, and the second large and ever increasing.

How could it be otherwise? The Irish and the English are two peoples. The Irish have never been and are not now reconciled to English rule. English statesmen have admitted that within twenty years. Sometimes from weariness and lack of hope Ireland gives up for a while the struggle to be free. But hope revives, and strength returns, and always the seeds of fire burn. Always the seeds of fire burn.

There are differences of opinion as to how the ultimate Republic may best be achieved, and as to how long it will take the country to reach the final goal. There are men who have substituted peaceful means in place of the force they once used as an instrument in securing it. But all these men remember the words of Pearse: that the national demand of Ireland is fixed and determined; that that demand has been made in every generation; that young generations receive it as a trust from their fathers; that they are bound by it; that they have not the right to alter or abate it by one jot or tittle; that any undertaking made in the name of Ireland to accept in full settlement of Ireland's claim anything less than the generations of Ireland have stood for is null and void, binding on Ireland by neither the law of God nor the law of nations.

Nationalist leaders in Ireland who weary of the struggle have other words of Pearse's to warn them of their fate if they are tempted to compromise with England: "Separation is the national position," said Pearse, and proved it from Irish history. "Whenever an Irish leader has taken up a position different from the national position he has been repudiated by the next generation. The United Irishmen repudiated Grattan. The Young Irelanders repudiated O'Connell, the Irish Volunteers repudiated Redmond."

Pearse's words are as true now as when he wrote them the Christmas before the Rising of 1916. On the walls of Kilmainham Gaol, where Robert Emmet waited for his death, where the English imprisoned O'Connell and Parnell in the days of their power, where Pearse and thirteen other martys of Easter Week were executed by the English, someone has painted in letters defiantly large the inevitable challenge: "WE SHALL RISE AGAIN . . . THE RE-PUBLIC TO VICTORY."

Those who love Ireland hope that her ultimate freedom may be gained without further shedding of blood. Such a hope is not impossible of fulfillment, though past events have shown that Ireland wins concessions from England painfully and dearly, and only when the yielding saves England from a greater loss. The Irish Volunteers of 1779 won Free Trade for Ireland by the menace of their cannon pointing at the Dublin Parliament. O'Connell won Emancipation for the Catholics because the English government knew it was not safe to withhold it. The country was on the verge of war. Gladstone disestablished the Church of Ireland because Fenian activities of the late sixties had shown him that something must be done to soothe the country. He considered the disestablishment of the Church a bargain. The Irish Free State was a compromise settlement for the Republic demanded by the elected representatives of the Irish people in 1919.

The great spiritual exaltation which began with the Easter Rising culminated in the Proclamation of the Irish Republic by Dail Eireann in 1919. The emotion was sustained during the ensuing two years of Anglo-Irish war, but was sapped by the strain and bitterness of the civil war which followed the announcement of the signing of the Peace Treaty. Still, bit by bit, the separation between England and Ireland is widened. The Oath of Allegiance was abolished in May, 1933, the Senate in May, 1936. By the Election of June, 1937 a new constitution was adopted for Ireland which became effective six months after the election. It drastically altered the country's legislative structure, and omitted all mention of a King or the British Commonwealth of Nations.

By the new constitution the territory of Ireland is asserted to be "the whole of Ireland, its islands and territorial seas," but "pending the reintegration of the national territory," in other words, the ending of the partition of Ireland by the existence of the English-controlled state of Northern Ireland, the new state, Eire, will legislate for the old Free State area.

Grave political problems and carefully nurtured religious prejudices will have to be overcome before that reintegration of the national territory can be accomplished.

In some ways, the mere passing of time is helping the cause of a united Ireland. Gradually, the native Irish element is gaining on the planter stock of the six counties which make up Northern Ireland. In some counties election majorities by the planters can be secured only by gerrymandering. Also, peace and increasing prosperity in the southern twenty-six counties show how false were the English assertions that the departure of the English government from Ireland would bring anarchy and ruin.

Time helps Ireland further by the continued breaching of the "wall of paper" which England long used to separate Ireland from the rest of the world. More and more it is becoming known that Ireland is not the unruly child of England which English propaganda has pictured but that the Irish are a people with a separate nationality, and that the Anglo-Irish relation has been that of conqueror and captive. As a result, the policy of the English government toward Ireland has had to be amended, to the greater dignity of both countries.

So, slowly and steadily, Ireland moves toward her inevitable final victory, inevitable because the Dear Dark Head is still without her crown, and while she is her children will never stay at peace for long. It was in speaking of Ireland of Fenian times that John Stuart Mill said that rebellions never really become unconquerable until they become rebellions for an idea. Ireland's rebellions have been that for four hundred years.

The scholars of Ireland, in the days when the island was a pleasant garden of learning, used to gather related facts into groups of three, and call them Triads. "Three sparks that kindle love," they recorded: "a face, demeanor, speech. Three preparations of a good man's house: ale, a bath, a large fire. Three fair things that hide ugliness: skill in a serf, wisdom in the misshapen, good manners in the ill-favored."

The day came when I had to leave Ireland. As the ship relentlessly bore me westward, and the thin gray line on the horizon that was the last I could see of Irish shores narrowed and disappeared, I comforted myself by following the example of the old scholars, and by fixing in my mind small memories and pictures of Ireland.

Three pleasant whitenesses I remembered: the clean whiteness of cloth bleaching on hedgetops, the young whiteness of lambs beside their mothers, the fragrant whiteness of hawthorn in bloom.

Three beautiful blues: the blue eyes of Connemara women, the blue of faraway hills, the blue of the sea from the Wicklow headlands.

Three helpful wheels: the wheels of donkey carts carrying turf, the wheels of spinners drawing out yarn, the wheels of water mills grinding grain.

Three rugged things: the rocks of Aran, the mountains of Mayo, the courage of Connaught farmers.

Three Irish trees: the drooping willows of Clonmacnoise, the oaks of Columcille's Derry, the arching elms over the river walk at Slane.

Three curves of loveliness: the sweep of the Shannon to the sea, the rolling lines of low, pastured hills, the curve of the lake at Glendalough.

Three things that are eternal in Ireland: love of God, love of liberty, love of country.

Three endearing names for Ireland: Kathleen ni Houlihan, Dark Rosaleen, Dear Dark Head.

SOURCES

→»)《←

Foreword

P. 7, line 6.— "for the delectation of fools."—Translated by Dr. Joseph Dunn, from the colophon at the end of the *Táin Bó Cúalnge*.

Chapter 1. Nuada of the Silver Hand

P. 16, line 27.—"took possession of the province."—From the translation by John Fraser, of "The Battle of Moytura," in *Eriu*, vol. 8, 1915.

P. 17, line 10.—"in entertaining the assemblies of the court."— Quoted from Eugene O'Curry, *Manuscript Materials of Irish History*, pp. 248–50, and Whitley Stokes's translation of "The Second Battle of Moytura," *Revue Celtique*, vol. 12, p. 69.

P. 18, line 7.—"before they were subdued."—The early chapters of Eoin Mac Neill's *Phases of Irish History* contain a critical exposition of prehistoric Ireland. *The Book of Ballymote* places the battle of Moytura about fifteen centuries before Christ, but this is not accepted by most historians.

P. 20, line 9.—"rulers of the land."—Same as first note for this chapter.

P. 20, line 12.—"Scota and Gaedhal Glas."—The early chapters of Abbé Mac Geoghegan's *History of Ireland, Ancient and Modern*, translated from the French by Patrick O'Kelly, give an account of these legendary invasions, with references to many older books on the same subject.

Chapter II. Macha of the Red Hair

P. 21, line 17.—"Sweetness of its stringed music."—Eugene O'Curry, *Manners and Customs of the Ancient Irish*, vol. 3, p. 240, from the *Book of Invasions*.

P. 21, line 21.—"Goblets for brown ale."—*Annals of the Four Masters*, Age of the World 3656.

P. 22, line 1.—"now gaily stained."—*Annals of the Four Masters*, Age of the World 3664.

P. 22, line 11.—"Seven occupations had a king."—Eugene O'Curry, *Ancient Laws of Ireland*, vol. 4, p. 334.

P. 22, line 27.—"three centuries before Christ."—Translated from the *Book of Leinster* by Eugene O'Curry in *Manuscript Materials*, p. 527. The *Book of Ballymote* places Macha about 285 B.C.

P. 25, line 4.—"usurped the throne."—Adapted and condensed from Whitley Stokes's translation of "The Destruction of Dind Rig," in *Zeitschrift für Celtische Philologie*, vol. 3, 1901, from the *Book of Leinster*.
The synchronizations of the *Book of Ballymote* place the death of Labriad Loingsech at 221 B.C.

P. 26, line 11.—"every chief harper had to be knowing."— O'Curry, *Manners and Customs of the Ancient Irish*, vol. 3, p. 214.

P. 27, line 20.—"to reach the highest rank."—P. W. Joyce, *A Social History of Ancient Ireland*, vol. 1, p. 430.

P. 27, line 25.—"the secret language of poets."—*Ibid.*, p. 432.

P. 28, line 1.—"only of silver or bronze."—*Ibid.*, p. 447.

P. 28, line 7.—"chief poet went to Scotland to study."—Adapted and condensed from Whitley Stokes's translation of "The Colloquy of the Two Sages," *Revue Celtique*, vol. 26, from manuscripts in the *Book of Leinster* and the *Book of Lecan*.

Chapter III. Conor Mac Nessa, King of Ulster

P. 30, line 18.—"King of Ulster."—Adapted and condensed from Whitley Stokes's translation of "Tidings of Conor Mac Nessa," in *Eriu*, vol. 4, from the *Book of Leinster*.

P. 32, line 13.—"into Conor's presence without a welcome." —W. M. Hennessy's translation of *The Intoxication of the Ultonians*, in "Todd Lecture Series," Royal Irish Academy.

P. 33, line 6.—"in the manner of its making."—Same as first note for this chapter.

P. 33, line 31.—"foster son to Conor Mac Nessa."—Dr. Joseph Dunn's translation of the *Táin Bó Cúalnge*, p. 49.

P. 35, line 9.—"Queen Maeve, and her husband Ailill."—Adapted and condensed from portions of *Táin Bó Cúalnge*, translated by Dr. Joseph Dunn.

P. 42, line 11.—"the druid named the girl Deirdre."—This version of the legend of Deirdre is adapted from five early *Tales of Deirdre*, translated and published as follows: Douglas Hyde's translation, published in *Zeitschrift für Celtische Philologie*, vol. 1; Whitley Stokes's in *Irische Texte*, series 2; Alexander Cameron's in *Reliquiae Celticae;* T. O'Flanagan in *Transactions of the Gaelic Society of Dublin*, 1808; A. A. Carmichael in the *Transactions of the Gaelic Society of Inverness*, 1887, XIV.

P. 46, line 17.—"the brainball to burst from him, and he died."— *Death Tales of Irish Heroes, Royal Irish Academy*, "Todd Lecture Series," vol. 14. Translation by Kuno Meyer.

Chapter IV. Pagan Fires

P. 47, line 16.—"that God gives all that."—The *Instructions of King Cormac Mac Art*, translation of Kuno Meyer in "Todd Lecture Series," vol. 15, Royal Irish Academy and also in *Ancient Irish Poetry*.

P. 48, line 25.—"but one acorn on the oak."—*Annals of the Four Masters*, Age of Christ 94.

P. 49, line 6.—"again put the nobles in power."—Geoffrey Keating, *History of Ireland*, pp. 291 *et seq.*, translated by John O'Mahoney.

P. 51, line 7.—"every ridge of land."—*Silva Gadelica*, vol. 2, p. 97, translation by Standish H. O'Grady.

P. 52, line 2.—"must surely be the son of a king."—*Ibid.*, pp. 288, 357.

P. 53, line 2.—"to help the beautiful slave girl."—Keating, *History of Ireland*, p. 275, plus Edward Gwynn's translation of *The Dindsenchus*, "Todd Lecture Series."

P. 53, line 27.—"in the household of the king."—George Petrie, *History and Antiquities of Tara*, pp. 31 *et seq.*, plus Edward Gwynn's translation of *The Dindsenchus*, "Todd Lecture Series"; plus Keating, *op. cit.*, 302*ff.*

P. 54, line 16.—"sit under his own shield."—Eugene O'Curry, *Manners and Customs*, vol. 1, p. 15.

P. 55, line 2.—"according to the old tales."—*Irische Texte*, series 3, p. 204.

P. 56, line 2.—"caldrons of brass."—*Silva Gadelica*, vol. 2, p. 402, translated by Standish H. O'Grady.

P. 56, line 32.—"and the old king replying."—Condensed from Kuno Meyer's translation of *Instructions of King Cormac Mac Art*, "Todd Lecture Series," vol. 15, 1909, and in Kuno Meyer's *Ancient Irish Poetry*.

P. 60, line 30.—"was the cause of his death."—*Annals of the Four Masters*, Age of Christ 266.

P. 61, line 15.—"as he had himself ordered."—Quoted from Stephen Gwynn, *Fair Hills of Ireland*, from his translation of the *Seanchas Na Roile*.

Chapter V.   Finn Mac Cool and the Finna

P. 62, line 16.—"and kept order and rule in the land."—"Notes on the Feena-Erin," by Lord Walter Fitzgerald, *Journal of County Louth Archaeological Society*, vol. 1, no. 4.

P. 64, line 21.—"he was no man for Finn."—*Silva Gadelica*, vol. 2, p. 100.

P. 65, line 24.—"sloes turned from red to black."—The materials of this paragraph from *Gods and Fighting Men*, by Lady Gregory, p. 207; *The Lays of Finn*, Part II, pp. 371-4, published by the Irish Texts Society, and translated by Gerard Murphy; and from *Silva Gadelica*, translated by Standish H. O'Grady.

P. 66, line 21.—"ripples vexing the breast of a boat."—*Gods and Fighting Men*, translated by Lady Gregory, and *Lays of Finn*, translated by Gerard Murphy.

P. 67, line 8.—"then passed on to battle."—*Celtic Review*, vol. 1, p. 356, and *Revue Celtique*, vol. 2, p. 89.

P. 67, line 26.—"each man loosed two swift, fierce hounds."—*Lays of Finn*, vol. 2, p. 217. Translation by Gerard Murphy.

P. 68, line 3.—"as wife for one of his men."—Same as first note for this chapter.

P. 68, line 16.—"never recovered their great power."—*Ibid.*

P. 68, 22.—"the three daughters of Conara the Odd."—*Lays of Finn*, vol. 2, p. 329.

P. 68, line 29.—"Crimora followed him in grief."—James Mac Pherson, *Fragments of Irish Poetry*.

P. 69, line 16.—"Says Standish O'Grady's translation."—*Silva Gadelica*, vol. 2, p. 383.

P. 70, line 17.—"the leaves of the oak from the beech."—"Pursuit of Diarmuid and Grainne," *Transactions of the Ossianic Society*, vol. 3, 1857, translation by Standish H. O'Grady, and Richard O'Duffy's translation for the Society for the Preservation of the Irish Language.

P. 71, line 4.—"to be an exile all my days."—*Revue Celtique*, vol. 33. Translation by J. H. Lloyd, O. C. Bergin, and G. Schoepperle.

P. 71, line 23.—"the desire of his heart and soul of her."—"Pursuit of Diarmuid and Grainne." Same as note for p. 70, line 17.

P. 72, line 31.—"men their equal in the time of fight."—Standish H. O'Grady's translation of *Lament of Oisin after the Fenians*.

Chapter VI.   The Coming of Patrick

P. 74, line 17.—"was killed by treachery."—*Annals of the Four Masters*, pp. 366*ff*; and Keating, *History of Ireland*, p. 372.

P. 74, line 26.—"when peace was made after a contested election."—Sylvester O'Holleran, *General History of Ireland*, p. 293.

P. 75, line 29.—"and nearly as many at night."—Keating, *op. cit.*, p. 374.

P. 76, line 20.—"a tale that the years have made famous."—This version of Patrick's coming is based on material in Keating's *History of Ireland*, Whitley Stokes's translation of the *Tripartite Life of St. Patrick*, and *Lives of the Saints* from the *Book of Lismore*.

P. 85, line 21.—"their voices could be raised in praise of God."—Rev. John Healy, *Ireland's Ancient Schools and Scholars*, p. 65.

Chapter VII. Dove of the Church

P. 88, line 26.—"St. Ciaran's Plain of Crosses."—G. Hanson, *Early Monastic Schools of Ireland*.

P. 89, line 4.—"which was the cause of his exile."—This version of the life of Columcille is based on material in Adamann's *Life of St. Columba*, Manus O'Donnell's *Life of Columcille*, translation by A. O'Kelleher and G. Schoepperle; *Lives of the Saints* from the *Book of Lismore*, translation by Whitley Stokes.

P. 91, line 1.—"her women noble, of good rearing."—Lady Gregory, *A Book of Saints and Wonders*.

P. 95, line 3.—"upon the line where he had stopped."—Keating, *History of Ireland*, p. 441.

P. 96, line 2.—"music of the lament."—Lady Gregory, *A Book of Saints and Wonders*.

Chapter VIII. Quiet Gardens

P. 97, line 20.—"and the love of letters."—H. Zimmer, *The Irish Element in Mediaeval Culture;* G. Hanson, *Early Monastic Schools of Ireland*. .

P. 98, line 28.—"every seventh day of the week."—Hanson, *op. cit.*, p. 7.

P. 99, line 7.—"also sat under Irish teachers."—John Lanigan, *Ecclesiastical History of Ireland*, vol. 3, p. 150, and the Rev.

E. J. McCarthy's translation from the French of the Count of Montalembert's *Life of St. Columbanus*.

P. 99, line 18.—"their occupations varied."—William F. Skene, *Celtic Scotland*, vol. 2, p. 101.

P. 100, line 21.—"happily do I work under the green-wood."— Adapted from Kuno Meyer's translation in *Ancient Irish Poetry*, and Whitley Stokes's translation in *Thesaurus Paleohibernicus*.

P. 100, line 25.—"and our cat has escaped from us." (And other colophons and marginalia in this chapter)—Charles Plummer, *Colophons and Marginalia of Irish Scribes*.

P. 101, line 20.—"the name meaning Friends of God."— W. Reeves, "Culdees," *Transactions of the Royal Irish Academy*, 1874, vol. 24.

P. 102, line 1.—"lifted up in praise and thanksgiving."—Adapted from Kuno Meyer's translation in *Ancient Irish Poetry*.

P. 103, line 11.—"lent to the music of heaven."—*The Monastery of Tallaght*, translated by Edward Gwynn and Walter Purton, in *Proceedings of the Royal Irish Academy*, 1911–12, sec. C.

P. 104, line 32.—"save her feet only."—L. Gougaud, *Christianity in Celtic Lands*.

P. 105, line 8.—"let her be buried in the bog of Leighlin."— Whitley Stokes's translation of *Lives of the Saints*, p. xiii. This story is also retold in the lovely chapter on Irish scholarship, "Fortunatus to Sedulius," in Helen Waddell's *The Wandering Scholars*.

P. 106, line 9.—"restrains them from their course."—Kuno Meyer, *Ancient Irish Poetry*.

Chapter IX.   And Then the Vikings Came

P. 108, line 1.—"to plunder neighboring coasts."—Charles Keary, *The Vikings in Western Christendom*.

P. 108, line 28.—"weep for the enslavement of his people."— *Ibid.*, p. 143.

P. 109, line 18.—"this quickly striking terror."—The general story of this period is based on Eoin Mac Neill's *Phases of Irish History*, *The Annals of Clonmacnoise*, *The Annals of Ulster*, *The Annals of the Four Masters*, and James H. Todd's translation of *Wars of the Gael and Gall*.

Chapter X.   *"We Have Found a Golden Cup"*

P. 129, line 4.—"To save yourself, young man, you must flee."—Jonas of Bobbio, *Vita Columbani*, quoted from *St. Columbanus*, by the Count of Montalembert, English translation from the French, by the Rev. E. J. McCarthy.

P. 129, line 24.—"ruins of the old Roman Civilization."—*Ibid.*

P. 131, line 2.—"the chapel bell rang to call the monks to prayers." —*Regula S. Columbani*, quoted by Montalembert.

P. 131, line 10.—"a wolf sniffed at his garment, and left him unharmed."—Helen Concannon, *Life of St. Columbanus*.

P. 132, line 7.—"the air of the hall was filled with it."—Margaret Stokes, *Three Months in the Forests of France*.

P. 132, line 26.—"allowed their passengers to land."—Montalembert, *op. cit.*

P. 133, line 18.—"but it is full of serpents."—Montalembert, *op. cit.*, p. 50.

P. 134, line 3.—"from them countless others branched out."—Montalembert, *op. cit.*, p. 224; Helen Waddell, *The Wandering Scholars;* G. Hanson, *Early Monastic Schools of Ireland;* and L. Gougaud, *Christianity in Celtic Lands*.

P. 134, line 32.—"Charlemagne himself was no great scholar."—James B. Mullinger, *Schools of Charles the Great*, and W. Turner, *Irish Teachers in the Carolinian Revival*.

P. 135, line 20.—"men who were at court served God prosperously."—Ussher's *Works*, vol. 4, p. 466. Parts of this work specially translated for *Dear Dark Head* by Dr. William Cornog.

P. 135, line 26.—"the stream of exiles seems unending."—G. Hanson, *Monastic Schools*, p. 81.

P. 136, line 27.—"money bestowed by the kings and princes of Ireland was almost unbounded."—"Irish Monasteries in Germany," Wattenbach's article translated from the German by W. Reeves in the *Ulster Journal of Archaeology*, 1859, pp. 227, 247, 295-315.

P. 137, line 15.—"Supported by the writings of Marianus."— *Ibid*.

P. 137, line 20.—"radiance of his shining fingers."—Bolland, *Life of Marianus*.

P. 137, line 28.—"gave all my might to letters."—*Monumenta Germaniae Historica*, quoted by Helen Waddell in *The Wandering Scholars*.

P. 138, line 19.—"other divine gifts as my Master Marianus."— Wattenbach-Reeves, *op. cit.*, p. 245.

P. 139, line 1.—"the happenings of the year 1050."—*Annals of the Four Masters*.

P. 139, line 22.—"violent and vindictive life of the time."— *Annals of Florence of Worcester*, year 1139 *ff*., Geoffrey of Monmouth, and Roger de Hoveden.

P. 140, line 1.—"relics of Celtic literature in the world today."— Douglas Hyde, *Literary History of Ancient Ireland;* and Margaret Stokes, *Early Christian Art in Ireland*, p. 92.

P. 140, line 8.—"and all their melodious comrades."—Edward Bunting, *Ancient Music of Ireland*, and Francis O'Neill, *Irish Minstrels and Musicians*, Chapter IX.

P. 140, line 13.—"strike the humming strings with sweet sound." —*Memorials of St. Dunstan*, pp. 256-7. Specially translated from the Medieval Latin by Dr. William Cornog.

P. 140, line 26.—"lived together in one group."—Introduction to *Life of St. Malachy of Armagh*, by St. Bernard of Clairvaux, edited and translated by J. J. Lawlor.

P. 141, line 1.—"were either ignorant or negligent."—*Ibid.*, p. 18.

P. 141, line 8.—"found it suited him well, and ambled pleasantly."—*Ibid.*, p. 70.

Chapter XI. *"Trembling Sod"*

P. 143, line 25.—"King of Meath, would be away."—"The Annals of the Four Masters, Loch Cé, Ulster, Clonmacnoise, and Tigernach," *Revue Celtique*, vols. 15–18; *Chronicum Scotorum;* Campion and Hanmer in Ware's *Ancient Irish Stories*, Keating, *op. cit.*, pp. 614*ff;* "The Book of Howth" in the *Calendar of Carew Manuscripts*, and Giraldus Cambrensis' *The Conquest of Ireland*, in Holinshed's *Chronicles*, for all this period. Special points, and points likely to be questioned, will be noted specifically.

P. 144, line 18.—"traverse Ireland in safety alone."—*Annals of the Four Masters*.

P. 145, line 8.—"assured of the king's license and favor on that behalf."—Campion in Ware's *Ancient Stores of Ireland*, vol. I, p. 80.

P. 145, line 21.—"not only for her beauty."—For the genealogy of the Geraldines and for the Welsh background of the time as it relates to Ireland see Clark, *Earls and Earldom of Pembroke*, p. 7; Hayman, *Unpublished Geraldine Documents*, p. 64; *The Earls of Kildare and their Ancestor*, by the Duke of Leinster, p. 3; Giraldus Cambrensis, note p. 47 (1587 ed.); Warrington's *History of Wales*, vol. 2, p. 372; *Chronicles of Florence of Worcester*, note p. 227; Brady, *History of England*, p. 271; *Britannia* by Wm. Camden, p. 754; *Chronicles of the Princes (Welsh Chronicle)*, p. 213; Woodward's *History of Wales*, p. 250; History of Wales, Powell-Wynn, page 100; *Panton Papers—Royal Tribes of Wales*, p. 33; *Annals Cambrae*, years 1070, 1171; Keating, *History of Ireland*, (O'Mahoney translation) p. 617.

P. 146, line 16.—"but as a private person."—Giraldus Cambrensis, *op. cit.*

P. 147, line 5.—"whose business it was to spy out the resources of the land." Giraldus Cambrensis, *op. cit.*, Chapter III.

P. 152, line 1.—"I give you, and hold under your favor."—Hanmer in Ware, *op. cit.*, p. 252.

P. 154, line 16.—"no vessels were to sail after him to the island."—*Annals of Roger de Hoveden*, year 1172.

P. 155, line 4.—"lesser kings and chieftains."—Keating, *op. cit.*, note p. 631.

P. 156, line 1.—"were conspiring against the king."—Giraldus Cambrensis, *op. cit.*, Book I.

P. 156, line 11.—"men-at-arms and common archers."—*Ibid.*, Chapter XXXVII.

P. 157, line 29.—"before dividing it among the common soldiers."—*Ibid.*, Book II, Chapter X.

P. 160, line 10.—"the real reason why the English came to Ireland."—Oliver J. Thatcher, "Some Studies Concerning Adrian IV," in the *Decennial Publication* of the University of Chicago, series 1, no. 4, for a nonbiased article in the scientific manner, with bibliographies of both sides of the question.

P. 160, line 12.—"was an after-thought by the English."—*Ibid.*

P. 161, line 15.—"but to try fortune, and seek adventure."—Giraldus Cambrensis, *op. cit.*, Book II, Chapter XXIII.

P. 162, line 28.—"The Annals of Loch Cé confirm this."—*Annals of Loch Cé*, 1200.

Chapter XII.   *"Warme Neste"*

P. 165, line 13.—"the king's scullery and treasures."—*State Papers, Calendar of Inquisitions Post Mortem*, vol. III, pp. 3, 6, 10, 18.

P. 165, line 20.—"its courts of law."—Olive Armstrong, *Edward Bruce's Invasion of Ireland*, p. 19, 20.

P. 166, line 16.—"wherever the king might command."—*Calendar of Documents Relating to Ireland*, May 4, 1297.

P. 166, line 21.—"awaiting the king's orders."—*Ibid.*

P. 166, line 29.—"the port of Skinburness, near Carlisle."—*Ibid.*, Dec. 12, 1298.

P. 167, line 4.—"some competent office or bailiwick."—*Ibid.*, May 8, 1299.

P. 167, line 8.—"on the feast of St. John next ensuing."—*Ibid.*, Feb. 14, 1300.

P. 169, line 30.—"and filch the country from them."—by John Mc Graith, *Triumphs of Turlough*, Irish Texts Society Publication, nos. 26, 27, translation by Standish H. O'Grady. Also T. J. Westropp, "External Evidence of the Wars of Turlough," in *Transactions of the Royal Irish Academy*, vol. 32, sec. C., 1903.

P. 170, line 29.—"by an unknown writer, says that he did."—"An Irish Account of Bruce's Invasion," in the *Journal of the County Louth Archaeological Society*, vol. 1, no. 2.

P. 171, line 17.—"may easily yield ourselves a prey to them."—*Proceedings of the Royal Irish Academy*, vol. 37.

P. 172, line 7.—"and corn destroyed."—*Annals of Clonmacnoise*, year 1315.

P. 173, line 4.—"were required to ride on saddles."—Rev. Denis Murphy, "The Pale," in *Journal of the County Kildare Archaeological Society*, vol. 2, p. 53.

P. 174, line 1.—"Irish works of art wrought from fine gold."—Alice Stopford Green, *The Making of Ireland and Its Undoing*, Chapters I and II.

P. 174, line 10.—"before the Irish trade was throttled."—Holinshed, *Chronicles*, vol. 6, p. 35, 1610 ed.

P. 174, line 19.—"a sight that combined so much variety and beauty."—James Hardiman, *Galway*.

P. 175, line 28.—"had ridden to a day of pillage or battle."—*Catalogue of Irish Manuscripts in the British Museum*, edited and translated by Standish H. O'Grady.

P. 176, line 3.—"less sensible of pressure or opposition than other where."—W. M. Hennessy, Article on the Curragh, in *Proceedings of the Royal Irish Academy*, vol. 9, 1867.

P. 176, line 17.—"and given gifts at parting."—*Annals of Clonmacnoise*, year 1352.

P. 177, line 1.—"saving her body alone."—*Annals of the Four Masters*, note p. 972.

P. 177, line 22.—"as Irish as the Irish themselves."—*Tribes and Customs of Hy-Many*, edited by John O'Donovan, p. 136.

P. 177, line 27.—"without such decay, increaseth."—Edmund Spenser, *View of the State of Ireland*, p. 524.

P. 179, line 23.—"to acquaint them with the good fortunes of his house."—Duke of Leinster, *The Earls of Kildare*, p. 65.

P. 181, line 12.—"the richest Earls' houses under the crown of England."—Holinshed, *op. cit.*, Chapter VI.

P. 182, line 19.—"so that they join not together."—J. O. Halliwell-Phillips, *Letters of the Kings of England*, pp. 244-63.

P. 184, line 3.—"to prey in the bottom of each man's conscience."—Holinshed, *op. cit.*, vol. 6, p. 48, 1610 ed.

P. 184, line 17.—"he wished himself, especially of an evening, in her arms."—J. O. Halliwell-Phillips, *op. cit.*, p. 310.

P. 184, line 25.—"declared himself supreme head of the Church in England."—Gilbert Burnet, *History of the Reformation of the Church of England and Ireland.*

P. 185, line 26.—"to fortify his own strong Maynooth."—Holinshed, *op. cit.*, vol. 6, pp. 287 *et seq.*

P. 186, line 18.—"especially concerning his life."—*Calendar of Carew Manuscripts*, vol. 1, p. 74. Also in *The Earls of Kildare*, where most of the documents relating to the Kildares are published.

P. 187, line 4.—"old hosen and shoes, and old shirts."—*Carew*, vol. 1, Feb. 3, 1537.

P. 187, line 27.—"than otherwise to gain great goods."—*Ibid.*, vol. 2, p. lxix.

P. 188, line 30.—"phrases as insulting as possible to the old Church."—*Ibid.*, vol. 1, p. 55.

P. 189, line 6.—"without payment of two hundred pounds."—*Calendar of State Papers Relating to Ireland*, vol. 1, April 14, 1538.

P. 189, line 17.—"all virtue and honesty is almost banished from you."—*Carew*, vol. 2, July 31, 1537.

P. 189, line 28.—"a chide to them and their canons."—*Ibid.*, vol. 2, April 8, 1538.

P. 190, line 19.—"and an Ave for the souls of the dead."—*Calendar of State Papers Relating to Ireland*, vol. 2, Part 2, p. 564.

Chapter XIII.   Nemesis

P. 193, line 30.—"such a ruin to England as I am afeared to think on."—*Carew*, vol. 1, p. 302. Sept. 11, 1560.

P. 194, line 15.—"Procure, too, the Earl of Desmond."—*Ibid.*, p. 297, May 28, 1560.

P. 195, line 5.—"to allure them further to our service."—*Ibid.*, vol. 2, May 22, 1561.

P. 195, line 26.—"head-pieces and shirts of mail."—*Annals of the Four Masters*, year 1557.

P. 196, line 11.—"active to search woods and morasses."—*State Papers of Henry VIII*, April 6, 1543.

P. 196, line 13.—"had hard going against these men."—T. Gainsford, *The Glory of England*, p. 144.

P. 196, line 19.—"there will be done to him what others can."—*Calendar of State Papers Relating to Ireland*, Aug. 23, 1561.

P. 196, line 28.—"at whom the English gazed with wonder."—*Camden's Annals*, year 1562.

P. 196, line 31.—"the title of Earl of Tyrone."—*Camden*, year 1567.

P. 197, line 12.—"with no result."—*Calendar of State Papers Relating to Ireland*, Nov. 2, 1562.

P. 197, line 21.—"if he came to any government he would never return."—*Ibid.*, Sept. 22, 1562.

P. 199, line 5.—"and with this sword I will keep them."—*Ibid.*, p. 233.

P. 199, line 16.—"so did the English-held town of Dundalk."—Holinshed, *Chronicles of Ireland*, p. 116.

P. 199, line 24.—"help the English in the subduing of Shane."— *Annals of the Four Masters*, year 1567.

P. 200, line 23.—"with loss of goods and lands during life."— *Carew*, vol. 1, p. 340.

P. 200, line 29.—"the O'Neills shouted as they rushed to combat." —P. W. Joyce, *A Social History of Ancient Ireland*, vol. I, p. 148.

P. 201, line 8.—"and there is none to nick them out."—Douglas Hyde, *A Literary History of Ancient Ireland*, p. 521.

P. 201, line 13.—"or anything that was English."—*Calendar of Carew Manuscripts*, vol. 1, pp. 214–15, Feb. 7, 1549.

P. 201, line 23.—"Now she would make them outcasts."— Douglas Hyde, *op. cit.*, p. 520, and *Carew*, vol. I, p. 214.

P. 202, line 17.—"kerne by the thousand to his aid."—Paul Flynn, *The Book of the Galtees*, p. 139.

P. 202, line 23.—"and his brother were imprisoned in Dublin Castle."—For all this period, Wm. Camden, *History of Queen Elizabeth;* Stanihurst in Holinshed's *Chronicles; Annals of the Four Masters; Calendar of Carew Manuscripts; Calendar of State Papers Relating to Ireland;* and *Book of the Galtees*.

P. 203, line 20.—"and that the Pope bore all the charges."— *Calendar of State Papers Relating to Ireland*, and *Carew*, March 23, 1579.

P. 205, line 7.—"will never agree with none of your adversaries without your consent."—R. Cox, *Hibernia Anglicana*, Part I, p. 361.

P. 205, line 18.—"a wonderful navy is prepared in Italy."— *Carew*, vol. 2, Nov. 25, 1579.

P. 212, line 6.—"I do not know one dangerous man of that sect left."—*Ibid.*, vol. 2, p. 442. Apr. 18, 1587.

P. 213, line 4.—"if he can escape with his life."—*Ibid.*, vol. 3, p. 174.

P. 213, line 9.—"Council of Ireland complained to London of a cleric."—*Calendar of State Papers Relating to Ireland*, vol. 1574–1585, pp. 509, 517.

P. 213, line 20.—"all Ireland stirred at the news."—Lugaid O'Clery, "Introduction" to *Life of Hugh Roe O'Donnell*.

P. 215, line 28.—"and of a high dissembling subtile and profound wit."—Fynes Moryson, *Rebellion of Hugh, Earl of Tyrone, and the Appeasing Thereof*, in *Itinerary*, Part II, Chapter I.

P. 216, line 21.—"asking aid from the Spanish King."—Quoted from the "Introduction" to O'Clery's *Life of Hugh Roe O'Donnell*.

P. 217, line 32.—"to be oppressed by those vile rebels."—*Carew*, vol. 3, pp. 284-5, Dec. 1, 1598.

P. 218, line 24.—"command you to pass thither with great speed."—*Ibid.*, vol. 3, p. 315, July 19, 1599.

P. 222, line 17.—"though defeat and destruction might come of it."—*Annals of the Four Masters*, year 1601.

P. 224, line 14.—"the requiem of Hugh O'Donnell, and Irish liberty."—The materials for the description, but not the idea of the double death, from O'Clery, *Life of Hugh Roe O'Donnell*, p. 327.

Chapter XIV.   *The Flight of the Earls*

P. 225, line 17.—"like the carcase of a goose broken up."—Luke Gernon, *Discourse of Ireland*, in C. L. Falkiner, *Illustrations of Irish History and Topography, Mainly of the Seventeenth Century*.

P. 225, line 20.—"hath now not one in rebellion."—*Calendar of State Papers Relating to Ireland*, Sept. 2, 1603.

P. 227, line 22.—"and then the rest will shortly follow."—*Calendar of State Papers Relating to Ireland*, Sept. 2, 1603.

P. 228, line 18.—"to meddle with the religion of God."—*Calendar of State Papers Relating to Ireland*, vol. 1603–1606, p. 217.

P. 229, line 1.—"bring the mayor back again to his house."—Barnaby Rich, *Remembrance of the State of Ireland*, 1612.

P. 229, line 32.—"till it pleased the judges to set them at liberty."—*Archivium Hibernicum*, vol. 5–6, p. 64.

P. 231, line 11.—"Sir John Davies was pleased to relate."—Quoted from John Mitchel, *Life of Hugh O'Neill.*

P. 231, line 13.—"by means of the garrisons they had good espial in Tyrone."—*Calendar of State Papers Relating to Ireland,* Apr. 4, 1606.

P. 231, line 19.—"who may reveal her husband's secrets."—*Calendar of State Papers Relating to Ireland,* Feb. 18, 1606.

P. 232, line 3.—"he had made his province the best governed in Ireland."—*Ibid.,* 1607, p. 159.

P. 232, line 16.—"the truth of the charges."—*Ibid.,* Jan. 23, 1607.

P. 232, line 27.—"to seize the government."—*Ibid.,* May 27, 1607.

P. 233, line 8.—"O'Neill and O'Donnell were in danger of their lives."—C. P. Meehan, *The Fate and Fortunes of the Earls of Tyrone and Tyrconnell,* p. 113.

P. 233, line 17.—"and sailed into Lough Swilly."—*Calendar of State Papers Relating to Ireland,* Sept. 2, 1607.

P. 234, line 3.—"the two merlin falcons who had found refuge in the rigging of their craft."—T. O'Cianan, *The Flight of the Earls,* translated by the Rev. Paul Walsh.

P. 234, line 25.—"nor genealogies heard attentively."—*Catalogue of Irish Manuscripts in the British Museum,* edited by Standish H. O'Grady, vol. 1, p. 397.

P. 235, line 5.—"recompensed in the district without charge to the king."—*Calendar of State Papers Relating to Ireland,* Sept. 9, 1607.

P. 235, line 9.—"tainted with suspicion of treason."—*Ibid.,* p. 266.

P. 235, line 19.—"shadowed as persistently as they had been at home."—*Ibid.,* p. 265.

P. 236, line 12.—"The rest were simply uprooted."—For a general discussion of the Plantation of Ulster see Sir John Davies's *Letters;* P. W. Joyce, *Concise History of Ireland;* George Hill, *The Plantation of Ulster* and *Plantation Papers.*

P. 236, line 31.—"free themselves from such a just punishment."—*Calendar of State Papers Relating to Ireland,* Oct. 30, 1609.

P. 237, line 15.—"poets' and minstrels' bedclothes thrown to litter cattle."—*Catalogue of Irish Manuscripts in the British Museum*, vol. 1, p. 374.

P. 237, line 22.—"as it was the English fear."—C. P. Meehan, *The Fate and Fortunes of the Earls of Tyrone and Tyrconnell*, pp. 359, 402.

P. 237, line 27.—"wrote one of his countrymen who was with him."—*Ibid.*, p. 406.

P. 238, line 14.—"and the tolling of a hundred bells."—*Ibid.*, p. 445.

Chapter XV. Poverty and Potatoes

P. 240, line 1.—"wrote Lord Esmonde in 1629."—*Calendar of State Papers Relating to Ireland*, 1629, p. 539.

P. 241, line 12.—"Ireland paid, and had but little in return."— Richard Bagwell, *Ireland Under the Stuarts*, vol. 1, p. 197.

P. 241, line 18.—"not your blood at first, sleeping Ireland."— Sir John Temple, *History of the Irish Rebellion in 1641.*

P. 241, line 29.—"praying women cut down around a cross."— Rev. Denis Murphy, *Cromwell in Ireland*, p. 167.

P. 241, line 31.—"defenders brought down by English snipers."— J. T. Gilbert, *Contemporary History of Ireland*, Part 2, vol. 1, p. 426.

P. 242, line 1.—"before the paymasters' empty coffers."—Rev. Denis Murphy, *op. cit.*, pp. 38–41.

P. 242, line 8.—"the blare of trumpets."—J. P. Prendergast, *Cromwellian Settlement of Ireland*, p. 81.

P. 242, line 15.—"ladies starving on makeshift farms."—*Ibid.*, p. 177.

P. 243, line 1.—"drums beating, Ireland,"—*Ibid.*, p. 78.

P. 243, line 20.—"The hounds will find him, too."—Edmund Burke, *Laws against Popery in Ireland.*

P. 244, line 1.—"They were my means."—*Autobiography of Wolfe Tone*, p. xi.

P. 244, line 22.—"has been transacted here."—*Ibid.*, p. xvii.

P. 244, line 25.—"and there is nothing you can do."—The early pages of W. J. O'Neill Daunt's *Eighty-Five Years of Irish Life* give many authorities for this period. Also W. J. Fitzpatrick, *Life of Cloncurry*, p. 86; *Memoirs of Lord Holland*, p. 106; Lord Castlereagh, *Memoirs and Correspondence;* Lord Cornwallis, *Correspondence*, vol. 1, p. 46, vol. 3, p. 89; G. Locker-Lampson, *A Consideration of Conditions in Ireland in the Nineteenth Century.*

P. 244, line 31.—"and he was glad to shed it."—*Life of Robert Emmet*, from "Authoritative Sources," Irish Library, no. 1.

P. 245, line 30.—"hardly be left an oak in Ireland."—Lecky, *Ireland in the Eighteenth Century*, p. 336.

P. 247, line 3.—"Let Sir Jonah explain the phrase."—Sir Jonah Barrington, *Personal Sketches.*

P. 250, line 20.—"to the next merry meeting."—*Ibid.*, pp. 40 *et seq.*

P. 252, line 5.—"not the strength to perform it."—Jonathan Swift, *Letter to the Irish People*, p. 4.

P. 252, line 22.—"poverty no less pitiful."—John Bush, *Hibernia Curiosa*, p. 26.

P. 254, line 18.—"anything that could be wished."—De Latocnaye, *A Frenchman's Walk Through Ireland*, p. 210.

P. 255, line 15.—"which no leeches can cure."—Daniel Corkery, *The Hidden Ireland*, p. 9.

P. 256, line 17.—"lovemaking with a fair woman."—Adapted from Daniel Corkery's translation in *The Hidden Ireland*, p. 79.

P. 256, line 28.—"recite their own."—*Ibid.*, p. 100.

P. 257, line 8.—"the sweetness of a bell."—*Ibid.*, p. 231.

P. 258, line 6.—"it raised vision."—*Ibid.*, p. 142.

Chapter XVI. *"The Ragged Coat"*

P. 260, line 22.—"the rights of society."—Dublin *Evening Post*, Feb. 29, 1812. Quoted from Denis F. MacCarthy, *Early Life of Shelley.*

P. 261, line 1.—"in that unfortunate country."—*Ibid.*, p. 290.

P. 261, line 22.—"more prosperous than most Catholic families."—Mrs. Morgan O'Connell, *The Last Colonel of the Irish Brigade.*

P. 262, line 25.—"from byre to shed, and from shed to barn."—Daniel Corkery, *The Hidden Ireland*, p. 38.

P. 263, line 22.—"a relish for happiness."—*Journal of Daniel O'Connell*, p. 190.

P. 263, line 32.—"if ever I could put an end to it."—*Ibid.*, p. 62.

P. 264, line 15.—"one of his severe critics."—Charles G. Duffy, *Young Ireland*, p. 35.

P. 266, line 3.—"wouldn't color it."—J. Binns, *Miseries and Beauties of Ireland*, vol. 1, p. 184.

P. 266, line 22.—"if we could get good bread."—*Ibid.*, vol. 2, p. 9.

P. 267, line 24.—"did not intervene and forbid."—Thomas Carlyle, *Chartism*, p. 27.

P. 268, line 4.—"glorious and free nation."—James Grant, *Impressions of Ireland and the Irish*, p. 125.

P. 269, line 8.—"pockets of the Irish gentlemen."—The Duke of Wellington's *Dispatches and Correspondence.*

P. 269, line 21.—"degrade the mass of the Irish population."—John Campbell Campbell, *Life of John, Lord Campbell*, vol. 2, p. 27.

P. 271, line 1.—"weld the people into a powerful group."—Charles G. Duffy, *Young Ireland.*

P. 271, line 24.—"persisted in to all extremeties."—*Ibid.*, pp. 65*ff.*

P. 278, line 9.—"repeated the couplet two or three times."—*Ibid.*, p. 381.

P. 280, line 3.—"the toil and sweat that raised this food."—John O'Rourke, *History of the Great Irish Famine*, p. 52.

P. 281, line 2.—"admitted to be quite correct."—John Mitchel, *An Apology for the British Government in Ireland*, p. 6.

P. 281, line 29.—"give up his land before he was given relief."—
Ibid., p. 31.

P. 282, line 6.—"the tenant got nothing."—Wm. Bennett,
Six Weeks in Ireland, p. 40.

P. 282, line 23.—"whose industry produced them."—W. J.
Daunt O'Neill, *A Life Spent for Ireland*, p. 62.

P. 284, line 1.—"and pass you unheedingly."—*Annals of the Irish
Famine*, Mrs. A. Nicholson, p. 38.

P. 284, line 31.—"he coldly records."—Thomas Carlyle, *Re-
miniscences of My Irish Journey*, p. 217.

P. 285, line 14.—"all hope for the poor of Ireland was dead."—
John Denieffe, *Recollections of the Irish Republican Brotherhood*,
p. iii. Also O'Donovan Rossa, *Recollections; J. Devoy,
Recollections of an Irish Rebel;* John O'Leary, *Recollections of
Fenians and Fenianism.*

P. 287, line 10.—"just discontent of the whole people."—
Cardinal Manning, *Ireland and England*, p. 40.

P. 288, line 20.—"successful candidates were Home Rule leaders."
—Michael MacDonagh, *The Home Rule Movement*, p. 33.

P. 290, line 9.—"distinction was not long in coming to him."—
John H. Parnell, *Charles Stewart Parnell*, p. 130.

P. 290, line 23.—"fight for self-government."—Michael Davitt,
The Fall of Feudalism. Also Brian O'Neill, *The Fight for the
Land in Ireland.*

P. 291, line 11.—"creeping upon the threshold."—*A Short History
of the Land War in Drumlish.*

P. 292, line 27.—"published in 1888."—Wm. H. Hurlbert,
Ireland Under Coercion, p. 55.

P. 293, line 21.—"current at the time."—Sir Alfred Robbins,
Parnell—The Last Five Years, p. 132.

P. 294, line 24.—"to lead his party in Parliament."—Katherine
O'Shea Parnell, *Charles Stewart Parnell*, p. 164.

P. 295, line 5.—"almost a nullity."—John Morley, *Life of Wm.
Gladstone*, vol. 3, p. 436.

P. 295, line 22.—"human weakness of apology."—Katherine O'Shea Parnell, *Charles Stewart Parnell*, p. 186.

P. 296, line 10.—"perish in its coils."—John Morley, *Life of Wm. Gladstone*, vol. 3, p. 440.

P. 296, line 28.—"Parnell master in Ireland."—*Ibid.*, 457.

Chapter XVII.   Seeds of Fire

P. 299, line 1.—"they were always the rebels."—L. Mac Manus, *White Light and Flame*, p. 2.

P. 299, line 25.—"the wants of the hour."—Douglas Hyde, *What Ireland Is Asking For*, in *Literary Ideals in Ireland*, edited by Lady Gregory, p. 56.

P. 300, line 24.—"the story of the national soul."—AE in the introduction to Standish O'Grady, *The Coming of Cuchulain*.

P. 302, line 19.—"was not to be blotted out."—Mary Brigid Pearse, *Home Life of Padraig Pearse*, p. 111.

P. 304, line 4.—"work houses are full of paupers."—*An Tsean Bhean Bhocht*, 1897.

P. 304, line 30.—"the moment comes for slipping the leash."—George Lyons, *Some Recollections of Griffith and His Times*, p. 19.

P. 306, line 21.—"goodbye to the English interest in Ireland forever."—Quoted from Eoin Mac Neill, *The Ulster Difficulty*, p. 15.

P. 307, line 4.—"controlled by Roman Catholics."—Stephen L. Gwynn, *John Redmond's Last Years*, p. 96.

P. 307, line 12.—"the bulletin had been sold by 1914."—R. G. S. King, *Ulster's Protest—Her Industrial, Political and Imperial Reasons for Refusing to Submit to Home Rule*, p. 7.

P. 308, line 4.—"poverty would be their lot."—Pamphlet, *The Lesson of Craigavon*.

P. 308, line 15.—"his dear friend and patron."—E. Marjoribanks, *Life of Sir Edward Carson*, p. 5.

P. 310, line 20.—"must in the end be in harmony."—AE, *Nationality and Cosmopolitanism in Literature*, in *Literary Ideals in Ireland*, p. 83, edited by John Eglinton.

P. 311, line 32.—"he never changed his mind."—Desmond Ryan, *James Connolly, His Life Work, and Writings;* Nora Connolly O'Brien, *The Unbroken Tradition* and *Portrait of a Rebel Father*.

P. 313, line 21.—"and fight for lost causes."—Mary Brigid Pearse, *Home Life of Padraig Pearse*, p. 14.

P. 314, line 9.—"slavery is one of them."—Reprinted from p. 98, *Political Writings and Speeches of Padraig Pearse*, by kind permission of The Talbot Press, Ltd., Dublin.

P. 314, line 32.—"the Volunteer movement."—Bulmer Hobson, *History of the Irish Volunteers*, p. 20.

P. 316, line 28.—"allowed to jeopardise it."—P. S. O'Hegarty, *The Victory of Sinn Fein*, p. 15.

P. 318, line 30.—"safely under his foot."—Some details of the account of the Howth gun-running given by Darrell Figgis in *Recollections of the Irish War* have been questioned. Mary Spring-Rice, in *Log of the Howth Gun-Running in the Asgard*, in *Sinn Fein*, July 26, 1924, *et seq.*, gives a day-to-day account.

P. 321, line 28.—"before the war was over."—P. S. O'Hegarty, *The Victory of Sinn Fein*, p. 2.

P. 323, line 8.—"are written elsewhere."—Louis Leroux, *P. H. Pearse*, p. 305 *et seq.*

P. 324, line 23.—"there is no redemption."—*Workers' Republic*, Feb. 5, 1916.

P. 324, line 29.—"dear only to men of foul breeds."—Reprinted from p. 28, *Political Writings and Speeches of Padraig Pearse*, by kind permission of The Talbot Press, Ltd., Dublin.

P. 325, line 29.—"not gone well with their plans."—Dorothy Macardle, *The Irish Republic*, for detailed account of this period.

P. 328, line 9.—"a friend had written of him."—Darrell Figgis, *Recollections of the Irish War*, p. 84.

P. 336, line 7.—"rise up where patriot graves are found."—
The poems from which these fragments are taken may be
found in *Nineteen-Sixteen, An Anthology*, compiled by Edna
FitzHenry.

P. 337, line 2.—"strong in their deaths."—Dora Sigerson Shorter,
The Tricolor, p. 6.

P. 338, line 9.—"a symbol of a new unity."—Darrell Figgis,
Recollections of the Irish War, p. 59.

P. 338, line 26.—"demand a nation's right."—Rev. Michael
O'Flanagan, in *The Catholic Bulletin*, 1917.

Afterword

P. 346, line 7.—"the Irish Volunteers repudiated Redmond."—
Reprinted from *Political Writings and Speeches* of Padraig
Pearse, by kind permission of The Talbot Press, Ltd., Dublin.

P. 348, line 11.—"and called them Triads."—From *The Triads of
Ireland*, translated by Kuno Meyer, "Todd Lecture Series,"
vol. 13, Royal Irish Academy; also in Kuno Meyer, *Ancient
Irish Poetry*.

Index

375